A-Z
of
Natural Remedies

A-Z of Natural Remedies

General Editor

Amanda Sandeman

Dealerfield

This edition specially printed for:-
Dealerfield Ltd
Glaisdale Parkway
Glaisdale Drive
Nottingham
NG8 4GA

ISBN: 1-85927-081-6

NOTE TO READERS
This book is not intended to replace the advice and treatment of a
physician or other licensed health professional, but rather should be used
in conjunction with professional care. The author and Dealerfield Ltd
expressly disclaim any responsibility for loss or personal illness alleged to
have been caused, directly or indirectly, by the contents of this book.

Material previously published in 1988 as part of the encyclopedia set
Natural Choice (Orbis Publishing Ltd).

Editorial and design:
Brown Packaging Ltd,
255-257 Liverpool Road, London N1 1LX

Printed in The Slovak Republic

Contents

Evening Primrose

ALOE VERA

Soothing and healing skin tonic

Hailed as an important natural drug throughout history, aloe vera can be used as an effective skin toner and anti-burn remedy

There are three officially recognised varieties of aloe, a succulent, cactus-like plant belonging to the lily family. Recognisable by their long, pointed, fleshy leaves (usually prickly at the margin and tip), woody stems, and erect spikes of yellow, orange or red flowers, aloes can be grown conveniently as house plants and provide a handy remedy for a variety of ailments. The leaves of the plant are filled with a yellow juice which contains the bitter-tasting drug called aloes.

Aloe vera (also known as the Curacao or Barbados aloe) is native to the West Indies and, of the three varieties, it is most extensively used in modern medicine. Cape (native to South Africa) and Socotrine aloes are also grown but less widely used commercially.

MEDICINAL USES

Beneath the outer skin of the leaves is a layer of enlarged cells which contains the yellowish juice known as aloes. It is this juice which possesses the medicinal properties. For internal use, aloes is recognised as an emmenagogue (to promote suppressed menstruation). It is also known for its purgative properties and acts as a vermifuge (working against parasitic worms), destroying and expelling them from the gut. Cape aloes is the most potent purgative and vermifuge and is used for veterinary purposes.

Aloe vera acts externally as a soothing and healing gel, as well as a disinfectant and astringent. It helps to keep the skin healthy by stimulating the circulation and promoting the growth of new tissue. Minor cuts and burns, sunburn and insect bites can all be treated effectively with aloe vera. Some readers may remember having aloes rubbed onto their fingers to deter nail-biting by its strong, bitter taste.

Aloes are easily recognisable by their tall, woody stems and spiky flowers.

CULTIVATING ALOES

H ISTORY AND LEGENDS

In the West Indies, aloe vera grows both wild and in plantations.

Due to their preference for a hot climate, aloes must be kept indoors or in a heated greenhouse for best results. Growth is slow, and it is important not to over-water: do not forget, the aloe is a desert plant. Brown spots can appear on the leaves as a result of watering with tap-water containing fluoride, so use, if possible, rain-water or spring water. The leaves may also develop blemishes from bruising or direct sunlight (although the plant likes plenty of light).

Side shoots appear when the aloe needs re-potting; these should be removed and potted separately before replanting the parent aloe in a larger pot, otherwise they will sap the vitality of the parent plant. When potting, use a well-watered, sandy compost, and then do not water again for a while; this will encourage strong root growth.

Using aloe leaves

Older plants are medicinally more effective, and yield larger leaves for use on skin afflictions, than younger ones. Two to three years' growth should be allowed before harvesting the juice, but young plants will have some curative properties.

When collecting the juice, cut the leaves off close to the stem (the aloe will then seal off the cut). Choose a leaf from the base, as these are the oldest and have the highest medicinal value; this method is also the least disfiguring to the plant. The leaf can then either be arranged so that the juice drains into a cup, or sliced lengthways and the cut surface applied directly to the skin.

In West Indian aloe plantations, the aloes are grown in rows and the juice collected in March or April; in Africa, the juice is collected from wild plants by arranging the cut leaves round a hole, dug in the ground, in which is spread an animal skin – inner side uppermost – to collect the resin.

East India House in the 1600s.

The power of aloes was known to the Greeks as early as the fourth century BC. A legend tells how the great Aristotle requested that his pupil, Alexander the Great, conquer the aloes-producing islands of Socotra. In the tenth century, the herb was being imported into Europe via the Red Sea and Alexandria, but Moslem travellers reported that Socotra was still the only place cultivating aloes. East India Company records from the early 1600s show that aloes were being imported into Britain and by 1693 were being sold by London druggists.

The Moslems and the Jews of Cairo hang aloes in their doorways to protect the household from evil.

ALOE VERA – EXTERNAL REMEDIES

PRECAUTIONS

CUTS, SCRATCHES AND BRUISES
Apply fresh aloe juice to reduce swelling and speed healing.
ACNE
Apply juice daily. Skin may become dry, but only initially.
PSORIASIS
Aloe juice mixed with almond oil has been found to have a beneficial effect.
BURNS
Apply the cut surface of a leaf to scalds, fat burns, and acid burns. Pain is eased, healing is rapid and scarring is reduced. The gel seals the burn, thus preventing the entry of secondary infections. The same leaf can be used for several applications by scratching the cut surface each time to produce more gel.
DAMAGED HAIR AND DANDRUFF
Apply aloe juice to scalp and hair and leave overnight (if possible). It protects against the removal of natural oils from the hair and counteracts the detergent effects of shampoos.

DRY OR DULL SKIN
Use aloe cream at night, or as a morning moisturiser under make-up. Aloe is also available as a combined moisturiser and sun screen. Alternatively, fresh juice can be applied as a face pack for 15-20 minutes, and then washed off; this makes a marvellous skin tonic.

1 If used as a purgative, aloes should be combined with herbs such as fennel, ginger or caraway, as these are carminative (acting to stimulate and soothe digestion) and prevent gripping pains in the abdomen – a possibility when aloes is used alone.
2 Aloes act as an emmenagogue by stimulating the uterus, and it may cause contractions. It should, therefore, be avoided during pregnancy.
3 Aloes should be avoided by nursing mothers. This is because the active ingredients will pass through into the breast milk and may also purge the infant.

Herbalists would not recommend you to experiment with aloes as an internal remedy because it has a potent action and dosage requires careful monitoring. Purging is not a fashionable practice these days, and the use of aloes as an internal remedy has greatly declined.

ARNICA

Natural shock–absorber

Valued throughout Europe as a soothing treatment for both physical and mental traumas, arnica has been in use since the days of the Roman Empire

Anyone who has ever spent a summer holiday in the Alps will certainly have come across mountain arnica (*Arnica montana*), which grows abundantly in the high pastures. The plant is found throughout the mountainous areas of central and northern Europe, at altitudes between 1,200 and 2,800 metres (4000-9200 ft). Its flowers look rather like a paler version of the pot marigold, with its leaves grouped at the base of the stem.

The plant is also found in the mountainous regions of Canada and the northern USA and was a favourite herb with the early settlers. It is not native to the UK however, although it has been seen in Scotland, possibly having escaped from a cultivated garden. There is therefore little traditional use of arnica in Britain and it is missing from most of the classic herbal texts. Arnica has recently become commonly used in the home, however, principally as a homoeopathic remedy, or in the form of a cream as an external treatment for bruises, swellings and sprains.

FIRST AID

Arnica has such a diversity of uses that no home medicine chest should be without it, particularly if there are children in the house since it is ideal for treating the bumps and bruises of childhood. But if not handled properly it can also be extremely toxic and should be used with caution (see box).

European *materia medica* have listed mountain arnica as a valuable medicinal plant for centuries, it is used both in herbal medicine and homoeopathy. The flowers, leaves and roots are all used – both externally as ointments and lotions and internally in teas and tinctures, as well as homoeopathic pistules.

Arnica is also known as mountain tobacco, as the leaves were once smoked as a substitute for tobacco, and in France tradition has it that a phial of arnica carried in the pocket will help you give up smoking.

Europeans take arnica internally as a stimulant for the nervous sytem and circulation and also in treating atherosclerosis (clogging of the arteries) and high blood pressure. It can also be used in cases of paralysis and epilepsy.

The herb is sometimes given in very small doses during pregnancy, to help prevent varicose veins, but as it can also act as a uterine stimulant this type of treatment must be supervised by a trained herbal specialist.

In herbal texts arnica infusion for internal use is given as a maximum of 5 grams (2 teaspoons) of arnica leaves or flowers to one litre (2 pints) of water – a substantially weaker mix than for other herbs. Homoeopathic remedies are made from very diluted arnica tincture and because of arnica's possible toxicity, it is much safer to use such commercial preparations.

HOMOEOPATHIC HEALER

Arnica is probably one of the most widely used homoeopathic remedies. For bad falls and bruising it is best to combine homoeopathic arnica internally with an arnica ointment as an external remedy – but not if the skin is broken for it can cause severe irritation. It appears to relieve bruising by causing reabsorption of internal bleeding.

Sprains can be treated in exactly the

ARNICA COMPRESSES

As an alternative to ointments and lotions, a hot compress of arnica can be applied to bruises and boils. Add two tablespoons of arnica flowers (about 10-15 grams) to a litre (1¾ pints) of water and boil for five minutes. Then soak a compress in the infusion and apply while still hot. This should not be used if the skin is broken.

In Germany, beer rather than water was often used for arnica compresses. The French apply the same sort of compresses to soothe sore throats and treat laryngitis, while in the USA these compresses are used for stomach pains.

Arnica tincture still appears in the official French pharmacopoeia and is made by macerating 50g (2oz) of the flowerheads in 250ml (9 fl oz) of 60° alcohol in a stoppered jar for 10 days. The jar should be shaken from time to time and the tincture finely filtered or pressed.

Although the tincture should be stored at this concentration it must be substantially diluted before use: for compresses, add a teaspoon (5ml) of tincture to a tumbler of hot water.

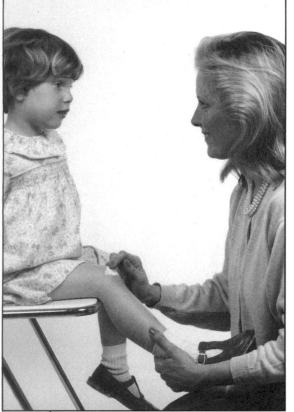

Arnica is ideal for bruised knees.

same way – internal homoeopathic doses of arnica plus an appication of arnica ointment to open wounds. Taking arnica tablets internally does help in cases of bleeding – be it from a cut, injury or even nosebleed. Homoeopaths also recommend arnica for black eyes – not ointment this time, but internal doses of the remedy which should be taken until the bruising and swelling subsides.

SOOTHING EFFECTS OF ARNICA

Homoeopathic arnica can also assist recovery from any sort of trauma or shock – be it mental or physical. Cases of physical exhaustion and weakness, or the insomnia that may result from over-tiredness can all benefit from arnica. To relieve fatigue and aching muscles relax in a hot bath that contains two teaspoons of arnica tincture. Similarly, a teaspoon added to a foot bath will ease tired feet.

In France, arnica is known as the *herbe des chutes* (a *chute* is a fall) because of its value in any sort of accidental upset. As well as being a useful remedy for shock it also assists the natural healing process and regular doses of homoeopathic arnica tablets (usually one tablet taken at half-hourly intervals is adequate) after an

operation really do speed recovery. It can just as readily be taken after a trip to the dentist, especially after an extraction and homoeopathic arnica is also often given immediately after childbirth, repeating the dose every 15 minutes until the mother feels comfortable. Not only does it help to relieve sore muscles and bruising but can also speed healing if there has been an episiotomy.

The German writer Johann von Goethe once claimed that his life was saved when he took arnica – a traditional European remedy for the treatment of fevers – while he was suffering from a particularly high fever which had failed to respond to any other form of treatment.

Although arnica has been known as a diaphoretic (stimulating perspiration) for centuries, recent research also suggests that it has an anti-bacterial action and can stimulate the immune system via the white blood cells.

KEEP YOUR HAIR ON

Among its many attributes arnica has also been credited with boosting hair growth. It is sometimes used in lotion or ointment form or added to the final rinse after shampooing. In cases where hair loss is mild, such as after an illness, arnica can stimulate the regrowth of hair.

Again, only diluted mixtures should be used (see compresses), but stop if there is any skin irritation.

ARNICA IN LABOUR

Arnica is often prescribed for the woman in labour. If the woman is suffering from exhaustion during a long labour, arnica can not only relieve the aches and pains of physical exertion, but also help the woman to overcome the shock and trauma experienced during the birth process.

Arnica is also invaluable after delivery as it enables the mother to recover from the experience more quickly and it can also help to reduce swelling and bruising and the discomfort of stitches.

Pregnant women should always seek professional advice before taking arnica, however – and recommended doses should never be exceeded.

HAZARDS OF ARNICA

Despite its obvious advantage, it must be remembered that arnica is poisonous in large, or undiluted, doses – it irritates the digestive tract and kidneys and excessive doses can lead to vomiting and dizziness. If arnica is taken internally, ideally it should be as a homoeopathic dose, or prescribed by a qualified herbalist or homoeopath – it is much better to opt for patent preparations than to risk brewing up arnica flowers yourself.

It should never be applied to broken skin so care must be taken, when treating bruises. Sensitivity to arnica can vary enormously between individuals and even if there is no wound some people quickly develop skin rashes with arnica ointments or creams. It is always wise to test it first on a small area of skin.

BACH FLOWER REMEDIES

Treating the person not the disease

A unique form of treatment from the wild plants of the countryside that tackles the negative emotions causing disease

The Bach flower remedies were developed by Dr. Edward Bach in the 1930's and have increased in popularity ever since. In the belief that all sickness is a product of negative states of mind, Dr. Bach used the essences of certain wild plants to treat the underlying emotional reasons for illness. After carrying out experiments over a number of years with numerous different plants, he made a final selection of 38 flowers and trees from which to extract the essence. These, Dr. Bach divided into seven groups, corresponding to emotions which he believed to be the most common negative states of mind occurring in human nature:

1 fear
2 uncertainty
3 lack of interest
4 over-sensitivity
5 despondency
6 loneliness
7 over-concern for the welfare of others

TREATING THE EMOTIONS

Dr. Bach believed in treating the patient's emotional state, not the disease, because every illness had its roots in the patient's character. He believed that, just as a minor worry, or irritating thought, will automatically cause a frown to appear on the face, so a continued, larger concern will have a correspondingly greater effect on the body – eventually causing physical illness to set in. The aim is to deal with the underlying emotional problem, before the physical symptoms set in.

Most people have suffered from indigestion or tension headaches at sometime in their lives, and many of today's major illnesses are closely related to emotional 'symptoms'. The nature of the medical condition is unimportant: if, for example, fear is present, a remedy to combat fear is what the patient requires.

PRESCRIBING YOUR REMEDY

The Bach flower remedies are available from most health-food stockists and herbalists. It is usual to self 'prescribe' the remedies but, for your initial prescription, it may be advisable to consult a flower remedies specialist (or naturopath), as most people find it difficult to be honest with themselves about their personality traits and their emotional state of mind.

As the remedies are quite harmless. they have no unpleasant side effects, and can, therefore, be taken with other treatments, such as homoeopathic tissue salts, or vitamin supplements.

THE RESCUE REMEDY

Dr. Bach also formulated a potent mixture of five of the remedies – Cherry, Plum, Clematis, Impatiens, Rock Rose and Star of Bethlehem – which he called the 'Rescue Remedy'. It can be used in a wide variety of situations such as after an accident, on hearing bad news, during childbirth, before important interviews, going on stage or taking a driving test. It helps to relieve feelings of panic and restores natural balance to the body. It is not, of course, a miracle cure, but a very useful emergency aid – the latter day equivalent of smelling salts.

The Rescue Remedy is available in liquid form or as a cream, which can be used for cuts, bites or stings. The liquid can also be given to pets after an accident or when they are disturbed.

HOW TO TAKE THE REMEDIES

The flower remedies are sold as 'stock' – that is, concentrated essences of the individual plants, preserved in brandy. Mix two or three drops of the remedy, or remedies using the dropper supplied with each bottle, with a little water and sip slowly. Hold the liquid in the mouth for a moment before swallowing. If no water is available, put several drops directly into the mouth and again, hold for a moment before swallowing. Repeat the dose three times a day, after meals, for several weeks until an improvement is noted.

The Rescue Remedy should be taken whenever necessary, directly from the bottle.

Bach's eventual selection of essences include holly, honeysuckle, wild rose and clematis.

YOUR GUIDE TO THE BACH FLOWER REMEDIES

The remedies are divided into seven groups which are classified according to the predominant emotion of the individual state of mind. Each essence is itself administered to treat a particular aspect of that emotion.

1 FEAR
Aspen
For vague fears that something awful will happen, or nightmares.
Cherry plum
Fear of losing control and doing something rash.

Mimulus
Fear, for unknown reasons, of speaking in public, or of accidents. For shy, timid types.

2 UNCERTAINTY
Cerato
For those who doubt their own ability, are lacking in self-confidence and always seeking others' advice.
Gentian
Easily discouraged. Good for children who find it difficult to keep up with others at school.
Gorse
Feelings of hopelessness and despair.

Hornbeam
Can't cope with present difficulties: always procrastinating.

3 LACK OF INTEREST
Clematis
Dreamy, absent-minded and preoccupied. Often forgetful.
Honeysuckle
Nostalgic or homesick. Recently bereaved or living on their own.
Wild Rose
Apathetic, resigned, unwilling to change.

4 OVER-SENSITIVITY
Agrimony
Puts on a brave face, but desperate inside.
Centaury
Weak-willed, 'human doormat', cannot stand up for self, easily swayed by others' opinions.
Holly
Jealous, suspicious, bad-tempered, aggressive.
Walnut
For adjusting to changes in life – teenagers going through puberty or women in the menopause. When severing ties – changing jobs or giving up a relationship.

5 DESPONDENCY
Crab Apple
Often ashamed of self, and feels unclean. Houseproud.
Larch
Expects failure, so doesn't even try. Feels inferior.
Oak
Brave, determined type who 'struggles on' whatever the odds.
Pine
Blames self for others' mistakes. Guilt complex.

6 LONELINESS
Heather
Talkative, self-centred bores.
Impatiens
Impatient and irritable. Wants everything done quickly. Hates slow people.
Water Violet
Appears proud and aloof. Does not become personally involved.

7 EXCESSIVE CONCERN FOR OTHERS
Beech
Intolerant and critical of others.
Chicory
Possessive, easily offended. Selfish, expects others to follow their high standards.
Vervain
Fanatical, incensed by injustice. Uptight and finds it hard to relax.

DR EDWARD BACH
Dr Edward Bach (1880-1936) gave up his Harley Street practice and moved to the countryside in 1930, where he believed he would be able to identify medicinal healing agents in the wildflowers growing in the meadows. He wrote:
'Among the type of remedies that will be used will be those obtained from the most beautiful plants and herbs to be found in the pharmacy of nature.'

BIOCHEMIC TISSUE SALTS

Nourishing the body's cells

Many everyday aches and pains respond simply and safely to inorganic substances that can be taken in pill form and that occur naturally in the human body

It has long been known that inorganic salts – substances of mineral origin – are essential for the healthy working of the human body. But it wasn't until about a century ago that a German doctor, W. H. Schuessler, suggested that some of these substances, which are found naturally in the body, had potent and special healing powers.

He called these the tissue salts, because they were found in the tissues of the body. At the time he listed 12. This has now been extended considerably by modern experts in biochemics – the healing therapy which uses tissue salts.

THE BASIC GUIDELINES OF BIOCHEMICS
Schuessler detailed very carefully what each of the salts did in the body and looked at various ailments that could be cured by using them as medicines. He formulated a set of rules that still make excellent sense today.
1 Disease does not occur if cell metabolism (the process at the very heart of cellular function) is normal.
2 Cell metabolism is in turn normal if the cells of the body receive the right kind of nourishment.
3 Substances that nourish the body are either of an organic nature (having an organised physical structure) or an inorganic nature as far as the body is able to discern.
4 If there is a deficiency of the inorganic material (mineral salt) that helps to make up the body tissues, the body cells may have difficulty in carrying out the normal processes of assimilating and digesting foods and excreting waste.
5 The body cells can be properly nourished, and their metabolism brought back to normal, by supplying the required tissue salts to the body in a finely divided form which the body can deal with and make use of easily.

Biochemics – the healing use of the

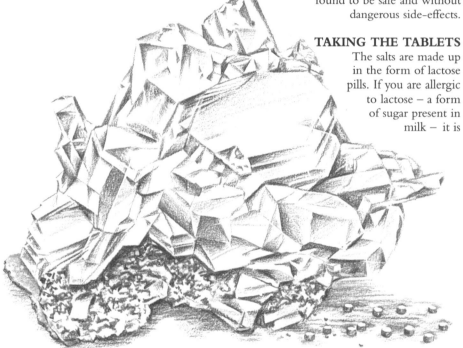

tissue salts – is really an extension of homoeopathy. The tissue salts are prepared in the same way as are homoeopathic remedies, but most of the original salts were included in the standard list of homoeopathic remedies many years before Schuessler expounded his biochemic therapy. In fact, Schuessler was greatly influenced by Samuel Hahnemann, the founder of homoeopathy.

SALTS – NATURAL BODY BUILDERS
In general, minerals have five main functions:
1 They are components of enzymes – protein substances which help to bring about certain biochemical reactions necessary for the body to function.
2 They are essential for nerve transmission.
3 They carry oxygen.
4 They form the building blocks that go to make healthy bones and teeth.
5 They are components of hormones.

The 12 original tissue salts (see box) were thought to be at the heart of all life systems, but with increasingly sophisticated methods of chemical analysis since Schuessler's day, another 30 have been identified by a an English expert, Dr Eric Powell, and other workers in the field have found more.

Although many a practitioner can attest to their effectiveness, no one knows exactly how tissue salts work. They probably function in the body much like other homoeopathic remedies, by stimulating the body's natural healing systems. After a century of experience with them, they have been found to be safe and without dangerous side-effects.

TAKING THE TABLETS
The salts are made up in the form of lactose pills. If you are allergic to lactose – a form of sugar present in milk – it is

SCHUESSLER'S 12 ORIGINAL TISSUE SALTS

Calcium fluoride (Calc. Fluor.)
Calcium phosphate (Calc. Phos.)
Calcium sulphate (Calc. Sulph.)
Iron phosphate (Ferr. Phos.)
Potassium chloride (Kali. Mur.)
Potassium phosphate (Kali. Phos.)
Potassium sulphate (Kali. Sulph.)
Magnesium phosphate (Mag. Phos.)
Sodium chloride (Nat. Mur.)
Sodium phosphate (Nat. Phos.)
Sodium sulphate (Nat. Sulph.)
Silicon dioxide (Silica)

probably sensible not to take them; otherwise, do not be put off, because the amount of lactose is very small indeed and should not cause problems except in the most highly sensitive people.

Choosing which salt to take requires some skill and experience, but there are commercial preparations on the market, some of which are combinations that have been found, by trial and error, to work better than single salts used alone. Tissue salts can be taken safely with other medications and are easy to take. Simply let the tablets dissolve under the tongue and use them as directed on the pack. Usually it is safe and effective to take them every couple of hours in the initial stages of an illness.

Biochemic tissue salts appear to act quickly in sudden-onset, short-lived conditions, but they may have to be taken for up to six months or more to produce results in chronic conditions. The turnover of the body's minerals in stores (as opposed to those in solution in the body's fluids) is slow and can take months. This is why results can take many months in long-standing ailments.

As with all do-it-yourself natural medications, it is vital to consult your doctor so that you know exactly what you are treating. This is of course, not necessary if the condition is a long-term one with which you are totally familiar, such as hay fever. And many such conditions respond well to the salts.

COMPLEMENTARY CURES
By and large, tissue salts are mainly used for everyday aches and pains. They are not intended to be used instead of medications prescribed by the doctor, but alongside them. Some people find that experience with the salts makes them confident to treat their common ailments without seeing a doctor, but if things are not improving or you are at all worried, do seek medical help.

About eight out of ten conditions that people go to their GP with are self-healing, yet we are all impatient to get better as quickly as possible. Often, medications prescribed by the doctor have undesirable side-effects and may do little good while the body goes about its self-healing process. Many users of tissue salts say that, in this waiting period, they prefer to take tissue salts than medications prescribed by their general practitioner.

CHECKLIST OF AILMENTS AND CURES

Some common ailments – and their biochemic remedies

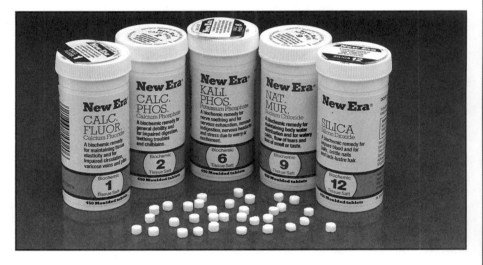

Acid regurgitation: Nat. Phos.
Acne: Calc. Sulph.
Anaemia: Ferr. Phos., Calc. Phos.
Anxiety: Kali. Phos.
Bronchitis: Ferr. Phos.
Burns: Kali. Mur.
Catarrh in ear, causing mild deafness: Kali. Sulph., Kali. Mur.
Colds – early stages: Ferr. Phos.
Colic in infants: Mag. Phos.
Cough – acute, painful, short and irritating: Ferr. Phos.
Cystitis: Kali. Mur., Ferr. Phos., Kali. Phos., Mag. Phos.
Dandruff: Nat. Mur., Kali. Sulph.
Depression: Kali. Phos., Calc. Phos., Nat. Mur.
Earache – with beating, throbbing pain: Ferr. Phos.
Fainting, tendency to: Kali. Phos.
Fatty food disagrees: Kali. Mur., Nat. Phos.
Fever – with chills and cramps: Mag. Phos., Ferr. Phos.
Gums – bleed easily: Kali. Phos.
Hair loss: Kali. Sulph., Silica, Nat. Mur.
Halitosis (bad breath): Kali. Phos.
Hay fever: Mag. Phos., Nat. Mur., Silica
Headache – at crown of head: Nat. Phos.
from mental work: Kali. Phos.
nervous: Kali. Phos.
Heartburn: Calc. Phos., Nat. Sulph., Silica.
Impatience and nervousness: Kali. Phos.
Irritability: Kali. Phos.

Laryngitis: Calc. Phos., Ferr. Phos.
Lumbago: Calc. Phos., 1/2 Ferr. Phos., Nat. Phos.
Menopausal symptoms – hot flushes: Ferr. Phos., alternating with Kali. Sulph.
Migraine: Kali. Phos., Nat. Sulph.
Nails brittle: Silica, Kali. Sulph., Calc. Fluor.
Nosebleed: Ferr. Phos.
Periods – heavy, too frequent and too profuse: Ferr. Phos.
heavy, with bearing-down pains: Calc. Fluor.
painful, relieved by heat: Mag. Phos.
Pimples on face: Calc. Phos.
Pregnancy: Kali Phos. and Calc. Phos. from 3-6 months before birth
Retching, with taste of food: Ferr. Phos.
Rheumatism: Ferr. Phos., Nat. Phos., Nat. Sulph., Silica

with swelling: Kali Mur.
Sciatica: Mag. Phos., Ferr. Phos.
Shyness: Kali. Phos.
Sleep, unrefreshing: Nat. Mur.
Sprains: Ferr. Phos.
Stings of insects: Nat. Mur. (applied locally)
Sweating at night: Nat. Mur., Silica, Calc. Phos.
Teething, with drooling: Nat. Mur.
Tiredness from overwork: Kali. Phos.
Travel sickness: Kali. Phos., Nat. Phos.
Ulcers in mouth, white: Kali. Mur.
Vaginal discharge – white, non-irritating: Kali. Mur.
scalding, yellow or orange: Kali. Phos.
yellow or greenish, slimy or watery: Kali. Sulph.
Varicose veins and ulcerations: Calc. Fluor.
Warts: Kali. Mur.

THE BITTER HERBS

From Paracelsus to the present day

This Scandinavian remedy which combines a variety of the bitter herbs is used principally for digestive problems

The old saying that if something tastes strong, it must be doing you good, is nowhere more true than in the context of bitter-tasting herbs and the herbal preparations which are made from them. The modern-day palate, used to bland flavours and taste sensations, is comfortable savouring sweet, sour and even salty foods. The reaction to a bitter-tasting substance is to block it out as quickly as possible – the 'spoonful of sugar' syndrome.

But as medical herbalists, Anne McIntyre, points out in her book, *Herbal Medicine*, 'Bitters are often referred to as 'bitter tonics' and, despite many people's dislike of them, for good effect they must be tasted.' There is growing evidence that the absence of bitter substances from our diet may be affecting our health – and not for the better.

HIDDEN RISKS IN EVERYDAY LIVING

Increasing awareness of the dangers of the so-called Western diet has been fostered by official and unofficial bodies.

The publishing of reports, articles in the press and the endorsements of Government ministers have all helped to create an understanding of the possible health hazards of a poor diet. It can be said that in general

people know now that too much fat, sugar and refined carbohydrate in the diet can cause ill-health and that several conditions such as obesity and lack of vitality and certain disorders such as cardiovascular disease can be linked to dietary causes.

DANGER IN THE AIR

Diet is something that most people can take responsibility for themselves and, where necessary, alter. More recently, concern is being voiced about the health hazards of something over which we have very little control – everyday environmental pollution. Walking or cycling to work may not be as healthy as we think, particularly if the route runs alongside heavy traffic conditions.

Fresh fruit and vegetables may be contaminated with traces of chemical pesticides either from crop-spraying or from the use of chemical fertilisers on the soil in which they are grown. Some fruit and vegetables are treated to give them a longer shelf life in supermarkets. The body can absorb all these chemical elements which, in turn, can lead to feelings of malaise, depression and, in severe cases, certain kinds of illness. Pollution can slowly start to build up in the body.

THE HISTORY OF THE BITTERS

Bitter tasting herbal elixirs have been used in herbalism for centuries. Paracelsus, the famous health philosopher and physician, recorded the formula for his Elixir of Life in the 16th century. It included the herbs aloe, myrrh and saffron. Aloe, well-known to generations of nail-biters, is a native of Africa and the sharp-tasting juice from the leaves is the part used (see ALOE VERA). Saffron was imported into the UK from the East many centuries ago and was once grown extensively in Essex around Saffron Walden. It is a member of the crocus family and the flower stamen are used by herbalists in the preparation of a number of different remedies. Myrrh is a shrub native to Arabia and Somaliland. The gum resin has an astringent and disinfecting action. Mrs Grieve in her book, A Modern Herbal, describes it as a tonic for dyspepsia and for exciting appetite and the flow of gastric juice.

The formulation put together by Paracelsus was recreated in the mid-19th century by a Swedish doctor, Klaus Samst, who extended the formula to include extracts from 11 herbs. Dr Samst is reputed to have lived to 104 and died after falling from his horse. Not even the bitters could prevent this!

A mature camphor tree grows by the side of a lake in Hangchow, China.

Internally-taken bitter herb elixirs.

TURF OUT THOSE TOXINS

The liver is the main detoxifying organ of the body and so it will be involved in any programme of detoxification and anything which can 'nudge' it into action must help. The expression 'feeling liverish' is generally understood, but what to do about it is something different – the feeling will last for a while and then, we hope, go away of its own accord.

It is in the context of detoxification that bitter-tasting herbs come into play, for it has been found that taking a regular and precise dose of bitters can help to stimulate the metabolism, encourage the secretion of digestive juices in the stomach and increase the flow of bile from the liver. Experience in using these herbs has shown that they should never be used alone but always in combination with other substances. Herbs which have a mild laxative effect are the most complementary.

The action of bitters also means that anyone who has digestive problems will find them beneficial to take on a regular

Three important bitter herbs are, from top to bottom, camphor, flake manna and carline thistle.

An aloe plant in southern Africa.

or occasional basis. For example, travelling abroad and coping with rich, unfamiliar foods can play havoc with the digestion – as can long business lunches or dinners. Hangovers are another problem which respond well – a dose of bitters first thing in the morning is more effective (and healthy than a 'hair of the dog').

TAKING THE BITTERS

If the taste is unacceptable (and it must be admitted that women find this more of a problem than men, for some reason), the bitters can be mixed with a fruit juice or herb tea or taken neat with a little honey. This in no way mitigates the action of the herbs.

For detoxification purposes, it is recommended that a course of bitters is taken twice a year – spring and autumn seem the most popular times – and that this is combined with a cleansing diet. To find out what this means and what foods are the most beneficial, Leslie Kenton's book, *The 10 Day Clean-Up Plan*, is a good reference guide.

For general digestive disorders, two teaspoonfuls of a bitters mixture can be taken twice a day. There is one word of warning. As would be expected, pregnant women or nursing mothers are not advised to take bitters. The same goes for anyone suffering from diarrhoea, intestinal obstruction or serious disorders of the liver.

TO THE PRESENT

Dr. Samst's formula came to light again this century when the Austrian herbalist, Maria Treban, was handed an old manuscript giving details of its preparation. Maria Treben uses the bitters mixture both internally and applied as a compress. Her book, *Health from God's Garden* sets out a surprising number of conditions which she believes respond to a course of bitters.

Perhaps this age-old remedy of bitter tasting herbs holds the answer to some of the problems caused by modern living conditions.

SUFFER FOR YOUR HEALTH

Strangely, the full benefits of bitter herbs do not occur if the remedy is given in a capsule to remove the taste – so put up with the nasty taste in the name of good health!

BORAGE

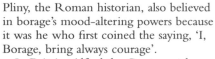

An age-old remedy that's right up to date

Its name may be a mystery, but there seems little doubt as to the usefulness of this ancient medicinal herb

Borage, or burrage as it is sometimes called, has been in use as a medicinal herb for so long that the derivation of its name has either been long-forgotten, or was never really known. The Arab physicians in medieval Spain knew it as *abou-rach*, meaning 'father of sweat', and used it to induce perspiration in people suffering from fevers. Another possible solution is that it gets its name from the Latin word *burra*, meaning 'high hair', because of its bristly leaves. Yet another theory is that the name is derived from the Latin *borrago* which, in turn, comes from the words *cor ago*, meaning 'I stimulate the heart'. Whatever the correct answer, it is clear that borage has been an important ingredient in herbal medicine since ancient times and is not often given the attention or credence that it deserves today.

GROWING BORAGE

Borage is very easy to cultivate. It thrives in poor, light, well-drained soil in direct sun or partial shade. Sow the seeds in spring, and you will have healthy, flowering plants by summer. The mass of cobalt blue flowers are not only lovely in themselves, but will attract the bees to your garden all summer long. Borage self-sows prolifically so, after the initial seeds planting, you could have a lifetime's supply of this historic herb that is as beautiful as it is useful.

OFFICIAL VERSION

Borage is easily recognised. It grows to between 30 and 70 cm (12 and 30 in) in height, has broad leaves with stiff hairs on both sides, and blue, star-shaped flowers that appear on the tips of the stems. The botanical name is *Borago officinalis*. The appearance of the word officinalis in the name of the plant indicates that it was recognised by the medieval medical profession as being as effective medicine. So much so, that the entry for borage in Culpeper's famous *Complete Herbal* (first published in 1653) gives more than 14 different medicinal used for the herb. Opinion seems to have been united on the subject of borage, and this 12th-century quotation, 'When talking of borage this much is clear, that it warmeth the heart and it bringeth good cheer', is typical of much that was written about this fascinating herb throughout the centuries.

Almost every historical description refers to its ability to bring happiness and comfort, and drive away melancholy. The ancient Greeks believed that borage, steeped in wine, was a sure remedy for depression. In ancient Egypt and Arabia, borage was grown as an ingredient for drinks intended to drive away sadness and bring back pleasant forgetfulness.

Best picked fresh from the garden, use borage seeds, stems, leaves or flowers.

Pliny, the Roman historian, also believed in borage's mood-altering powers because it was he who first coined the saying, 'I, Borage, bring always courage'.

In Britain, Alfred the Great must have taken borage because he described it as a 'maker of good blood', while Culpeper explained that borage was Nature's 'great cordial' and 'strengthener' because of its ruling astrological signs: Jupiter, for good fortune, and Leo, for bravery. He describes the leaves, flowers and seeds as being 'good to expel pensiveness and melancholy', and adds that borage is also good for 'those that are troubled with often swoonings, or passions of the heart'. Another well-known herbalist, John Evelyn, wrote, 'springs of borage are of known virtue to revive the hypochondriac and cheer the hard student.'

WHAT DOES IT DO?

Borage is rich in potassium and calcium and, as these are precisely the minerals that are used up most quickly by the body during stress, it is easy to see how its reputation for enhancing courage was gained. The plant contains a range of chemical substances, including saline mucilage, resins, tannins and volatile oil. Used externally, these ingredients make borage a soothing and healing application for skin irritations. Taken internally, it has a variety of actions, and these partly depend on the age at which the plant is picked for use. It is at its most soothing when young, and at this stage is often used in salads and soups, or cooked as a vegetable rather similar to spinach. It acts as a purifying agent, inducing sweating when it is in flower, and can be used as a diuretic (to stimulate the production of urine) when the seeds are ripening. The whole plant can be used, but the stem has the strongest concentration of active ingredients, then the leaves and lastly the flowers.

RAPID SPREAD

Borage originated in the Mediterranean area and the plant is thought to have been introduced into Europe by the Crusaders. It is known to have been cultivated in English gardens well before the 15th century because of its 'cordial qualities'. When the companions of Columbus landed on Isabella Island, one of the first things they did was to plant borage, thus ensuring its spread throughout the new world.

AN ALL-ROUND REMEDY

Among the health complaints for which borage has been used throughout its long history are: fever, poisonous bits, poor milk-flow in nursing mothers, depression, 'stale' system, debility after illness, anxiety, heated or fluctuating moods, red and inflamed eyes, sore throat, mouth ulcers, rheumatism and water-retention. Borage can be prepared in a variety of ways for chills, influenza and other fevers. The usual method is making a decoction by bringing a teaspoonful (3g) of

the dried plant to the boil in one litre (2 pints) of water, then allowing it to infuse for 15 minutes. Four of five cups of this borage tea can be taken each day. This also has a diuretic effect and can be used in cases of rheumatism. For the treatment of bronchial complaints, a stronger

The delicate, star-shaped borage flowers give individuality to a summer salad.

infusion is made then used as a steam inhalation. Borage is also used fresh, as part of a traditional, purifying cocktail, combined with watercress and dandelion leaves, and crushed to release juice.

IN THE KITCHEN

Raw borage leaves, with their subtle, cucumber-like flavour, are delicious in salads and sandwiches. Use whole or chop finely and add to yogurt or cream cheese. Ensure that the leaves you use are young and fresh ones, as the old ones are too bristly and dried leaves often lose their properties. The leaves can also be cooked as a vegetable, like spinach, and lightly buttered. In some areas of Italy, borage is used as a stuffing, again like spinach, for ravioli. Adding the leaves to spring cabbage at the end of cooking will give extra flavour. The attractive, blue flowers have the same refreshing cucumber taste as the leaves. They make an effective garnish sprinkled over salads or fruit and floating on summer wine or cider cups; when candied, they are used to decorate cakes or ice-creams.

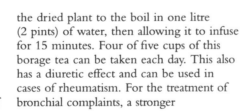

BORAGO

Borage has been found to yield an oil, known as 'oil of borago', that has an action similar to that of oil of evening primrose (see EVENING PRIMROSE OIL), as it is known to contain high levels of gamma linoleic acid but in a more concentrated form. This oil has, until recently, been used to mix with preparations based on evening primrose oil, but is now available on its own in capsule form.

CAMOMILE

Traditionally valued for its soothing qualities

In many European households, camomile is a standard item in the kitchen cupboard. French, German and Spanish children are often weaned on camomile tea to calm their childhood fears and help dispel nightmares

Similar in shape to the daisy, camomile (*Matricaria chamomilla*) is distinguishable by its dome-shaped centre and downward-pointing petals.

German camomile, Matricaria chamomilla, is recognisable by its white petals and domed yellow centre. A native to most parts of Europe and western Asia, it favours sunny positions and grows easily in chalky or sandy soil. Of all the varying types of camomile, this wild variety is said to be the strongest and it produces the best quality of essential oil.

GATHERING, DRYING AND STORING CAMOMILE

Like all flowering herbs, camomile should be harvested when the flowers have just opened – this is usually between July and September, although the time varies from year to year. Some herbalists suggest picking the flowers in the early morning on a fine day, just after the dew has dried, while others believe midday is the best time because the essential oils are at their peak. The traditional herbalists always collected their herbs on, or around the time of, the full moon, and camomile, being a herb of the sun, was collected on a Sunday.

In England, herbalists use only the flowers, whereas in many European countries, such as France, Germany and Spain the whole plant is collected and dried. It is sometimes easier to cut the whole plants and dry them in bunches, later separating the flower heads. A coarse comb can be used to speed the process. An airing cupboard, attic, spare room or dry shed are ideal places for the drying process, as long as the temperature is below 40°C (100°F). In a damp climate, drying can take a surprisingly long time, so allow six to eight weeks, except in the hottest of summers, when the drying is quicker.

Once dry, pack the flower heads into airtight containers – preferably not metal or plastic as this may affect

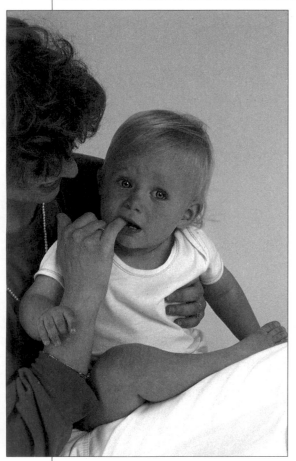

Camomile provides natural relief for babies suffering teething pains.

therefore a well-balanced, all-round remedy for the digestive system first relaxing, then healing and finally stimulating a healthy digestion.

BABIES AND CHILDREN

Camomile's strong and yet gentle action makes it an ideal remedy for babies and young children. The tea can be given in the feeding bottle, slightly sweetened with honey, or if the mother is still breast-feeding, she can take the tea herself and it will pass through to the baby in the milk. It is ideal for teething or irritable babies as it calms their nerves, soothes the pain and gives them, and the parents, a restful night. For older children, a nightly bath with camomile will settle them for bed. Better still, plant a camomile lawn and in summer allow the children to play on it while the baby sleeps nearby.

Camomile is ideal for over-sensitive children, and those with nervous stomachs, headaches, colic, nightmares and general timidity. In the language of flowers, camomile means 'patience in adversity' – perhaps for the mothers of such children.

A WARMING DRINK

For older people, camomile tea will help to ease constipation or stress-related bowel conditions, such as diverticulitis.

Soaking in a camomile bath makes a pleasant and soothing end to a busy day. The essential oil, present in the flowers, relaxes tired muscles and gives a restful night's sleep.

the taste – and store in a cool, dark place. It is important to keep camomile under airtight conditions, as it will reabsorb moisture very easily, and then mould will begin to develop.

ACTIVE INGREDIENTS

The main constituent of camomile is a volatile oil called azulene. This oil is released when the flower heads are crushed, or boiling water is added to them. You can see this for yourself when making a cup of camomile tea; the thin film of blue-green oil floating on the surface of the tea after brewing is azulene. It is this which gives camomile its strong distinctive fragrance.

Azulene is a relaxant, especially of the nervous and digestive systems. It slows and calms the nerves, without the deadening effect of tranquillisers which simply block feelings of anxiety. It relaxes the smooth muscle which lines the whole of the digestive tract, allowing food to move through it in a natural rhythm. It is this reduction of spasms in the gut that accounts for the fact that camomile eases colic in babies, and wind, dyspepsia, constipation or diarrhoea in adults.

The volatile oil also has an anti-inflammatory and antiseptic action, and the bitter component of the herb stimulates production of digestive juices. Camomile is

After your camomile bath, going to bed with a camomile pillow or tying a camomile herb sachet to the bedpost will mean waking up refreshed and ready to start the new day.

It has also been used in the treatment of migraine, irregular menstrual periods, peptic ulcers and colitis – all of which have been associated with stress.

It warms up the body and so benefits people who feel the cold badly in winter. It is also a good substitute for aspirin and other painkillers, which elderly people might find too harsh for their systems.

WOMEN AND CAMOMILE

For women, camomile provides a mild pain-killing action which helps ease menstrual cramps and the irritability of pre-menstrual syndrome. It is traditionally used for morning sickness in pregnancy, and for those odd aches and pains which can occur during the nine months. In bygone days, camomile was drunk during labour to both lessen the pain and give stamina to the mother. Menopausal women can benefit from the regular use of camomile tea, to ease tension and help with any sleeping problems that may occur.

ALLERGIES

Camomile can play an important role in the treatment of allergic reactions such as asthma and hay fever. It seems to act on he affected mucous membranes, reducing the body's reaction to the irritants and encouraging healing. It has an anti-histamine action and so reduces skin allergies and hay fever in particular. Inhalation of the essential oil of camomile flowers over a steam bath can be used to stop an asthma attack or ease it considerably.

A HERB OF THE SUN

The Elizabethans grew camomile in their knot gardens. Its bright yellow and white flowers contributed to the colour, fragrance and texture of the intricate geometric patterns.

Throughout the ages, camomile has been notable amongst herbs. It was revered by the Egyptians as a 'herb of the sun' as a treatment for fevers and chills. The Saxons chose it as one of their nine sacred herbs, and in medieval times camomile was strewn on the ground – its fragrant scent successfully marked the odours of a less hygiene-conscious age. The Elizabethans grew camomile in herb gardens and sowed it in perfumed lawns, and for the past 200 years its pretty white flowers and fern-like leaves have been decorating summer arbours.

In the early nineteenth century, farmers in Mitcham and Tooting, England grew fields of camomile and, at harvesting time in July and August, the whole village would participate, including the village children.

GOLDEN HAIR RINSE

A camomile hair rinse will leave your hair light, fragrant and shiny. It has mild bleaching properties and gives blond hair a golden sheen if used regularly over a period of time.
To make the rinse, pour one litre (two pints) of boiling water on to a handful of camomile flowers. Allow to soak for half a minute and strain. Use the rinse, warm, after shampooing and rinsing your hair normally. There is no need to wash the camomile hair rinse off before drying.

CAMOMILE PREPARATIONS

In the camomile preparations given below, it is no coincidence that they all involve the use of heat. This converts the medicinal ingredients into their active form. When heating, however, make sure to cover the preparation in order to avoid the loss of active components in the steam.

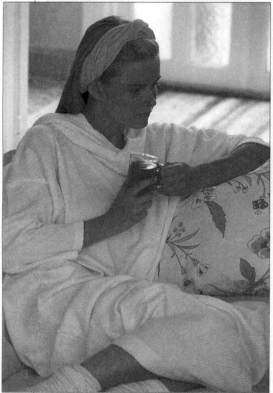

Adding honey to camomile tea hides the bitter taste.

CAMOMILE TEA
For digestive and nervous irritability.
Use up to two teaspoons of dried flowers per cup. Place these in a teapot, add boiling water, cover and allow to infuse for 10 to 15 minutes. Strain into a cup and drink warm.

Suitable containers in which to brew the tea should have a close-fitting lid – to prevent the loss of any volatile constituents – and be made of heat-resistant glass, glazed china or good-quality stainless steel. Containers made of aluminium will tend to affect the taste of the tea.

For those who find the slightly bitter taste of camomile tea unacceptable, half a teaspoon of honey can be added. This may be necessary in the case of children. As with all herbal teas, no milk is needed.

The best time to take this tea is before meals. It should be sipped slowly to give time for the stimulation of digestive juices and the regulation of muscle movement in the digestive tract ready for the ensuing meal.

CAMOMILE BATH
For exhaustion.
Scald four handfuls of dried flowers in a bowl, cover and allow to infuse. Strain and add the liquid to your bath water. Soak in it for 20 minutes, making sure that your heart is above the water line. Upon emerging, do not dry your skin, but wrap in a warm cotton bathrobe and blanket for about an hour, so that sweat is induced.

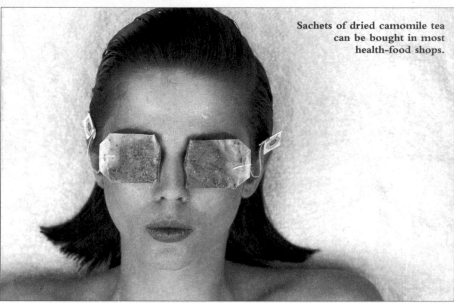

Alternatively, make a small muslin drawstring bag, fill it with camomile flowers and tie it under the hot tap. As the hot water pours through the bag it will rinse the oil into the bath.

CAMOMILE MILK
For aching eyes, rashes and skin irritations.
Soak one teaspoon (3g) of camomile flowers in 150ml (5 fl oz) of boiling milk for half a minute. Strain the liquid off, and soak a piece of clean cloth or a folded tissue in it. Place it over closed eyelids or on the irritable area of skin.

CAMOMILE FACIAL STEAM
For blackheads
Place a handful of camomile flowers in a bowl and cover with boiling water. Place a towel over your head and the bowl and steam your face for 10 minutes. Splash it with cold water to close the pores and pat dry.

CAMOMILE OINTMENT
For haemorrhoids.
Melt solid vegetable fat (not lard) in a bowl over a pan of boiling water. Pack in as many fresh camomile flowers as possible, cover and leave on a very low heat for about four hours. Strain the ointment, while it is still hot into a jar before the fat sets. Allow to cool and cover tightly. Store in a refrigerator and apply after each bowel movement.

Sachets of dried camomile tea can be bought in most health-food shops.

CAMOMILE OIL
For rheumatism and neuralgia (intense pain running along a nerve).
Pack a jar full of fresh camomile flowers, and cover with oil (sunflower oil is suitable). Close tightly and leave in a warm place, such as an airing cupboard, for three weeks, shaking the jar periodically. Press out the oil through a sieve and massage into the affected areas daily.

This oil can be used as a body massage to relieve physical tiredness. It is also said to remove unwanted body hair, but the hair is probably bleached slightly to make it less visible.

CAMOMILE INHALATION
For head colds and asthma.
Pour 500ml (1 pint) of boiling water on to a teaspoon (5g) of flowers. Lean over the bowl with a towel over the head, or with cupped hands round the top of the bowl, and inhale the steam.

CIDER VINEGAR

An organic cure for a wide range of diseases and complaints

A time-honoured, trans-atlantic folk remedy which has been used to treat a myriad of complaints from arthritis and hay fever to high blood pressure and excess weight

Cider vinegar lies at the heart of the folk medicine traditions of the farming state of Vermont in the USA. Today not only health-food stores, but most major supermarkets stock cider vinegar. The popularity of what was once a folk product, made simply by letting apple juice turn to vinegar naturally, owes a great deal to the book *Folk Medicine* written by a country doctor from Vermont, D C Jarvis, and first published in 1958.

Jarvis, whose family roots were in Vermont, underwent a conventional medical training, specialising in eyes, ears, nose and throat. However, he retained an enquiring and open mind when it came to traditional folk medicine, with which he was familiar through his family, and through his country practice.

Jarvis noted the long working life of many Vermonters, with many putting in a vigorous day's work on the farm when they were well into their seventies and even their eighties. They ascribed their prolonged vitality to a diet low in proteins such as meat and eggs, and high in carbohydrates such as root vegetables, fruit, leafy vegetables and berries. In addition, the Vermonters also placed a high degree of reliance on the regular intake of cider vinegar and honey (see HONEY). The practice was to take a couple of teaspoonfuls of each in a glass of water, at least once a day, although often the cider vinegar was used alone, or diluted with a little water, without the honey.

Jarvis was aware that there were long traditions of always serving something acidic with proteinous food, such as vinegar-dressed salads with cold meats; sorrel and other leafy, acidic vegetables with fish; cranberry sauce with poultry; pickles and chutneys with cheese and lemon juice or vinegar with beans or other kinds of pulses.

HEALTH SURVEYS
Applying scientific method to his studies, Jarvis enrolled the help of locals to carry out long-term surveys of health and illness as they related to certain specific conditions which could be monitored and altered by folk remedies. Chief among these conditions was the alkalinity or acidity of the urine. Litmus testing shows urine to have an acidic reaction when the body is fit and healthy, apart from an 'alkaline tide' that occurs just after eating. A number of bodily states can be reflected as an

PLUMBING INSPIRATION

Jarvis became interested in the effect of cider vinegar on calcium metabolism. The acid was capable of eradicating calcium deposits in domestic boilers, and local plumbers used it for this purpose. When his arthritic patients reported almost total relief after taking a course of cider vinegar, Jarvis surmised that the acid and potassium counteracted calcium deposits and helped the body control calcium use.

alkaline reaction in the urine, the tests normally being taken on rising in the morning (before drinking or eating), and just before the evening meal.

ANXIETY REACTION

Urine tests have indicated that states of fear or anxiety could cause an alkaline urine reaction. Other causes of an alkaline urine reaction include a high-protein, low-carbohydrate diet, the onset of complaints such as the common cold and childhood diseases such as chicken pox and measles, and conditions such as sinusitis, asthmatic attacks, and hay fever. In nearly all cases the regular administration of cider vinegar, which changed the urine reaction into an acidic one, was accompanied by an improvement in the medical condition. Symptoms either disappeared, or the attacks were extremely mild, and soon over. Where diet seemed to be the cause of the alkaline reaction, a shift to a higher

proportion of fresh vegetables and fruits, together with the cider vinegar supplement, soon restored the urine to the acidic state.

Not all acids have the required effect. It was noted that while a teaspoon of cider vinegar in a glass of water taken four times a day relieved arthritic pain in the course of a two-week treatment, a similar treatment with dilute hydrochloric acid actually increased the arthritic pains. It was also recommended that the intake of citrus fruits, such as oranges and lemons, should be kept to an absolute minimum as citric acid provoked an alkaline reaction, and could be harmful, especially for those whose metabolism has been conditioned by being born and bred in northern climates, where citrus fruits are not indigenous.

IMPROVED OFFSPRING

The Vermont farming folk applied the same remedies to their livestock as they applied to themselves. Cider vinegar was administered to pregnant women, and strong, vigorous offspring resulted in both instances. Potassium-deficiency in the Vermont region, due to lack of potassium in the top soil, was remedied by adding cider vinegar to the daily feed, as well as kelp (a type of seaweed) supplements. In the last week or two of pregnancy, cows received cider vinegar and iodine mixtures in their feed. Calves were strong, fully sized, on their feet within five minutes of birth, and bore a heavy coat of hair. Goats and chickens too benefited from potassium supplements in the form of cider vinegar, in that it improved both their general health and their fertility.

Jarvis studied all facets of Vermont folk

medicine, and recommended the use of honey, kelp, castor oil and corn oil. However, the principal place in the Vermont folk pharmacy is held by cider vinegar, which appears in a great range of applications.

As well as a general tonic, it is used as an important supplement for pregnant women, and as an antidote for neuralgic pain, headaches and migraine, sinusitis, high blood pressure, and arthritis. It has been used to quell stomach upsets as serious as food poisoning and to clear up inflammation of the kidneys. Cider vinegar washes and baths are believed to be far more beneficial than the use of soap, which is strongly alkaline.

The effects of cider vinegar on arthritis can be remarkable. The addition of it to cattle feeds has reduced the swollen and inflamed knees of some cows, as well as remedying milk yield problems and bovine infections.

HOME-MADE

The cider vinegar that features so predominantly in Vermont folk medicine is widely available, and is also easily made at home. Half-fill a non-metallic container with chopped apples, and top up with boiling water. Leave it uncovered until the tiny vinegar flies have done their work and turned the liquid sour – you should be able to smell the acid. Cover, and leave for a couple of weeks before straining thoroughly and putting in covered jars.

HONEGAR

Honegar is the trade name of a honey and cider vinegar mixture produced using British Cox and Bramley apples from Sussex and Kent orchards. The apples are matured in oak vats, and the vinegar is mixed with unpasteurized honey. Endorsements of Honegar have appeared in the national press from arthritis sufferers claiming remarkable relief from pain and immobility of arthritic joints after taking it for several months.

If you cannot find Honegar in your health-food store, write to the suppliers asking for the name of a stocklist near you:
Martlet Natural Foods, Horam Manor, Horam, Heathfield, East Sussex, TN21 0JA, U.K.

Cider vinegar, a tonic with great potential – look for organic brands.

FRAGRANT VINEGAR

Add one drop of rose, geranium, lemon, lime or orange oil per each 10ml of cider (or other) vinegar.

DANDELION

A natural cleansing
tonic, and stimulant
for a sluggish liver.

*Cursed by gardeners as a weed
in lawns and flower beds,
dandelion is, in fact, a
useful addition to the
medicine chest*

Few children can have grown up without experiencing the pleasure of telling the time by puffing away the downy seed-head of this common wildflower. Yet even though the dandelion is remembered fondly as part of a charming childhood game, its medicinal uses are often sadly neglected.

The dandelion grows naturally all over the northern hemisphere, thriving in meadows and on practically any scrap of waste ground. Flourishing most of all in sunshine, it flowers nearly all year round – provided there is no frost – a fact that accounts for its widespread, and seemingly continual, presence.

DANDELION THE CLEANSER
The dandelion plant is beloved of herbalists and practitioners of folk medicine. The whole plant – the flowers, leaves and the root – can be utilised in various ways. Dandelion has been regarded for centuries

as a stimulant for a sluggish liver: it is also thought to act as an overall, cleansing 'tonic': the salts in dandelion neutralise the acids in the blood, hence its cleansing action on the pancreas, spleen and the female sexual organs. In addition, the application of dandelion juice to warts is a

traditional remedy, while the leaves were used as a curative in ancient China, crushed as a poultice and applied to boils and abcesses.

DIURETIC ACTION
Dandelion's most important function is as a diuretic. By flushing out impurities in the blood, liver and kidneys, it helps to reduce water retention and swollen ankles (diuretics increase the flow of urine from the body and so tend to be used for heart and rheumatic complaints, amongst others). Most diuretics used in orthodox health care have the unfortunate effect of robbing the body of potassium. This is not the case with dandelion, for it naturally contains a high level of potassium and thus makes supplementary potassium unnecessary. Furthermore, its high potassium, sodium, iron and vitamin content makes dandelion especially beneficial in the treatment of anaemia.

NATURAL PICK-ME-UP

Herbalists recommend fresh dandelion leaves (taken in food or drink) as a remedy for poor appetite – such as often occurs through illness or anxiety. The very bitterness of the leaves, it is claimed, stimulates the digestive juices. Dandelion is also compounded with burdock as a traditional remedy for poor appetite or digestion. This combination is available in the form of a ready-made drink at many health-food shops.

Chopped and grated two-year-old dandelion root – a preparation that acts primarily as a tonic – is frequently used for liver ailments. The root is particularly effective in the treatment of cirrhosis of the liver, as it improves considerably the efficiency of the liver's detoxification process.

The grated root has also been shown to benefit certain rheumatic conditions, and the juice of the root has proved helpful in lowering blood sugar levels, thus making it a worthwhile remedy for those suffering from certain types of diabetes.

The dandelion clock from which seeds are blown after the flower has gone.

Lastly, the root can be used in the treatment of gallstones and non-obstructive jaundice, as well as chronic dyspepsia, chronic enteritis and gastritis.

DANDELION IN THE KITCHEN

The dandelion has numerous culinary as well as medicinal uses: the root, for instance, can be crushed and ground to make dandelion coffee. This palatable, though somewhat bitter, beverage provokes none of the unpleasant bodily reactions associated with ordinary coffee or tea. The stimulant caffeine, present in both tea and coffee, can cause an assortment of unwanted conditions, from raised blood pressure and indigestion, to the impairment of normal liver function. In fact, coffee made with dandelion has a positive

LION'S TEETH

Dandelion leaves are shiny and hairless. The leaf margins are cut into jagged teeth – sometimes sub-divided – which point either upwards or backwards. This may have given rise to the popular belief that the dandelion is so named because of the leaf's close resemblance to a canine tooth of a lion. The name dandelion is thus thought to be a corruption of the French 'dent-de-lion' (lion's tooth).

According to other sources, however, the dandelion is not so named on account of its appearance. These sources attribute the name to a fifteenth century surgeon who was reputedly so impressed by the plant's ability to heal certain illnesses that he declared that it was 'as strong and powerful as a lion's tooth'.

The distinctive leaves of the dandelion which resemble rows of jagged teeth.

toning effect on the liver, and helps to keep the bowels healthy.

Fresh dandelion leaves make a nutritious, readily available addition to salads, soups and even sandwiches. Young, fresh leaves only should be selected, otherwise they may taste unpleasantly bitter. Furthermore, the 'tops' (the flowers and the freshest looking leaves) can be infused to make a curative tea which is useful for

biliousness and swollen ankles. Use a handful of the tops to 575ml (1 pint) of boiling water. Leave to 'brew' for about 10 minutes, strain, and stir in a teaspoonful of clear honey. This drink can be taken several times a day.

GATHERING DANDELIONS

The best time to collect dandelion roots is between June and August when they are at their bitterest; but gather only large,

DANDELION COFFEE

Dandelion roots should be dug between June and August. Wash them thoroughly – two ancient recipes suggest the easiest way to wash the roots is to 'put them in a net under a waterfall', or to 'leave them in a basket in a running stream'. If this sounds impractical, rinsing the roots under running water in your sink will do just as well.

Dry the roots in a gentle heat until bone dry, either in sunlight or an airing cupboard. Roast the roots slightly in a cool oven until brown, then chop and grind them: the grounds are used to make dandelion coffee. Simmer approximately 5ml (1 tsp) of the dried, ground root in 150ml (5 fl oz) water for a few minutes, then strain and add milk to the liquid.

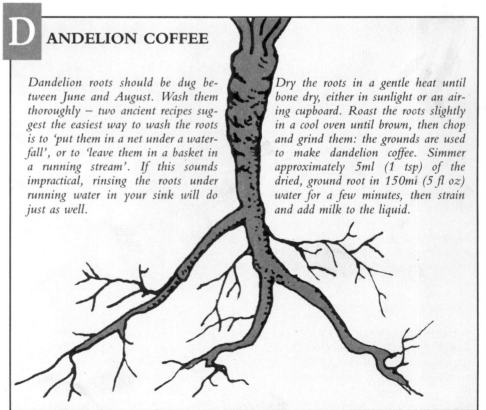

ANDELION TEA

Put 50g (2oz) chopped, fresh dandelion herb – or 25g (1oz) dried, powdered leaf – into a non-metallic pot. Pour over 500ml (1 pint) of boiling water, cover and leave to brew for approximately 10 to 15 minutes. Three small cupfuls a day of this potassium-rich infusion will help to alleviate water retention and reduce swollen ankles.

fleshy, well-formed roots from the older plants. Dig the roots in wet weather (not when there is a frost) as this is when their healing properties are greatest, but take care to avoid breaking or damaging them while digging. The roots can then be dried whole or split lengthways. This is a slow process which usually takes about two weeks.

Dandelion leaves should be collected when young, and can be used dried (overnight in a warm airing cupboard) or fresh. As they can be picked all year round, use them fresh when possible.

DANDELION SALADS

Using your hands, rather than a knife, shred three or four fresh dandelion leaves per person (tearing is preferable to cutting, as more flavour is retained). Grate or dice a tart eating apple, and sprinkle this over the top of the leaves: add a little vinaigrette dressing to prevent discolouration. Top the apple and dandelion leaves with chives, or with chopped nuts, sultanas or dates.

This nutritious salad can be served with dandelion beer as a delicious light meal. Pick several handfuls of fresh young dandelion leaves (preferably in April). Rinse them well in cold running water and mix with lemon juice, olive oil, half a teaspoonful of nutmeg, diced smoked tofu and hard-boiled eggs. Serve with lightly toasted wholemeal bread.

Make a crisp salad with a difference using fresh dandelion leaves instead of lettuce. Nasturtium flowers as decoration add a vibrant touch of colour.

WHAT'S IN A NAME?

An ancient English document called the '*Doctrine of Signatures*' puts forward the theory that the characteristics of a plant – its colour, shape or habitat, for example – give clues as to its uses.

Therefore the dandelion, with its bright yellow flowers of a 'bilious hue', is associated with liver and gall-bladder complaints.

Similarly, even the common name of a plant can be of use in fathoming its medicinal qualities. In Tudor England, for example, the colloquial term for dandelion was 'piss-a-bed' – referring of course to dandelion's diuretic property. The colloquial French name for dandelion, 'pis-en-lit' – a literal translation from the English – also reflects this property.

Dandelion's latin name *taraxacum*, is possibly derived from the Greek *taraxos* meaning disorder and *akos* meaning remedy. Again, this alludes to the curative powers of this plant.

DANDELION SPREAD

To make this spread, you will need a cupful of young dandelion leaves. Wash gently and pat dry on a clean tea towel, then place them in a blender. Add half a cupful of cottage cheese, and a quarter of a cup of chopped nuts: blend together until smooth. Add enough mayonnaise to make the mixture easy to spread.

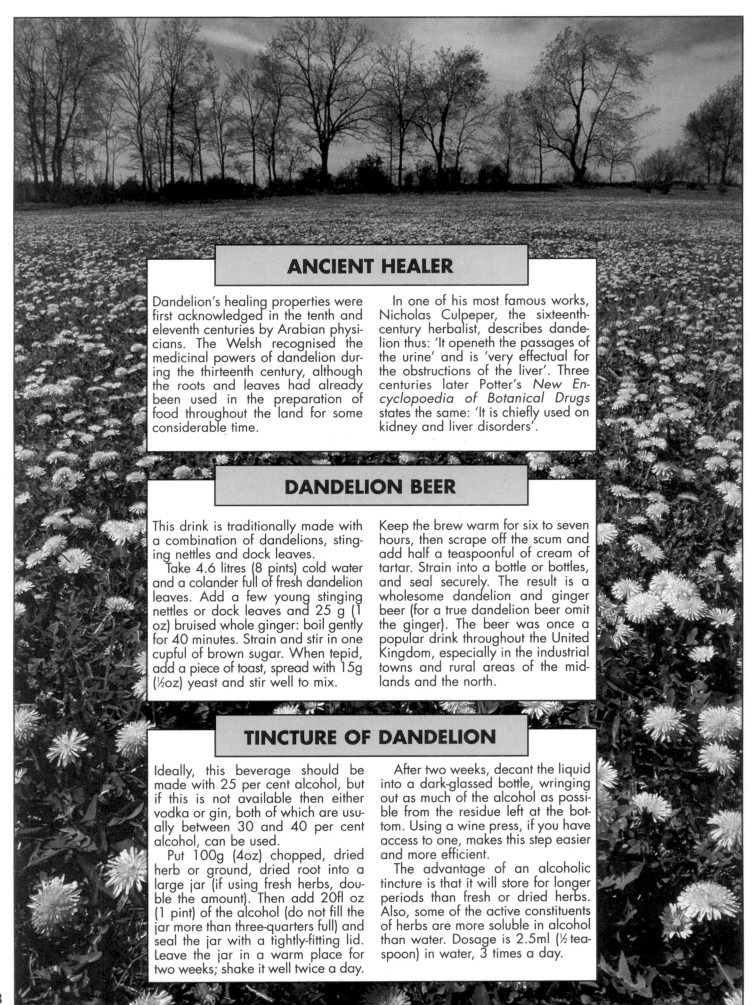

ANCIENT HEALER

Dandelion's healing properties were first acknowledged in the tenth and eleventh centuries by Arabian physicians. The Welsh recognised the medicinal powers of dandelion during the thirteenth century, although the roots and leaves had already been used in the preparation of food throughout the land for some considerable time.

In one of his most famous works, Nicholas Culpeper, the sixteenth-century herbalist, describes dandelion thus: 'It openeth the passages of the urine' and is 'very effectual for the obstructions of the liver'. Three centuries later Potter's *New Encyclopoedia of Botanical Drugs* states the same: 'It is chiefly used on kidney and liver disorders'.

DANDELION BEER

This drink is traditionally made with a combination of dandelions, stinging nettles and dock leaves.

Take 4.6 litres (8 pints) cold water and a colander full of fresh dandelion leaves. Add a few young stinging nettles or dock leaves and 25 g (1 oz) bruised whole ginger: boil gently for 40 minutes. Strain and stir in one cupful of brown sugar. When tepid, add a piece of toast, spread with 15g (½oz) yeast and stir well to mix.

Keep the brew warm for six to seven hours, then scrape off the scum and add half a teaspoonful of cream of tartar. Strain into a bottle or bottles, and seal securely. The result is a wholesome dandelion and ginger beer (for a true dandelion beer omit the ginger). The beer was once a popular drink throughout the United Kingdom, especially in the industrial towns and rural areas of the midlands and the north.

TINCTURE OF DANDELION

Ideally, this beverage should be made with 25 per cent alcohol, but if this is not available then either vodka or gin, both of which are usually between 30 and 40 per cent alcohol, can be used.

Put 100g (4oz) chopped, dried herb or ground, dried root into a large jar (if using fresh herbs, double the amount). Then add 20fl oz (1 pint) of the alcohol (do not fill the jar more than three-quarters full) and seal the jar with a tightly-fitting lid. Leave the jar in a warm place for two weeks; shake it well twice a day.

After two weeks, decant the liquid into a dark-glassed bottle, wringing out as much of the alcohol as possible from the residue left at the bottom. Using a wine press, if you have access to one, makes this step easier and more efficient.

The advantage of an alcoholic tincture is that it will store for longer periods than fresh or dried herbs. Also, some of the active constituents of herbs are more soluble in alcohol than water. Dosage is 2.5ml (½ teaspoon) in water, 3 times a day.

DEVIL'S CLAW
An ancient African herbal cleanser and detoxifier

Devil's Claw has been used in South West Africa for centuries and more recently in other parts of the world against rheumatic conditions and other ailments

The complete Devil's Claw plant (left) comprises flowers, roots and tubers, the last being used as a herbal remedy. The plant gets its name from the seed pods (above).

Devil's Claw (*Harpagophytum procumbens*) is a plant native to South West Africa, which grows in the Kalahari Desert and the grasslands of Namibia. Its name, Devil's Claw, derives from the claw-like shape of its seed pods, which are about the size of a hand and have 'fingers' armed with vicious-looking, hook-like thorns. (These often get embedded in the mouths of grazing animals, preventing them from eating.) The plant has fragile, creeping stems and, when the rains come, produces trumpet-shaped flowers, rather like those of the bindweed, which are a red-violet colour.

To survive the long periods of drought that affect the areas where it grows, Devil's Claw puts down roots as far as a metre (1 yard) into the soil, and produces brown tubers at different levels underground, which store water. It is these secondary roots which are used as a herbal remedy.

HISTORY AND RESEARCH

Devil's Claw has been used for centuries by the natives of Namibia for various ailments, including malaria, stomach troubles, gall-stones, rheumatism and arthritis. Women in labour drink Devil's Claw tea, which is thought to help to ease the process of giving birth, and the root is applied to wounds to stimulate healing.

Its discovery by the West began early this century when a German doctor observed that a tribal witch-doctor cured a very sick patient with the root. He sent samples to some laboratories in Germany, and research in Europe (particularly in Germany) and in America has gone on ever since.

In 1958, the root's anti-inflammatory action was demonstrated. One trial by a German professor resulted in the discovery that, after the use of Devil's Claw for five weeks, arthritic joints became freely movable again and swelling was reduced. He, and other doctors, noted that the healing process continued after treatment had ceased. A Dr Siegmund Schmidt prescribed it over a period of a year for more than a hundred of his rheumatic patients and found that it gave valuable support and that, in some cases, orthodox drugs could be dispensed with entirely. He further concluded that Devil's Claw 'stimulates the detoxifying and

AVAILABILITY AND USAGE

Devil's Claw, and combination remedies containing it, are available from health food stockists in a variety of forms:
• dried
• in filter bags
• as tablets
• as capsules (dried, ground or as an extract)
• ground and preserved in a liquid
   To prepare Devil's Claw tea from filter bags, boiling water should be poured over the bag and left to infuse overnight. The next day, a third of the liquid should be taken ten minutes before each meal: morning, lunch-time and evening. It tastes very bitter. To avoid this, Devil's Claw tablets or capsules can be taken instead or, alternatively, the fresh-ground root in a liquid suspension.
   A recommended dosage is three 250g capsules (or their equivalent in another form) taken three times a day before meals during the painful phase of rheumatism, reducing to four a day when the pain is lessened. This should be continued for three or four weeks, followed by several weeks' break. The remedy should be discontinued if there is no improvement after one month.
   Two or three tablets, crushed to a paste with hot water, can be used as an external arthritis application.
   Follow recommended dosages carefully and do not take Devil's Claw for more than three weeks unless under the instructions of a naturopath or GP.

Cutting fresh roots in the desert. They will be preserved in a wine base.   © Ortis

protective mechanisms of the body'. It has recently been discovered that the root contains some 40 constituents.

MEDICAL APPLICATIONS

Many sufferers from rheumatism, which affects the soft tissues, and rheumatoid arthritis, which affects the joints, have found Devil's Claw of benefit: documentary evidence indicates that six out of ten arthritis patients obtain relief from this remedy. It has an anti-inflammatory action, reducing pain, swelling and stiffness of inflamed joints and muscles, seems to cleanse and detoxify the body and stimulates the body's immune system. (Dr A Vogel, a Swiss naturopath, particularly recommends Devil's Claw for

counteracting modern-day pollution.) Devil's Claw can be used in combination with a wholefood diet and relaxation therapy, both of which seem to have a beneficial effect on rheumatic conditions.
   Devil's Claw helps the body to excrete excess fluid, and has been used to treat kidney, liver and bladder disorders and certain intestinal and circulatory problems. It can be soothing to skin irritations.
Our thanks to Ortis for their help in providing the photographs.

DEVIL'S CLAWS COMBINATIONS

Natural ingredients combined with Devil's Claw to relieve rheumatism and rheumatoid arthritis include: herbs, like garlic or white willow, chosen for their cleansing or anti-inflammatory properties; cod-liver oil, which is rich in vitamins A and D and essential fatty acids; mineral-rich kelp; vitamin B_6; and vitamin B_5 (pantothenic acid) (see GARLIC; KELP; WHITE WILLOW BARK).

CAUTION FOR DIABETICS

Diabetics should not take Devil's Claw except under strict medical supervision, since it can significantly lower the dose of insulin they need – thus they run the risk of overdosing with insulin.

Devil's Claw comes as tablets, capsules and in liquid suspension.

The body's natural painkiller

*Being in constant pain can be a life-destroying experience.
But there is hope. Painkilling compounds are found in many natural
substances. Herbs, foods and minerals can be
sources, so too can our own bodies*

Notable among herbal pain relievers are the opium poppy, the Californian poppy, aconite, wild lettuce, yellow jasmine, and Jamaican dogwood. Homoeopathic compounds for pain relief are derived from animal and mineral sources, as well as from plants. Examples include cuttle fish (SEP – Sepia Officinalis), arsenic (ARS – Arsenicum Album), and magnesium carbonate (MAG-C – Magnesia Carbonica). But it can come as a surprise to discover that our bodies, too, have the capacity to manufacture analgesic chemicals of their own. One amino acid in particular, Phenylalanine, often referred to by its chemical name, DLPA, has been shown to have far-reaching effects in pain control. A great deal of time and research has been aimed at discovering the nature and mode of action of the endorphins and encephalins – pain releaving brain chemicals whose release is encouraged by prolonged aerobic exercise. Low levels of serotonin, a chemical neurotransmitter responsible for transporting messages between groups of brain cells, and a natural mood elevator, have been linked with a reduced pain threshold.

Adrenalin and noradrenalin are hormones released during stress and exercise by the adrenal glands. These are partly responsible for the lack of pain many people experience after a serious injury – the type of injury that often follows a sudden burst of extreme stress which has, in turn, been caused by a fight or other emergency requiring vigorous activity.

ACID TEST

All these compounds – endorphins and encephalins, neurotransmitters and stress hormones – are proteins synthesized by the body from the amino acid building blocks that make up proteins. We obtain these from the protein foods we eat – meat, fish, eggs, dairy products and vegetables – which are broken down during digestion in the small bowel into their constituent units and absorbed into the bloodstream.

Amino acids play numerous vital biochemical roles, from helping to repair and replace old and damaged tissues, to acting as a source for the synthesis of enzymes, hormones and other cellular chemicals. Around 16 major amino acids have been discovered, and they are labelled from the point of view of dietary requirements, as either essential or non-essential. The latter, for instance tyrosine, alanine and aspartic acid, our bodies can make for themselves. The essential amio acids, which cannot be synthesized by the body, include tryptophan (see NATURAL CALMATIVES), from which serotonin is made, and phenylalanine, which gives rise to both tyrosine and to adrenalin and noradrenalin.

INDIVIDUAL ACTIONS

It has been found possible to isolate amino acids, like vitamins, minerals and trace elements, in the form of supplements and to use them to produce specific beneficial effects. Tryptophan, for instance, which is now available both as a supplementary dietary nutrient and as a drug, can relieve depressive illnesses, act as a sedative, encourage sleep and increase the body's pain threshold. Phenylalanine (also known chemically as DL-phenylalanine or DLPA), has proved beneficial in the treatment of

PMS PRESCRIPTION

Some recent studies and research indicate that pre-menstrual tension symptoms may also be associated with the release of endorphins. In the United States, many women have been successfully treated for PMS just by strictly adhering to a vitamin-and mineral-rich diet, together with supplements of DLPA.

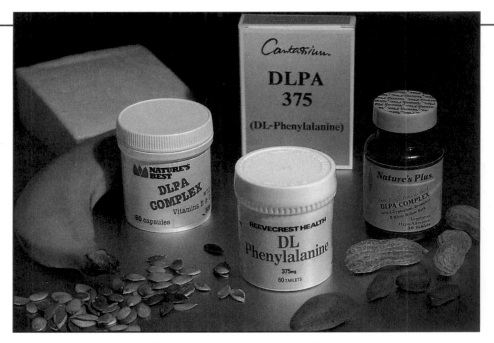

Everyday food items such as bananas and peanuts are rich in DLPA, but for specific treatment and pain relief, DLPA supplements are probably more helpful.

chronic pain and other disorders.

DLPA is broken down by the body in a chain reaction, the successive stages of which run through tyrosine, L-dopa, dopamine, adrenalin and noradrenalin. Besides its actions as a pain reliever, various different research programmes have shown that this natural nutrient can relieve depression, improve memory and mental alertness, increase sexual interest, suppress the appetite and also be of assitance in the treatment of Parkinson's Disease.

Dopamine, for instance, the next stage on from L-dopa, has been known since the 1960s to relieve Parkinsonism. It has to reach the next stage, L-dopa, for this effect to be realised, and the drug L-dopa has become the mainstay of clinical treatment for this condition. L-dopa is prescribed instead of dopamine itself, because dopamine does not cross the blood-brain barrier. Adrenalin and noradrenalin play vital roles besides those of stress hormones. They are released by nerve endings and brain cells, where they act as neurotransmitters mediating both sympathetic nervous activity and brain impulses.

UNSUITABLE TREATMENT

Sympathetic nerves increase the rate and force of the heart beat; raise the blood pressure; suppress the action of the digestive organs; dilate arteries to muscles, including the coronary arteries supplying the skin and abdominal organs; stimulate the sweat glands and hair root muscles in the body; and dilate the pupils. Some of these effects make DLPA unsuitable in cases of migraine, depression treated with monoamine oxidase inhibitor (MAOI) drugs, (for example pargyline, phenelzine, procarbazine, isocarboxazid), phenyl-ketonuria (PKU), and heart disease.

It is generally thought that an increased production and release of adrenalin and noradrenalin in the brain and other body

tissues probably accounts for DLPA's ability to relieve chronic pain. Increased brain levels are responsible for DLPA's anti-depressant effects since, in common with serotonin, adrenalin and noradrenalin are also mood mediators. Low levels of adrenalin and noradrenalin have been discovered in a number of depressed patients, and the MAOIs act as antidepressants by raising the level of both neurotransmitters and dopamine in brain tissue.

DIETARY SOURCES

Natural sources of DLPA include cheese, non-fat dried milk, pickled herrings, peanuts, avocado pears, bananas, lima beans, almonds, and sesame and pumpkin seeds. Supplements are available as tablets from health food stores, but check with your doctor before taking them if you are pregnant or being treated for high blood pressure. Like other natural nutrients, DLPA is safe to take provided you do not suffer from any of the complaints that contra-indicate its use, and take the specified dose. Reported adverse reactions include raised or lowered blood pressure and migraine headaches, and the chances of these occurring are increased by taking supplementary tyrosine concurrently, which should therefore be avoided. But comparative research indicates there is less risk of toxicity from DLPA than from even vitamin C and one of the other 'side-effects' experienced included a surge in energy and activity.

KNITTERS' CHOICE

Mrs Bertha Pocock, aged 52, went to her doctor complaining of 'never being free from pain' as she has suffered from osteoarthritis for the past 10 years.

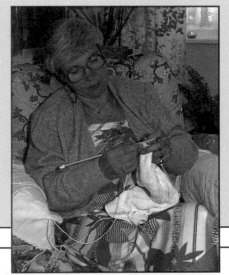

Her GP had prescribed several varieties of anti-inflammatory drugs for her condition but the side-effects caused her to abandon treatment after recurrent bouts of stomach pain and diarrhoea. Various other nutritional supplements had been tried but no benefit had been gained from Devil's Claw, and neither fish oil extract nor green lipped mussels were satisfactory since she was allergic to fish.

Finally her doctor recommended supplements of DLPA. These were taken after breakfast every day and, after a month, Mrs Pocock told her doctor that she was very much better. She was able to walk further, and she was sufficiently improved to resume her previous hobby of knitting.

WHAT TO EAT

Cheese, peanuts, avocados, bananas, herring and sesame seeds are all good dietary sources of DLPA.

ECHINACEA

Purple panacea

The purifying and anti-bacterial properties of echinacea make it a valuable herbal treatment, both internally and externally

Echinacea is a relatively unknown plant, yet it is an important remedy in many areas of herbal medicine. It is perhaps better known in the UK as an ornamental plant, of which there are white, yellow and purple species. The two species used in herbalism are both purple – *Echinacea angustifolia*, and to a lesser extent *Echinacea purpurea*, both possess healing powers, which are contained in the roots.

Echinacea is a native of the United States where it grows in the Western prairies. In Europe it is cultivated as an attractive garden plant. Sometimes called the purple coneflower, *Echinacea purpurea* has a stout, bristly stem with tapering, hairy leaves, but its most distinctive feature is its purple flowers. These are in the form of downturned petals surrounding a cone of pointed bracts, the shape of which is reflected in its generic name – echinacea comes from the Greek for hedgehog. It was given this name by the famous 18th-century Swedish botanist Linnaeus, while Rudbeckia was given in honour of the Rudbecks, the father and son who carried on Linnaeus's work in Sweden.

PATENT PURIFIER

Like many American plants, echinacea was known to the native Indians, who used it for a variety of applications, including the treatment of snake bites. In Mexico, it is also valued as a traditional medicine, to prevent and cure infections and inflammation.

Echinacea, under various names, was much in evidence in the 19th century, and referred to in some medical journals. It was the main ingredient of a patent medicine called Meyer's Blood Purifer – one of the many 19th century cure-alls for which exaggerated claims were made. However, echinacea was also used by physicians as a blood purifier, and for reducing fevers. Modern research has shown that it does possess quite remarkable healing properties.

Echinacea root is what is known in herbal medicine as an 'alternative'. Basically, this means it has the ability to alter the whole system. It affects the processes of metabolism to produce gradual and beneficial changes in the body, so that it functions more efficiently – the absorption of nutrients is improved, as well as the elimination of toxins. If this elimination is impaired there can be a build up of poisons within the body. A more familiar term for an alternative is blood purifier, and echinacea is one of the best available to herbalists – other herbs of this type include nettles (see STINGING NETTLE), burdock and red clover.

IMMUNE SYSTEM BACK-UP

Echinacea is also a very effective antiseptic. As a preventative it improves the body's resistance to infections of all kinds, and helps deal with existing infections, including those in the blood stream. It is of particular value for chronic infections and inflammation caused by toxic conditions, helping the body to heal itself by stimulating the white blood cells which fight infection. It is effective against bacterial and viral attacks, not so much by killing them as by reinforcing the body's own immune system. For this reason it may be useful in treating viral infections such as glandular fever and ME (myalgic encephalomyelitis).

FROM INSIDE OUT

One of echinacea's classic uses is as an internal remedy for skin problems. When there is infection, and elimination of the toxins is impaired, this can disturb the balance of body fluids, and septic conditions may arise, in the form of boils, abscesses, carbuncles or tissue inflammation. A course of echinacea tablets or a herbal blood purifer can help clear these up.

Other skin conditions, for example acne, dermatitis and eczema, can also be helped. Skin troubles such as these may have a variety of causes, among them stress,

NATURAL FIRST AID

Echinacea can be used in a variety of first aid treatments. One dusting powder available combines tinctures of the plants arnica and marigold (calendula) – both renowned healing herbs, (see MARIGOLD; ARNICA) with echinacea and other natural ingredients. This powder can be used for minor burns, sore patches of skin and for slow-healing wounds that need to be kept dry. Echinacea is also included in a number of homoeopathic ointments specifically for burns, combined with herbal tinctures such as St John's Wort, and marigold. To repel insects, and soothe bites, try a remedy called pyrethrum compound, which includes echinacea amongst its natural ingredients (see HOMOEOPATHIC FIRST AID).

Make your own honey–sweetened decoction, or buy one of the many commercial preparations.

For best results, the roots of echinacea are unearthed in autumn, after flowering.

allergies, or a poor diet with too much junk food. The basic causes do have to be tackled as well but a herbal remedy like echinacea can be used as part of the holistic approach.

Echinacea's antibiotic and cleansing properties may be of benefit in treating low grade respiratory infections, colds, tonsillitis, and catarrh. Echinacea may also be applicable to chronic inflammatory conditions such as rheumatism. Externally, it can be applied to wounds, infections, minor burns, or used as a mouthwash.

MIX AND MATCH
Echinacea is available as the dried root, or powdered in tablets or capsules. Certain tablets are specifically recommended for skin troubles. It is also widely used as an ingredient in combination herbal remedies,

ALTERNATIVE ANTIBIOTIC

Recent research undertaken in Germany has found that echinacea contains a chemical with strong anti-bacterial properties. Described as an anti-microbial, it can destroy or resist the micro-organisms that cause disease. For those who do not wish to take antibiotics, echinacea therefore provides an effective alternative. In recent years some General Practitioners have been prescribing a particular well-known herbal remedy for infections of the upper respiratory tract. This is a product that combines a well-tried trio of garlic, echinacea and medicinal charcoal. This remedy is particularly recommended for the relief of both catarrh and sinusitis.

such as liquid or tablet forms of blood purifying mixtures. In these it is combined with diuretic or other purifying herbs – burdock, clivers and yellow dock. These provide excellent blood–purifying formulas that are especially helpful for skin problems. In conjunction with other herbs it can be effective against infection anywhere in the body, for example, with yarrow or bearberry it can be an effective treatment for cystitis.

Echinacea is used in some herbal remedies for catarrh and hay–fever, when it is teamed with various natural ingredients and herbs like garlic. It is also available in a catarrh cream, applied directly to the nose, which contains plant tinctures with oils of peppermint, thyme and eucalyptus. Together with cutting out dairy products, which encourage the production of mucus, many people find echinacea, in conjunction with other recommended herbs, very useful.

MAKE YOUR OWN
Roots like echinacea are prepared by boiling in water – what is called a decoction. To make a decoction of echinacea, simmer 30g (1oz) of the dried root in 550ml (1 pint) of water for about 25 minutes. Strain and drink sweetened with honey, or use as a lotion. If you find the taste too unpalatable then take tablets or capsules. Standard recommended dosage is 0.5 to 1g of dried root equivalent three times a day.

SKIN CHANGES
Hormonal changes experienced during the teenage years, during and after pregnancy and the menopause can have a detrimental effect on the skin, and echinacea can be particularly helpful during these times. Echinacea improves the circulation of blood to the skin, as well as increasing resistance to infection which is particularly useful during adolescence when spots and blemishes can appear.

ELDER

A cold remedy from the hedgerows

Many myths, tales and traditions testify to the value of this pretty shrub as a herbal remedy

Elder (*Sambucus nigra*) is a familiar sight in many fields, hedgerows and gardens. Its clusters of powerfully scented, creamy-white flowers and small, dark berries are recognisable to most people – especially to connoisseurs of home-made wines. In the past, all parts of this plant – bark, leaves, roots, flowers and berries – were utilised; today, however, herbalists tend to concentrate on the elder's flowers and berries for their curative properties.

LOCATING ELDER

Indigenous to Europe, Western Asia and West Africa, elderflowers are grown commercially mainly in Europe, where they are collected in early summer. In the UK, this herb can be gathered from the wild – away from roadside and cropspray pollution. Since the 1986 accident at Chernobyl, prices for dried elderflowers have quadrupled due to plant contamination in some areas.

MEDICINAL USES

Elder is a specific for the common cold and respiratory infections. The main property of both the flowers and berries as a diaphoretic (inducing gentle perspiration in feverish conditions). They also act as an anticatarrhal (reducing mucus production), antitussive (reducing coughing) and expectorant (expelling respiratory mucus), which renders them useful in cases of influenza, nasal catarrh and deafness, sinusitis and pulmonary infections. The berries have been quoted as a mild laxative and anti-neuralgic (reducing nerve pain), as well as a valuable source of vitamin C. In general, the action of the flowers and berries is described as 'cleansing by improving elimination of wastes via skin, kidneys and bowel'.

The leaves, bark and root have a stronger purgative action than the berries, and the root is an emetic – so all are best avoided as internal remedies.

The elder tree flowers from May to July and produces berries not long afterwards, in the early autumn.

COLLECTING THE FLOWERS AND BERRIES

Gather the flowers on a dry, sunny day when they are in full bloom, and their medicinal contents are at a peak. Pick the whole umbrella of flowers and place in a paper sack or cardboard box. At home, comb the flowers off the stalks; fully-opened clusters will loosen as they warm up in the collecting bag. If they do not loosen easily, snip across the underneath of the cluster of flowers with a pair of scissors. Do not leave the stalks on, as drying time will be longer and the dried stalk can give a bitter taste.

When collecting the berries, choose fully ripe bunches. Pick them on a dry, autumn day, otherwise the berries will soon grow mould, and place them in a cardboard box so that the ripe fruits are not squashed. Provided that the berries are clean, washing is not essential. Strip the berries off the stalks with a fork, making sure to avoid any green berries as they will add a bitter flavour and produce a laxative action.

FOLKLORE AND TRADITION

The name 'elder' comes from the Anglo-Saxon word aeld, which means 'fire'. The shrub's common name is pipe tree, or bore tree, because the young, straight, hollow branches were used for blowing air into the embers of a dying fire, for woodwind pipes or flutes and for children's pop-guns.

It is a shrub with many magical and mythological connections. A dryad called the Elder-tree Mother was said to dwell in its branches; when the wood was cut to make furniture, the spirit was supposed to follow and haunt the owners. Some old people still refuse to burn elder wood and, in some areas, doff their caps at the plant as a mark of respect to the Elder-tree Mother.

Shakespeare refers to the elder in *Cymbeline* as a 'symbol of grief' and in *Love's Labours Lost*, Judas hanged himself on an elder. There is also a biblical reference suggesting that the cross of Calvary was made of elder, hence its reputation as an emblem of sorrow and death. In bygone days, the Russians hung up elder leaves to drive away evil spirits, and the Sicilians believed that elder sticks would kill serpents and ward off robbers. In England, a piece of elder tied in three or four knots was carried as a charm against rheumatism, and green elder branches laid in the grave during the burial ceremony were believed to protect the dead relative from evil spirits.

ELDER RECIPES

Recipes for elderflower and elderberry wine can be found in most wine books and are not, therefore, included here. Instead, a selection of other uses is given below, highlighting the versatility of this common shrub.

ELDERFLOWER TEA

For colds, influenza and sinusitis, elderflowers can be combined with peppermint, yarrow or hyssop (plus a little honey if desired) and taken as a hot tea at bedtime. These herbs will give restful sleep while cleansing the body and, on waking, the sufferer will feel better and be well on the way to recovery.

ELDERBERRY ROB

A 'rob' is a vegetable juice thickened by heat. Made with elderberries, it is a useful cordial for colds as the berries contain viburnic acid, a substance which induces perspiration.

Simmer 2.3 kg (5lb) of fresh, ripe, crushed berries with 450g (1lb) of sugar. Strain and evaporate the juice to the thickness of syrup. Bottle and store.

25-30ml (1 fl oz) in a glass of hot water, taken at night, will soothe chest complaints.

ELDERFLOWER OINTMENT

For chapped hands and chilblains, melt some solid vegetable fat in a basin over a pan of boiling water, and pack in as many fresh flowers as the liquid fat will hold. Cover and simmer for two hours. Strain it, when hot, into a container, allow to cool and cover. The ointment should be stored in the refrigerator.

ELDERFLOWER WATER

Pack a heatproof jar with elderflowers and pour on boiling water. Allow to cool slightly and then add 5ml (1 teaspoon) of isopropyl alcohol (obtainable over the counter at most chemists). Cover with a cloth and leave in a warm place for several hours. Cool, strain and bottle. This natural toilet-water soothes sunburn and has been said to clear freckles. If mixed with glycerin and borax and applied at night and in the morning, it keeps skin soft and fair. Alternatively, a small muslin bag of elderflowers can be soaked in the bath water to soothe skin irritations. Cold elderflower tea can also be used to bathe eyes when they are irritated or tired.

EVENING PRIMROSE OIL

The evening primrose could turn out to be one of the most valuable finds in plant and medical history

Every now and then there does seem to be a pot of gold at the end of the rainbow, in this, a pot of gold from the seeds of the evening primrose. This 'miracle plant' has long been a part of traditional herbal medicine and now modern medical research is demonstrating that there is a scientific basis for its success.

Unlike other notable healing plant extracts, evening primrose oil (EPO) is used to treat diverse and widely differing illnesses. These range from rheumatoid arthritis to benign breast disease, multiple sclerosis to eczema, from strengthening brittle nails to relieving he symptoms of premenstrual syndrome.

HEALING SEEDS
Evening primrose can be cultivated as an attractive garden plant. It is a biennial plant, having a two-year life cycle. During its second year the stem shoots up from a small rosette of leaves to a height of about two metres (2 yards), before flowering from June to September or October. It is only after flowering in its second year that the plant produces its valuable seeds. In addition, it has a very nourishing parsnip-like root which can be eaten as a vegetable.

500 seeds are needed to produce just one EPO capsule. The oil has to be uncontaminated by anything that could block its specific function, so companies are competing to produce the purest oils. There are, however, some combinations – for instance with zinc, fish oils, and various vitamins – that are proving especially beneficial for specific ailments.

The oil is usually sold in 250mg and 500mg capsules, and can also be obtained in a 'dropper' bottle for mixing into your own face creams, or for rubbing into babies' skins (a quick and easy way for them to absorb the oil) as

required. It is also now available as an ingredient in many skin products.

The only strong caution being expressed about EPO is directed at people with temporal lobe epilepsy, who may find that high dosages of EPO make them worse, rather than better. Also, if you find that EPO is giving you headaches, taking the capsules with food (and not late at night) should prevent this. Finally, some people experience a slight nausea, but this usually disappears after the first few days.

There are over 1000 different strains of evening primrose, many of which can be seen growing wild. *Oenothera biennis* is the type preferred by manufacturers for making the valuable oil. This is extracted from the seeds after flowering.

It was not until this century that scientists started to examine EPO closely. In 1919 the discovery of its rare gamma-linolenic acid (GLA) content was reported

in Germany, and the effect of GLA on cell generation and cholesterol levels was soon monitored.

Then, in the 1960s, British scientists began to discovered the life-enhancing uses to which EPO could be put. And as medical research strides forward, so does the botanical search for better varieties of evening primrose with higher seed yields containing higher concentrations of GLA.

Evening primrose oil manufacturers grow many types of plant in order to breed new, disease-resistant strains that yield higher concentrations of the all important gamma-linolenic acid.

GOLDEN HARVEST

In the seventeenth century the evening primrose arrived in Europe as a 'stowaway' from its native North America. It travelled across the Atlantic as seeds contained in the sacks of soil used as ballast by the cotton cargo ships. These sacks were dumped on nearby wasteland and evening primrose took root.

Botanists, who also brought specimens of the plant to Europe, labelled it *Oenothera biennis* – part of the willow-herb family. Despite its name it is not related to the primrose family (*Primulacaea*), rather it came to be called evening primrose because it only opens its primrose-yellow flowers between six and seven in the early evening.

The North American Indians valued this plant both as a food and medicine. They used it for coughs, bruises and, as a poultice, for open wounds. Its soothing and healing properties soon revealed themselves to herbalists, and it became known as 'King's cure-all'. During the reign of Charles I it was prescribed as cooling and astringent, good against 'bloody fluxes', 'loosenesses', gonorrhoea and 'nocturnal pollutions', 'hot tumours' and inflammations.

HOW EVENING PRIMROSE OIL WORKS

Evening primrose oil (EPO) is usually taken in capsule form as a nutritional supplement to a normal diet. EPO works by:

- supplying gamma-linolenic acid (GLA)
- helping make protaglandin E1 (PGE1)
- bypassing faulty enzyme processes

GLA is an essential fatty acid which is also known as Vitamin F. It is required because the fatty acid is necessary for the processes that makes prostaglandins, the body's metabolic regulating system. Prostaglandins are needed for the normal function of involuntary muscles, including the heart, the lungs, the intestines and blood vessels. Normally, the body creates its own GLA from linoleic acid which is contained in foodstuffs like liver kidneys and vegetable oils. However, many

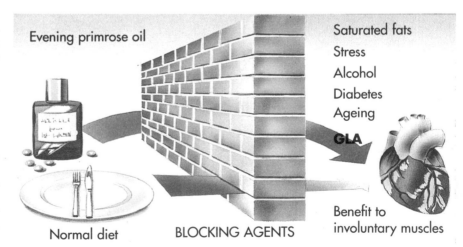

Evening primrose oil

Normal diet   BLOCKING AGENTS

Saturated fats
Stress
Alcohol
Diabetes
Ageing
GLA

Benefit to involuntary muscles

factors like foods rich in saturated fats or cholesterol, stress, alcohol, ageing or diabetes impede the body from successfully making its own GLA. EPO works by providing a ready-made supply of GLA that bypasses any difficulty the body had in making its own.

(The only other ready-made supply of useful quantites of GLA is a mother's breast milk.) It is for this reason that EPO is useful in treating a wide range of ailments for they all seem to share a common complaint, a deficiency in essential fatty acids.

WHAT EPO CAN DO FOR YOU

It is now understood that the conditions for which evening primrose oil (EPO) could be effective are due, at least in part, to a deficiency of essential fatty acids (EFAs), and therefore often to a follow-on deficiency of prostaglandin E1 (PGE1). Research is showing that EPO could be useful for the following.

SKIN, HAIR, NAILS
EPO is recommended by leading beauty experts to counteract effects of ageing. Weak nails and hair loss have also responded well.

BENIGN BREAST DISEASE
Symptoms include painful swelling and 'granular' lumps. Causes still uncertain, but EFA and PGE1 deficiencies both seem to be indicated. EPO relieves many symptoms – over a period of time.

HEART DISEASE
Reduces blood cholesterol levels, thereby lessening risk of high blood pressure and heart disease.

ECZEMA, ASTHMA, ALLERGIES
EPO is often recommended for sufferers of these ailments as it contains GLA. Babies can have the oil rubbed into the soft parts of the skin where it will be quickly absorbed. Only a little oil is used as it is strong for infants. (Babies often develop these conditions when switched from GLA-rich mother's milk to cow's milk.)

RHEUMATOID ARTHRITIS
Is thought to be useful in helping reduce the symptoms of crippling inflammation.

PRE-MENSTRUAL SYNDROME
Includes fluid retention, bloatedness, aches, depression, irritability, weepiness – sometimes for two weeks out of every month. Low EFA levels probably cause an excess of the female hormone, prolactin. EPO can restore balance.

HYPERACTIVITY
Probably caused by PGE1 deficiency which affects brain and behaviour patterns. EPO can correct this imbalance.

MULTIPLE SCLEROSIS
Still very much an unknown quantity, but is possibly a virus causing damage to the body's immune system and cell structure. EPO may be helpful in relieving symptoms but, as yet, this is not certain.

OBESITY
If the enzyme involved in burning excess calories is inactive, EPO can help reactivate it.

P RE-MENSTRUAL SYNDROME

What is pre-menstrual syndrome (PMS)? Most women can provide a good part of the answer to this long list of ailments that many have to endure for up to half of every month. These include: water retention and bloatedness, weight gain, swollen ankles and other joints, skin problems, headaches, muscle aches, lack of concentration and co-ordination, diminished sex drive, tension, insomnia, food and alcohol cravings, lethargy, irritability, weepiness and severe depression.

What causes pre-menstrual syndrome? Lack of essential fatty acids is now considered to be a main offender. This results in a deficiency of prostaglandin E1 (PGE1) which causes a hormonal imbalance that brings about those symptoms once dismissed as 'women's' problems.

Hospital trials and doctors have found that a course of evening primrose oil (EPO) helps many women. Treatment usually begins a few days before the symptoms start.

Other factors are helpful in the relief of PMS. Zinc and vitamin C help in making PGE1, and vitamin B_6 is known to be an essential regulator of the menstrual cycle. Deficiency of vitamin B_6 is not uncommon, particularly in women taking the oral contraceptive pill.

Although EPO should do much to help, there are additional ways of relieving PMS

1 Cut down on saturated fats. Remember, these are EFA-conversion 'blockers'.

2 Cut down on salt – it is probably increasing your water retention.

3 Tea and coffee also block absorption of essential nutrients. Cut back as much as you can.

4 Try and reduce your sugar intake. It is probably contributing to your water retention, your weight gain and your depression. Eat little and often. An increase in B vitamins (use a B-vitamin complex plus magnesium and chromium supplements) will help control sugar cravings.

5 Relax. Try a course of relaxation exercises – you can join a class, or take yoga lessons, or buy a relaxation tape or video cassette. A warm bath to which you have added a few drops of essential oil of ylang-ylang, plus a drop of lavender oil or clary sage, will leave you feeling much better. Melissa oil is another wonderful relaxant, and geranium is 'uplifting'.

6 Go easy on yourself. You have got enough to contend with. Do not put yourself on any ferocious new regimes. One step at a time.

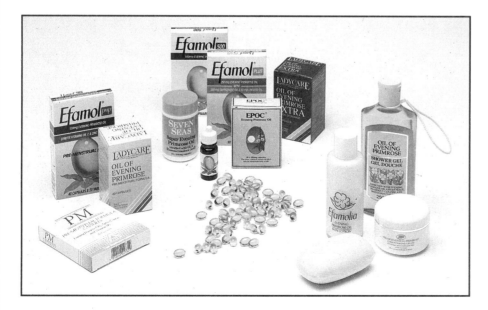

BUYING EPO

It takes 5000 seeds of the evening primrose plant to make just one capsule of evening primrose oil. This is now available in many different forms. Pure EPO is sold in both 250mg and 500mg capsules and as a liquid in 'dropper' bottles. An ailment such as eczema can be alleviated by applying EPO, either from the bottle or by breaking open a capsule, directly on the affected area. EPO can also be found in combination with other beneficial 'ingredients', for instance, with zinc, oil of borage, safflower oil, agnus castus, and vitamins B, B_6 and C. For sufferers of premenstrual syndrome specially prepared packs, combining a range of components, can be obtained.

FEVERFEW

A herbal remedy for migraine

This humble member of the daisy family, used by early herbalists and medical practitioners, has recently been rediscovered as an effective treatment for migraine

In 1772, J. Hill, a herbalist, noted the qualities of feverfew as a cure for headaches: 'In the worst headache there is no more efficacious remedy'. Its place of origin has been traced to the Balkan peninsula, but how, or when, its introduction to western Europe occurred remains a mystery. Mention of its use as a herbal remedy was made, however, as early as 1653 by Nicholas Culpeper in his book, *Complete Herbal*: 'The powder of the herb taken in wine with some Oxymel purges both choler and phlegm, and is available for those that are short winded and are troubled with melancholy and weariness or sadness of spirits'.

Although it is a **specific** for (possesses distinct properties for the relief of) migraine, feverfew also has other functions: as a **diuretic**, to increase the flow of urine; as a **febrifuge**, to reduce fevers; and as an **anti-spasmodic** in a similar way to camomile, to which feverfew is closely related. A herbalist would not, however, prescribe feverfew for the treatment of these individual disorders (other herbs being more suitable), but as a general remedy for migraine.

THE PLANT

Feverfew is easily grown on all soils, although it prefers a well-drained, sunny position. It can be obtained as seed, and develops into a strong-smelling acrid bush up to 45cm (18in) tall, and bears white-petalled daisy-like flowers with yellow centres throughout the summer. There are two varieties of the herb: an ornamental, golden-leaved type, which is of doubtful medicinal value, and the medicinal plant, with dark-green leaves. It is a perennial – dying back in the autumn, but reappearing in spring.

TAKING FEVERFEW

The traditional method of taking feverfew is to eat the leaves fresh from the plant, the usual dosage being up to two large or four small leaves daily. For best results, feverfew should be taken regularly for a period of several months. To this end, you will need to find ways of ensuring supplies of the fresh herb throughout the winter months. One preservation technique is to make a syrup from the leaves; this should be done, however, without boiling the herb as heat will destroy its active constituents. The syrup can be made, therefore, by boiling the sugar and water first, allowing this mixture to cool, and then adding the fresh herb. Alternatively, the fresh leaves can be chopped like mint and mixed with honey; this acts as a preservative and improves the taste by countering the

Tanacetum parthenium, **known commonly as feverfew (or featherfoil – because of the feather-like shape of its leaves), is a summer-flowering member of the daisy family.**

HOW FEVERFEW WORKS

The active constituents of feverfew include cosmosiine, borneol, partenolide, volatile oil, and sesquiterpine lactones.

The Lancet (a medical magainze for doctors) describes the action of feverfew as blocking the formation of prostaglandins, substances which occur naturally in the body and are connected with pain initiation. One of the functions of prostaglandins is to assist in the contraction of involuntary muscles in the body, including those of the arteries and blood vessels in the brain; it is the constriction of these vessels which contributes to the pain experienced in headaches and migraines. By inhibiting the production of prostaglandins the muscles relax, the blood vessels dilate and the pain is eased. Feverfew may also be effective in other cases which respond to aspirin-type drugs (which also inhibit prostaglandin synthesis).

bitterness of the herb, which some people may find quite unpalatable. The leaves may also be frozen in ice.

RISKS

An important point to remember in the use of feverfew is that the plant occasionally causes a contact skin reaction in those handling the downy leaves, and if the fresh leaves are eaten some people develop blisters in the mouth. For this reason, and because of the bitter pungent taste, it is usually eaten sandwiched between pieces of bread. The herbalists of old also used feverfew 'to promote suppressed menses' (to restore the regularity of menstruation): for this reason it would be unwise to take feverfew during pregnancy.

Many people grow their own feverfew and take it without experiencing any such side-effects, but if you are worried, try a commercially-made preparation of feverfew.

HERBALISTS

Herbalists usually prepare feverfew in the form of a tincture – a liquid extract of the leaves, prepared by cold maceration (softening by soaking) in a mixture of water and alcohol. This is combined with extracts from other medicinal plants which have tonic effects on the nervous system, or which treat associated symptoms, thus giving an individual prescription tailored to the needs of each patient. Dried, powdered leaves can be pressed into tablets, and those are available at most health-food shops; the powder may also be found packed into gelatine tablets.

MIGRAINE RESEARCH

Recent reports from herbalists suggest that the effect of feverfew on migraine symptoms in particular has been quite remarkable. Some people experience an almost immediate improvement in their migraine pattern, whilst others show a steady reduction in the frequency and severity of attacks.

A series of questionnaires and clinical trials carried out in studies on feverfew by Dr P. J. Hylands, and revealed at the 1985 Symposium on Herbal Medicines held by the London College of Phytotherapy (the treatment of diseases using plants), testifies to these results. Dr Hylands discovered that 37 per cent of migraine sufferers who were experiencing an average of one or two attacks per month found that with feverfew their headaches disappeared altogether; 75 per cent found that their attacks became less frequent and less painful.

FISH OILS

Good for the brain, good for the joints

Oils extracted from, or eaten in, fish have proved effective in arresting arthritis and heart diseases. Its efficacy as an alternative remedy has been clinically tested, and the message is clear: 'eat more fish'

Although life has evolved over millions of years, and man and other animals have adapted to living on the land, much evidence remains of our earliest origins from the sea. The sea can evoke our strongest emotions and has inspired many great musicians, artists and poets. Many of us feel a simple yet strong need 'to see the sea' from time to time. Physiologically, our blood – like the sea – is a solution of sodium chloride, together with various other substances, in water.

Astrologers maintain that as the seas' tides are governed by the gravitational pull of the moon, so our 'inner seas' are, in part, regulated by the pull of planetary influences. The sea also provides us with vital nutrients which are not easy to obtain from non-marine sources. Seaweed is the richest source of natural iodine available, and many sea plant and animal extracts are used as effective alternative remedies for a variety of ailments, for instance, kelp to treat

thyroid problems, as well as gastric and duodenal ulcers (see KELP); the green lipped mussel to treat arthritis (see GREEN LIPPED MUSSEL) and spirulina for protein deficient diets. More recently, researchers' interest has focused on fish and the properties of their oils.

COD LIVER OILS

Cod liver oil holds a place of honour among well-known folklore remedies. As with other traditional remedies, fish oil first became established as worthwhile simply because it worked. Fishermen in Scotland, Iceland, Norway and Greenland have used it for centuries to help protect their health during periods of long exposure to intense cold. Our grandparents and their forebears took cod liver oil daily to relieve complaints such as rheumatism, aching muscles and stiff joints.

The first clinical tests carried out on fish oils were done by Samuel Kay, a doctor at the Manchester Infirmary in

FISH OIL AND THE BRAIN

Docosahexaenoic acid (DHA) is a vital component of the membranes (cell walls) of every cell of certain body organs and it is found in particularly high concentrations in the brain. It appears to be necessary for normal brain function and very subtle 'wave' changes have been found in the brains of some vegans who avoid all animal products, including sea food and fish.

Together with other polyunsaturated fats, DHA seems essential for the normal development of the brain of the unborn baby. A recent UK study showed that mothers who have very low levels of polyunsaturates, including plant oils, Evening Primrose Oil (EPA) and DHA, give birth to smaller babies. Breast milk supplies some DHA to the developing child, so it is possible that the quantity present is affected by the mothers' diet.

DECLINING FISH DIET

Mackerel – one of the oil-rich fish which has declined in popularity.

In past centuries fish was very common in the British diet, and heart disease was a rarity. Herring, mackerel, sprats and other oily fish were consumed daily and in large quantities as they were cheap and plentiful. Sir William Osler, a famous British physician in the 1890s, said that throughout his years of consultant medical practice, he had only seen a handful of patients with heart disorders.

Fish eating (and with it the fishmonger) has declined sharply in western societies, and when fish is consumed it is usually the white kind – plaice, cod and haddock – which contain relatively little oil.

Figures compiled in 1980 show that the total amount of herrings caught in the UK during 1979 was 5000 metric tonnes, compared with 276,000 metric tons which were caught in 1938. Over the same period white fish catches, such as haddock and cod, had also declined dramatically from 513,000 to 243,000 metric tonnes.

F | ISH AND NUTRITION

Nutritional experts are now urging us to eat more oily fish such as herring, mackerel, pilchards, sardines, salmon, whitebait and tuna, or to take a daily fish oil supplement in pill form to protect ourselves from heart disease. Since many people unfortunately dislike fish, and its availability in fresh form has declined, a fish oil nutritional supplement enables us to gain the benefits of EPA without having to eat the fish that contains it.

Fish oils once derived from the livers of cod and halibut to provide supplements, are now made mainly from the fish flesh. Fish liver oil is very rich in vitamins D and A, and both vitamins can prove toxic when too much is taken.

Giving children cod liver oil is an old tradition well worth carrying on. But limit the daily dose to 2.5ml (½ teaspoon) oil – or 5ml (1 teaspoon) emulsion – more can be toxic.

the UK from 1752 to 1784. At that time 227-273 litres (50-60 gallons) were dispensed annually. Dr Kay reported that '. . . its good effects are so well known among the poorer sort (of people) that it is particularly requested by them for almost every lameness. Except bark, opium and mercury, I believe no one medicine . . . is likely to be of better service.'

A German physician, Schenk, carried the research further and cod liver oil began to be used for treating rickets, a bone disease that causes serious deformities due to vitamin D deficiency. Rickets was rife in England during the 1890s and nine out of ten malnourished children suffered from it. By the 1920s more was known about essential dietary nutrients and doctors were aware that cod liver oil was rich in some that other foods often lacked – namely vitamins A and D and polyunsaturated fats. Doctors were soon urging parents to give cod liver oil to their children as a form of prevention, rather than a cure. Up to the 1950s, children were given a daily spoonful of cod liver oil for its high content of vitamins and to ward off winter coughs and colds. It was sometimes mixed with malt or orange juice for extra nourishment and to disguise its unpleasant taste.

In 1956 research into the non-vitamin ingredients of cod liver oil was sparked off by the discovery that many tuberculosis patients benefited from taking it. The usefulness of polyunsaturated oils derived from plants and fish, including cod, had already become established and research into the full range of their properties finally began in earnest.

Further research revealed that cod liver oil was effective in lowering blood cholesterol levels. Fish oil seemed to hold the secret, and this was further suggested by the discovery that the blood of Eskimos contained two special essential fatty acids (EFAs) in which the Western diet is deficient, since it includes relatively small amounts of fish from which the EFAs are derived.

This Tokyo fish market shows the huge variety of fish that is central to the Japanese diet. The high fish intake is part of the reason why, although most Japanese people have the life-style of an industrialised society, they also have one of the lowest heart disease rates in the world.

Eskimos get most of their food from the sea. The fat of cold water marine animals, unlike land animals, contains special polyunsaturated fats.

LEARNING FROM ESKIMO EATING HABITS

Heart disease has become an increasingly serious problem since the 1930s. The death rate from heart attacks is higher in the UK than anywhere else in the world and 200,000 men and women die from them annually – many well before retirement age. The problem has been studied widely. Population studies in the 1960s revealed that Greenland Eskimos, who eat a great deal of saturated animal fat, rarely suffer from heart or arterial disorders. Moreover, it seems to be that a healthy heart and circulation is associated in some way with a high consumption of fish.

Two Danish scientists, Jorn Dyerberg and H. O. Bang, travelled to Greenland to study Eskimos in their own environment. Investigations into their diet, including an analysis of many food samples, revealed that the Eskimos consume a high proportion of fish oil – directly from fish and from the fat of other marine animals, such as seals, which in turn feed upon fish.

An analysis of samples taken by the Danish scientists showed that Eskimos' blood is far less prone to clot than that of other races and contains a lower level of certain fats than would be expected on such a high fat diet.

Dr Hugh Sinclair, a British nutritional expert who accompanied Dyer and Bang to Greenland to study the Eskimo diet, carried out a now famous experiment on his return to the UK. For 100 days he lived exclusively on an Eskimo diet of raw fish, shell fish, seal meat, blubber and water. The results showed that diet was responsible for the properties of Eskimos's blood and that, by eating similarly, Dr Sinclair could change his blood to resemble theirs. The flipside of the argument was that when Eskimos emigrate to the USA or Europe and substitute a modern Western diet – which has been termed a 'cardiologist's nightmare' – for their traditional diet the effect is lost and they suffer as many heart attacks and related complaints as Westerners.

ESSENTIAL FATTY ACIDS

Research has identified that fish oil contains eicosapentanoic acid (EPA) which protects against heart and arterial disorders and docosahexaenoic acid (DHA) which is thought to be essential for the normal development of the unborn baby's brain. Both are essential fatty acids (EFAs).

EPA and DHA originate in sea algae, minute plants upon which the fish feed. The food chain consists of larger fish and other sea creatures eating one another in turn – and ultimately being eaten by man. EPA, like all essential fatty acids, helps to keep the cell walls throughout the body healthy, including those of the heart, circulatory system and red blood cells. Most importantly, EPA produces hormone-like substances called thromboxane and prostacyclin, which reduce the tendency of thrombosis (blood clotting), and it lowers the level of low density cholesterol (blood fat) – a major risk factor in atheroma (arteries becoming clogged with fatty deposits). At the same time, levels of the high density, protective type of cholesterol are raised.

Other fatty acids, present in saturated and some unsaturated fats, give rise to harmful prostaglandins which encourage the laying down of atheromatous plaques. When insufficient EPA is present to counteract their effect, they are free to cause maximum harm within the circulatory system.

Clinical studies using supplementary fish oil to treat heart disease have proved its value – both as a form of treatment and as a form of protection. It has been found to be effective in lowering high blood pressure and in reducing the severity of angina (chest pain) caused by diseased coronary arteries. It is also likely to prove useful in treating peripheral vascular disease which affects the arteries of the lower limbs.

The scientific findings not only show that fish, especially oily fish, is vital for the heart and joints, but that there is truth in the old saying 'fish is good for the brain' (see Box). In fact, it helps all the body's cells throughout our lives.

FISH OIL AND ARTHRITIS

Fish oil is highly beneficial in treating arthritis – another scientific proof of an age-old remedy. Elderly arthritic folk still swear by their daily spoonful of cod liver oil 'to oil their joints' and this, in fact, is exactly what they are doing.

Clinical tests at a Scottish medical school were carried out using Evening Primrose Oil (EPO) (see EVENING PRIMROSE OIL) alone and in combination with fish oil, to treat patients suffering from rheumatoid arthritis who were taking NSAIDs (non-steroidal anti-inflammatory drugs). The results revealed that 94 per cent of patients taking EPO and 100 per cent of patients taking EPO with fish oil, rated themselves as better. Only 33 per cent in the placebo (dummy) group felt any improvement. Osteoarthritis sufferers could also benefit from fish oil.

These results occurred despite drastic reductions in drug dosage – 59 per cent of the participants in both the EPO and the EPO plus fish oil groups were able to stop taking their drugs completely. In addition, 24 per cent in the EPO group and 35 per cent in the combination group were able to halve their drug dose. Only 28 per cent of those in the dummy group could stop taking their drugs altogether and only 6 per cent reduced the dose by half.

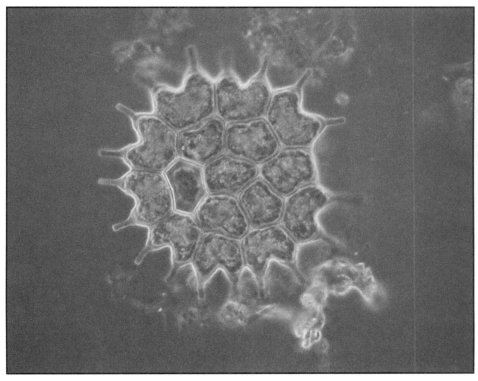

A microscope picture of a species of green algae. The vital fatty acids in fish oils originate in marine algae.

GARLIC

Highly valued throughout the ages as one of the most effective medicinal plants

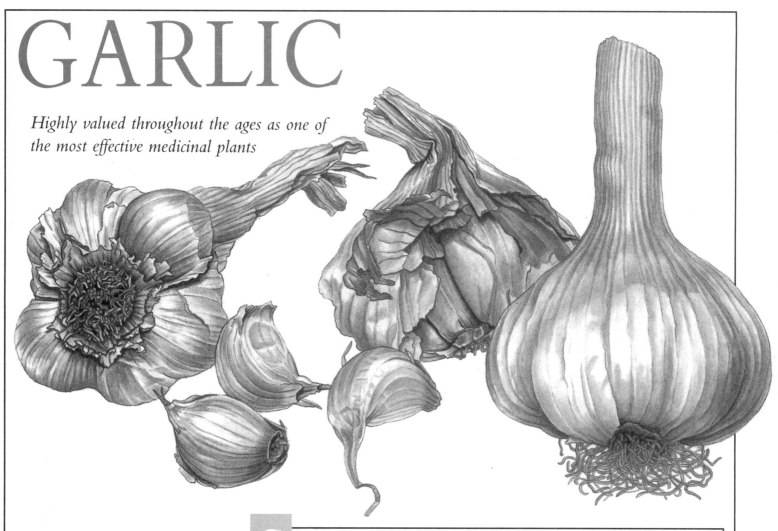

Garlic is one of the earliest recorded plant medicines and its use can be traced back 5000 years, but it wasn't until the mid-nineteenth century that the search began to try to discover what makes garlic such a powerful herbal medicine.

In 1844 Professor Wertheim isolated what he believed to be the main component of garlic oil – diallyl sulphide – but he missed several other sulphur compounds, particularly diallyl trisulphide, and he was unable to isolate the cause of garlic's distinctive pungent aroma. Similar work was also being carried out by American scientists. They discovered that whole, undamaged garlic tissue contains a sulphur compound which reacts, when crushed, to form a new compound which they named 'allicin'. This is the active ingredient of garlic and, they suspected, the source of the smell. They found it to be an unstable compound which, after a short while, changes into other basic sulphur compounds. Thus, allicin is the source of most of garlic's healing and therapeutic powers, and even though it breaks down very quickly into other sulphur-bearing chemicals, its power is not reduced.

This was not the complete story, however, as two Swiss scientists isolated the precursor of allicin – a sulphur-rich amino

G ROWING GARLIC

Although the majority of garlic that can be bought from supermarkets and greengrocers comes from hot Mediterranean countries such as Italy and France, it can also be grown in colder climates and can easily be grown in the garden.

Garlic is easy to cultivate, but needs a long growing season, plenty of sun and a light, sandy soil that has not been freshly manured

Select the outside cloves from the garlic bulb and plant at a depth of 2cm (1in), spacing the cloves 20cm (8in) apart and in rows 30cm (12in) away from each other. Harvest the garlic in summer after the leaves have died off and turned yellow. Dry the bulbs thoroughly in the sun and store in a dry, frost-free place until needed.

A useful tip for the keen gardener is to plant garlic among rose trees or bushes to deter greenfly.

In World War I garlic was used as an antiseptic to cleanse wounds.

acid they called 'alliin'. They found that there was an enzyme, allinase, which changes alliin to allicin. Crushing or cutting the garlic clove brings the amino-acid and the enzyme together and sets up a chain reaction.

The Parisian medical journals of the mid-nineteenth century contain reports of three cases of cholera that were treated effectively with garlic, and in 1918 the results of a clinical trial conducted on tuberculosis victims in America was published. For two years 1000 patients were given every modern drug treatment available – and garlic. The report from the hospital concluded: 'Garlic gave us our best results'. Similarly, in World War I garlic was used as an antiseptic and applied to wounds to cleanse and heal. Another doctor used it to treat cases of dysentery

GARLIC HAIR RINSE

Hair prone to dandruff will benefit from a garlic lotion. It will also improve the hair and stimulate growth.

Crush a clove of garlic and place in a small jar with a mixture made up of equal quantities of vodka and stilled water. Leave to infuse for three days and then strain and store in a screw-top jar.

The lotion should be used once or twice a week by moistening a cotton wool pad with the lotion and gently rubbing over the scalp. This treatment is best carried out at night so that the hair can be washed thoroughly the next morning to remove the smell.

G ARLIC (ALLIUM SAVITUM)

The word garlic is derived from two Anglo-Saxon words – 'gar' meaning a spear and describing the long, thin leaves of the plant, and 'leac' meaning pot herb.

Garlic is a hardy perennial belonging to the onion family. Other members include leeks, chives, scallions and shallots, all distinguished by a pungent aroma and flavour.

The garlic bulb consists of eight to twenty individual cloves enclosed in a silky membrane and grows to a height of 60cm (24in). The flowerhead is a cluster of small purplish-white flowers.

Garlic belongs to the onion family, as do leeks and chives.

caused by the poor sanitary conditions in the trenches.

The list of minor, and occasionally major, illnesses that had been successfully treated with garlic is long and impressive but, in the late nineteenth century new, synthetically-produced drugs started to appear which gave hope to many people suffering from diseases and herbal medicine began to decline. Now, the pendulum is beginning to swing in the opposite direction and there is a resurgence of public interest in natural remedies.

MODERN MEDICINAL USES OF GARLIC

Even though its effectiveness as a treatment for colds and flu has been recognised by herbalists through the ages, it is only lately that conventional medicine has acknowledged its value. Recently the Department of Health and Social Security in the UK has granted full product licences to various garlic preparations, enabling manufacturers to make certain claims concerning their products' benefits to health.

Garlic is a powerful destroyer of fungi in the body. Research carried out in Poland found that garlic juice was a more powerful killer of fungi than any synthetic medication. It can be used to combat candida albicans (thrush) and intestinal parasites such as threadworms, and if you are travelling abroad it is worth taking garlic with you to prevent stomach upsets – an added bonus is that the midges will leave you alone.

The effect that garlic has on the blood

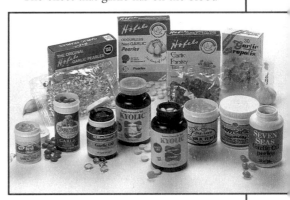

Many garlic preparations are licensed to make health claims.

has also attracted attention. In 1981 the Clinical Pharmacology Research Unit at Oxford tested the blood of a group of people who had been given garlic to help prevent the formation of blood clots. Their favourable findings were published in the British medical journal, *The Lancet*. This evidence was backed up by an American study which found that garlic contains several anti-coagulant agents.

GARLIC FOR HEALTH

Each garlic bulb contains valuable nutrients. Various B vitamins are present in quantifiable amounts as well as vitamins A and C. Also, 10 different sugars have been identified, together with a proportionally high level of trace minerals including zinc, calcium, manganese, copper, aluminium, selenium and germanium. These last two trace minerals are attracting attention because of the effect they are thought to have on strengthening the immune system, and consequently, their possible value to AIDS sufferers.

AIOLI

Aioli, or garlic mayonnaise, is superb served as a dip with a selection of sliced vegetables such as carrots, celery, peppers, cauliflower and cucumbers.

Crush 16 peeled garlic cloves in a mortar until reduced to a pulp. Add the yolks of three eggs and a pinch of salt and stir with a wooden spoon. Drop by drop, add 300ml (11 fl oz) of olive oil, stirring all the time as the mixture begins to thicken. When all the oil has been added and the aioli is very thick, add another 300ml (11 fl oz) of olive oil in a slow trickle. This will further thicken the aioli. Add a little lemon juice to taste and serve.

Aioli may be served as a dip with a wide variety of raw vegetables.

THE LEGEND OF THE VAMPIRE

Throughout time, superstition has credited garlic with the ability to ward off disease and evil spirits. The myth of the vampire, a resuscitated corpse that stalks the night for victims to feed off their blood, is perhaps the best known. The folklore of Eastern Europe credits garlic with the ability to ward off the vampire; the plant's pungent flowers are believed to provide protection if worn around the neck or placed at the window to keep the vampire from entering the room.

EATING GARLIC

Garlic is very versatile and can be used in a wide range of dishes to enhance the flavour. Cooking makes the taste of garlic less fierce, and adding it to soups and stews is an excellent way of increasing the amount in the diet.

The easiest way to increase garlic consumption is to take either garlic tablets (usually mixed with parsley which helps remove the smell from the breath) or in capsule form (perles) which contain essential oil of garlic. This method of encapsulating garlic oil was discovered some 50 years ago by a Dr Johann Hofel, an ardent food reformer. Provided these are swallowed with a cold drink, they will leave no taint of the smell on the breath.

To derive the best benefits from garlic it should be eaten raw – not a pleasant method as the taste can make the mouth sore by creating a burning sensation.

Garlic used in cooking adds flavour to a variety of dishes.

COMPLEMENTARY USES OF GARLIC

Garlic is used by herbalists to protect against the common cold, amoebic dysentery, typhoid and other infectious diseases. As an ointment it is helpful for rheumatism and swollen, painful joints. Smoothing oil of garlic on the chest and back helps relieve hoarseness, catarrh and coughs but, as well as making you smell unpleasantly, it can also have a reaction on sensitive skin – so use with caution.

If you are receiving conventional treatment from your doctor it is unwise to use herbal medications without first taking professional advice.

THE HISTORY OF GARLIC

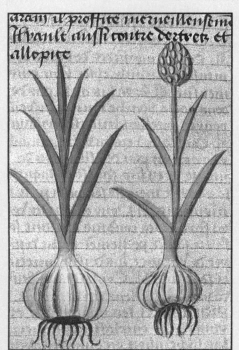

Garlic was prized highly by the ancient Egyptians; garlic bulbs, still perfectly preserved, where found in the tomb of Tutenkhamen.

of botanical specimens sent back from this region to Russia for identification. One plant was named *Allium Longicuspis* because of its similarity to the garlic plant we know today. To date, no one has challenged this theory and, because Central Asia was, even in ancient times, a key point for traders travelling to the East and West, it is easy to see how the plant could be found as far apart as China and Egypt.

The Egyptian pharaohs prized garlic very highly. Slaves building the pyramids were given a daily ration of garlic to keep them fit and strong for the back-breaking work of hauling the huge slabs of stone into position.

According to one source, the amount of garlic they ate, as well as onions and radishes (all important strength-giving foods, according to the Egyptians), is recorded around the base of the Great Pyramid. The slaves must have appreciated their diet for the first-ever industrial strike occurred when their garlic rations were withdrawn.

Garlic was used by the ancient Chinese, Greeks, Egyptians, Babylonians, and Indians. To these ancient people it was a plant sacred to the gods, and legends of its origins were mingled with stories about their deities.

However, it wasn't until the late nineteenth century that anyone could speculate, with a degree of authority, about the origins of garlic. A theory was put forward, based on the findings of Russian scientists, that the most likely place was Central Asia. The evidence for this was found amongst the hundreds

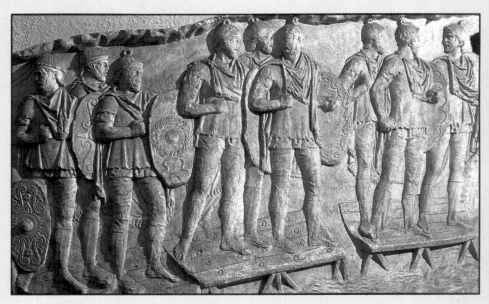

Romans believed in the strengthening properties of garlic and there is evidence it was issued to the troops in the field.

THE GREAT PLAGUE

In the seventeenth and eighteenth centuries, when plagues regularly swept across Europe, garlic was believed to give protection against them, a claim that appears to have some substance if the records of the College of Physicians for the Great Plague of 1665 are to be believed.

A tidy profit was to be had by some keen entrepreneurs who sold garlic at a guinea an ounce to people desperate to ward off the horrendous effects of the plague.

When Tutankhamen's tomb was opened they found six garlic bulbs still perfectly preserved, put there, presumably, to give the boy king strength for his journey into the afterworld. Even before this, another Egyptian tomb dating back to 3750BC was found to contain clay models of garlic bulbs.

The Romans, too, had great faith in the strength-giving properties of garlic and gave it to their troops.

But not all ancient Greeks, Romans and Egyptians were enamoured of garlic, for much the same reasons as we have ambivalent feelings about it today – the smell. It was considered a sign of vulgarity and scorned by the upper classes.

GINGER

Adding a spice to life

Gingerbread, ginger wine, ginger beer and preserved ginger are all familiar products. But ginger is more than a seasoning – its medicinal qualities have helped the sick throughout the ages

The *Zingiberaceae* botanical family to which ginger belongs includes three spices. Firstly there is turmeric, known in the past as Indian saffron, a spice that is used to give food a yellow colour. Cardamom is the second member of the family; its seeds are used in both curries and cakes. The third spice is ginger, the rhizome (root) of which has been widely used in cooking all over the world since earliest times. All three spices can also be used medicinally.

The ginger plant is a creeping perennial, growing to around one metre (1 yard) in height. Cultivated mainly in tropical countries, the Jamaican ginger is considered the best for culinary use. Ginger has many curative properties. Used on the skin, it can stimulate the circulation, and soothe burns. As a diaphoretic it encourages perspiration, so it can be employed in feverish conditions such as influenza, or colds. The root, which is the part of the plant most widely used in alternative forms of medicine, is rich in volatile oils, so ginger works well as a carminative – promoting gastric secretions. Colic and dyspepsia respond particularly well to ginger treatment.

ON THE GINGER TRAIL

In the 6th century BC Chinese medicine used ginger in about a quarter of all its mixtures. Ginger was also the key medicine of one of the fathers of medicine, Pedianos Dioscorides. He described it in *De Materia Medica*, his book on medical ingredients which remained in use for centuries. As physician to the Roman emperor Nero, Dioscorides may have used ginger 1700 years ago to warm the tired limbs of marching soldiers after a long day on the road. Rubbed into the skin, ginger produces a stimulating effect and, in a more sophisticated form, it is still used today by some experienced climbers who, when exposed to severely cold conditions, wish to get their circulation going.

After people realised the value of the spice, ginger was exported throughout the world. By the middle of the 16th century Europe was receiving more than 2000 tonnes per year from the East Indies, where it had first been planted by the Spaniard, Francisco de Mendoza. Ginger was soon playing a vital role in medical preparations and remedies of the time. *The History of Druggs*, written in 1712 by the two Frenchmen Lemery and Tournefort, recommended ginger for curing scurvy. In another publication, Lemery expressed the more traditional view that it helped wind, increased male potency and stimulated the appetite.

Another herbalist, Savory, suggested ginger as a remedy for gout, indigestion and flatulence at a dose of between 20 grains and a teaspoonful in any suitable carrier, such as honey. 'A weak infusion of ginger', he said, 'commonly called ginger tea, is an excellent beverage for people of dyspeptic and gouty habits and, combined with rhubarb, it forms a good remedy for the stomach, especially in the case where wind comes on before meals and the stomach is nearly empty'.

GINGER FOR BURNS

In a recent issue of the *Journal of New Chinese Medicine*, Dr Kai Liang-Ping writes that 'due to its potent taste and warming properties, fresh ginger is normally used as a diaphoretic (to induce sweating), and antitussive (to

A selection of foods and other spices which are commonly used together with ginger.

The *Zingiberaceae* family: ginger root (top), cardamom seeds (left) and turmeric (right).

GINGER'S ROOTS

The use of this fascinating healing spice is so widespread that it is hardly surprising that there is disagreement over the origins of its name. It could come from the Sanskrit *srngavera*, which some scholars believe gave rise to the Latin name *zingiber*, and the Greek *zingiberis*. Others believe, however, that the name may have originated in the mountains of Gingi in Hindustan.

stop coughs) or antiemetic (to prevent nausea and vomiting). Few people know about its use in treating burns, however; its effect in use far exceeds that of commonly used burn medicines'.

Dr Liang-Ping continues: 'Fresh ginger is a common kitchen spice which is readily available and easily applied. During my 20 years of practice, I have used fresh ginger in treating 400-500 cases of burns without a single failure. Ginger is mashed to release juice that is soaked up in a ball of cotton and applied to the burn area. Pain will be immediately relieved. Blisters and inflammation will subside. There will be no irritation, even when blisters are broken. Due to ginger's antibiotic activities, no ulceration will occur.'

A MOVING EXPERIMENT

In 1982 the medical journal, *The Lancet*, published a paper by Mowrey and Clayson about ginger's effect on motion sickness. This compared the effect of the powdered rhizome of *Zingiber officinale* with a standard pharmaceutical treatment and a placebo on 36 undergraduate men and women who said they were very susceptible to motion sickness. This condition was induced by placing the blindfolded subjects in a tilted, rotating chair. The reported degree of distress was checked every 15 seconds for up to six minutes by evaluating both physical and psychological changes. The conclusion was that ginger was more effective than the drug dimenhydrate in reducing motion sickness. None of the

subjects using the placebo, in this case chickweed, nor those taking dimenhydrinate, were able to stay in the chair for six minutes, whereas half of the subjects taking ginger stayed for the full time.

The article pointed out that an earlier study, in 1977, had also reported that ginger reduced gastric distress, and this is a continuation of the tradition, reported as long ago as 1597 in Gerard's *Herbal*. Ginger, in the form of ginger beer, ginger biscuits, or pieces of ginger (chewed), is also recommended as a remedy for morning sickness and travel sickness.

DIGESTIVE AID

Ginger is a carminative, which means that it helps the release of excessive gases from the digestive system where these can cause discomfort or pain. It has been used worldwide as an aromatic stomachic and pungent appetite stimulant, and in Chinese medicine it is recommended in cases of poisoning from bad water. But its effects on the digestive system are even wider. A Japanese team at Kyoto University, led by Dr Yamahara, studied ginger and its active constituents. They proved that two different substances in ginger called gingerols caused an increase in bile secretion. The experiments only worked, however, if the whole root or a solvent extraction was used. Infusing in water released constituents that had no effect.

A REMEDY FOR RHEUMATISM?

In 1989 two doctors from the Danish University of Odense presented a paper at a world conference on inflammation pointing out that ginger was used in the Ayurvedic system of medicine as a way of dealing with rheumatic disorders. The seven patients they tested reported relief from pain and associated symptoms after taking either five grams (1-2 teaspoons) fresh, or between a half and one gram (¼ teaspoon) of powdered, ginger daily. The patients said that their joints moved more easily, and their swelling and morning stiffness decreased, all without any noticeable side-effects. Two patients with muscular discomfort also found relief after taking ginger.

SHADES OF GINGER

The two main forms of ginger are white or black, and these result from different forms of processing. The white is washed, boiled, peeled and blanched, whereas the black is just washed and boiled before drying. To preserve ginger, young rhizomes are washed and boiled until tender, then boiled again with half their weight of sugar. This sugar preservation may be repeated as many as nine times to make preserved ginger.

Ginger for sale, with other spices, in China. A favourite of Chinese cuisine, Chinese research is also highlighting ginger's anti-burn properties.

GINKGO BILOBA

A tree of giant proportions

Ginkgo, possibly the world's oldest tree species, has recently aroused the interest of scientists, and research suggests it may be of great benefit in the treatment of circulatory and nervous disorders

Dating back some 200 million years, the Ginkgo biloba or Ginkgo tree has survived the various Ice Ages, several changes in climate and shown remarkable resistance to pests, diseases and pollution along the way. As a native of China, it was the Chinese who first recognised the potential of this healing tree and, since its spread westwards, these medicinal benefits have now, finally, come within our grasp.

CHINESE HERB

In Chinese herbal medicine Ginkgo is regarded as an astringent herb. This means it has a binding action, forming a protective coat on mucous membranes and exposed tissues, to heal and soothe inflammation, and act as a barrier to infection. Ginkgo was traditionally used for chest troubles, to relieve asthma, and for coughs and lung conditions. It has also been used in China for the treatment of problems associated with ageing and some circulatory conditions.

TRACING THE FAMILY TREE

The Ginkgo was brought to Europe from China, via Japan, in the 18th century. It is now a single genus with just one species grown throughout the world in mild climates, mainly as an ornamental tree. An attractive tree, with leaves that give it a feathery appearance, it can reach well over 30 metres (100ft) in height, and is often found in southern England, growing in large, public parks and landscaped gardens.

Being deciduous, the rich green Ginkgo leaves turn a clear yellow before they are shed in the autumn. As with holly, there are male and female trees. The male produces yellow catkin-like flowers, while the female bears acorn-like growths on long stalks. The fruits are non-edible but their ivory-coloured inner seed, similar to an almond, is sometimes used by the Chinese in cooking.

It is the unusual leaves that make Ginkgo biloba easily recognisable, although their fan-shape can resemble those of the maidenhair fern (*Adiantum*), and some people may know it better as the 'maidenhair tree'.

GBE – GINKGO BILOBA EXTRACT

Modern scientific research and clinical trials have involved the use of Ginkgo Biloba Extract – GBE, which is obtained from the leaves. Its most important constituents are believed to be bioflavonoids (or flavonoid glycosides) which are at their highest level in the yellow leaves of autumn. A standardised extract is carefully prepared from Ginkgo leaves gathered at this time, to ensure the best possible product.

Ginkgo grows mainly in temperate climates – here seen in Kew Gardens, London.

The leaves should be harvested in Autumn when flavonoid content is at its peak.

BIOFLAVONOIDS

Bioflavonoids are natural compounds present with vitamin C in plants and fruits.

According to research their main value is that they protect and strengthen the blood vessels, especially the tiny capillaries which carry vital food and oxygen to the body's tissues. They also have anti-inflammatory properties.

The bioflavinoids in Ginkgo appear to be more effective at blocking the production of free radicals than those occurring in other substances. Free radicals are molecules that can lead to tissue damage and inflammation and, in this way, ginkgo has a protective effect on cells and blood vessels.

REDUCING THE RISKS

Among other constituents, Ginkgo extract also contains substances called terpenes. These block the production of PAF (Platelet-Activating-Factor) in the body. Platelets are tiny particles in the blood involved in the clotting mechanism. In the early stages of clot formation the platelets may form a clump, which increases the risk of strokes or blood clots (thrombosis).

When arteries are diseased, platelets may settle on the walls of the blood vessels, which increases the possibility of clots forming and obstructing the blood flow. This affects the transfer of oxygen and blood to vital organs – leading to strokes or other serious impairments. By preventing the clumping of blood platelets, extract of ginkgo biloba can be of assistance in reducing the risk of such disorders.

ANTI-AGEING REMEDY?

Ginkgo biloba extract appears to have a particular potential in the treatment of some conditions associated with ageing.

As we grow older, fatty deposits (atheroma) are laid down in our arteries. This can lead to reduced blood supply, causing circulation problems, increasing risk of strokes, and impeding brain function. Extract of ginkgo biloba would appear to help such problems by its action on blood vessels, cellular function, and nerve transmissions – improving their overall efficiency.

In one year-long clinical trial over one hundred geriatric patients suffering from impaired blood supply to the brain were given extract of ginkgo biloba. In this trial, as in others, dosage was 40mg, three times a day.

The patients' symptoms, which included dizziness, short-term memory loss, tinnitus (ringing in the ears) and behavioural changes, showed a significant improvement, thought to be due to Ginkgo's action in increasing blood supply to the brain. The results were confirmed by using behavioural observation and EEGs (electroencephalograms), which measure brain activity.

From this trial it would seem that Ginkgo biloba may be beneficial in treating loss of memory and poor concentration, both common conditions among elderly people, and it could, perhaps, have potential in the treatment of Alzheimer's disease.

In Chinese herbal medicine, Ginkgo is known as 'Pai-Kuo'. Traditionally, both seeds and leaves have been used.

ALL IN ALL

In general, GBE's main function is in relation to the cardiovascular (heart and blood vessels) and nervous systems. Scientific and clinical studies suggest that the extract has a number of benefits:
• It increases blood supply to the brain.
• It inhibits clot formation.
• It improves the transmission of nerve signals in the brain and nerve cells.
• It increases cellular energy.
• It protects against the damaging effects of free radicals.

BUYING GBE

Ginkgo biloba extract is available in 40mg capsules, and in tablets that combine 30 mg of GBE with natural vitamin E (also beneficial for circulation).

Anyone suffering from a serious medical condition or prolonged symptoms should seek advice and treatment from a qualified practitioner.

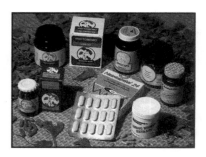

BRIGHT FUTURE

Extract of ginkgo biloba is known to boost the blood supply to the brain and other parts of the body. However, naturopaths, herbalists and scientists are currently making other dramatic claims about the substance.

Extensive research programs are now underway to investigate such claims that extract of ginkgo biloba can help to enhance memory skills – and, furthermore, even improve intellectual performance.

GINSENG

Elixir of life, miracle cure, the most potent aphrodisiac known to man?

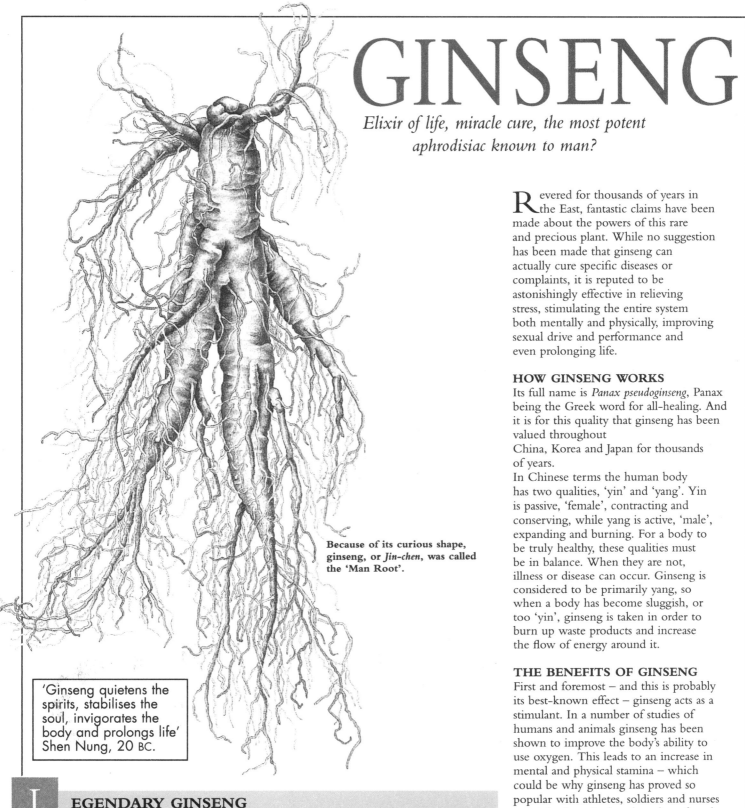

Because of its curious shape, ginseng, or *Jin-chen*, was called the 'Man Root'.

'Ginseng quietens the spirits, stabilises the soul, invigorates the body and prolongs life' Shen Nung, 20 BC.

EGENDARY GINSENG

For the Koreans, Chinese and Japanese, ginseng is more than just a useful remedy. It is a constantly recurring feature in the myths and legends of their country.

One legend tells how, long ago, a Chinese village called Shantan was troubled night after night by a mysterious wailing noise. Though frightened, the villagers eventually organised a torchlit expedition to find out where the wailing was coming from. They traced the cries to a large bush a mile outside the village, and when they dug the bush up, they found a huge root the size and shape of a man. The wailing stopped, and from that day on the root became known as ti ching, *spirit of the earth*.

Revered for thousands of years in the East, fantastic claims have been made about the powers of this rare and precious plant. While no suggestion has been made that ginseng can actually cure specific diseases or complaints, it is reputed to be astonishingly effective in relieving stress, stimulating the entire system both mentally and physically, improving sexual drive and performance and even prolonging life.

HOW GINSENG WORKS

Its full name is *Panax pseudoginseng*, Panax being the Greek word for all-healing. And it is for this quality that ginseng has been valued throughout China, Korea and Japan for thousands of years.

In Chinese terms the human body has two qualities, 'yin' and 'yang'. Yin is passive, 'female', contracting and conserving, while yang is active, 'male', expanding and burning. For a body to be truly healthy, these qualities must be in balance. When they are not, illness or disease can occur. Ginseng is considered to be primarily yang, so when a body has become sluggish, or too 'yin', ginseng is taken in order to burn up waste products and increase the flow of energy around it.

THE BENEFITS OF GINSENG

First and foremost – and this is probably its best-known effect – ginseng acts as a stimulant. In a number of studies of humans and animals ginseng has been shown to improve the body's ability to use oxygen. This leads to an increase in mental and physical stamina – which could be why ginseng has proved so popular with athletes, soldiers and nurses on night duty. And students have found that regular use of ginseng improves concentration and memory.

IS GINSENG AN APHRODISIAC?

More dramatically, ginseng's efficiency as a stimulant has earned it the reputation of being an aphrodisiac. For centuries, men in China and Korea have taken ginseng in the unshakable belief that it will enhance and preserve their sexual prowess. While scientists say that technically ginseng is not an aphrodisiac, they are agreed that its general stimulating effect on the body as a whole almost certainly filters through to sexual performance. This suggests that it could indeed be used as a treatment for impotence, low sex drive and infertility.

TURNING BACK THE CLOCK

One of ginseng's many Chinese nicknames, *tson mien huntan*, translates rather clumsily into English as 'the-regenerating-elixir-that-banishes-wrinkles-from-the-face'! Surprisingly, scientific research shows that this could well be true.

GINSENG AND STRESS

There has been much evidence to support the theory that ginseng helps the body to cope better with stress. It is now commonly believed that prolonged stress, whether physical or emotional, can be the cause of more serious disease.

When the body is exposed to stress, it automatically switches into a 'fight or flight' reaction. Unless this response is followed by immediate physical exertion, such as running about, screaming or shouting, to 'flush out' or use up the increased adrenalin, the body becomes severely taxed.

Ginseng has been shown to raise the threshold at which the body switches into its 'flight or fight' mechanism. This helps to eliminate, or at least alleviate, the harmful effects of stress.

POSSIBLE SIDE-EFFECTS

Ginseng is generally regarded as safe by most health departments, even when taken in large doses or over a long period. In fact, two or three kilograms (4-6lb) of pure ginseng would have to be eaten at one sitting for it to be considered harmful. Over-arousal can sometimes be a side-effect, and ginseng should not be taken with other stimulants, such as coffee or tea, neither should it be combined with herbal remedies containing iron.

RICHES, FAME, ROYALTY . . . AND GINSENG

Ginseng has always been associated with royalty and famous leaders in China and Korea. During the Han Dynasty, emperors would order their subjects to comb the Korean mountains in search of ginseng. Some were rewarded simply by being allowed to live, while others were paid the weight of the ginseng in gold or silver.

More recently, and less blood-thirstily, Mao Tse Tung and Chou en Lai were both known to take ginseng regularly throughout their lives.

Another well-known statesman, Henry Kissinger, is said to have relied on his regular intake of ginseng to keep him in good shape for his hectic, round-the-world schedule of meetings with world leaders.

HOW TO TAKE GINSENG

The raw root is the most active form, but its extremely high cost makes it too expensive for most people. Tablets or capsules are far cheaper, as well as being more accessible and convenient. Ginseng is also available in powdered extract form, as a tincture, and in tea or teabags. It can even be found in bubble bath and hand cream.

Traditionally, the more ginseng that is taken, the more long-term its beneficial effects. The need for regular dosage is also stressed. The definition of regular here is either one or more 'courses' a year, each lasting one month, or continuous long-term daily use of ginseng.

In both cases about one gram of ginseng should be taken daily. Alternatively, for a short-term tonic effect, the dose can be increased to two or three grams a day. In both cases it is best to take half the dose in the morning and half at night, preferably on an empty stomach.

GRAPE CURE

An age-old remedy for the prevention and cure of disease

Grapes are almost a complete food, not only can you live on them quite well for a long period of time, but doing so may well eliminate various bodily ills

Grapes were cultivated by the peoples of the Indus Valley as long ago as 4000 BC. In 140 BC the fruit was introduced to China by caravan traders in exchange for apricots and peaches. It is thought that the grape was introduced into the south of France and Italy by the Phoenicians, around 600 years BC. Following the discovery of America, wild varieties were also brought back to Europe, from which new varieties were developed.

Nowadays, dozens of varieties of red, white or black grapes are grown worldwide. They fall into two main groups: wine grapes and table or dessert grapes, though both types are suitable for eating. Once a seasonal crop, extensive commercial production and modern transport methods ensure that grapes are available all year round.

Rich in iron and various natural sugar, including fructose and glucose, grapes are a healthy addition to any diet. They also contain a number of minerals including potassium, sodium, calcium, magnesium and phosphorus. These minerals help to dissolve the build-up of toxic chemical deposits in the body while also stimulating their elimination. It is the grape's uniquely rigorous purgative action that is responsible for much of its curative and health-promoting effects.

ROYAL LEGEND

As far back as 1556, pamphlets and books that promoted the health-giving properties of grapes were published in all European languages. It is alleged that around this time several Royal Houses followed the grape diet as a cure for syphilis. During the 18th and 19th centuries grape cures (ampelotherapy) were widely used throughout Europe to rid the body of toxins and purify the blood, thereby, it was reasoned, eliminating the cause of disease. The 19th century English pioneer, reformer and dietician Dr Lambe, treated cancer with grapes.

In 1925 a South African naturopath, Dr Joanna Brandt, cured herself of abdominal cancer by following a strict grape-only diet. Following her own cure, Dr Brandt continued well into her 80s to successfully treat numerous patients suffering from cancer, often including those who were regarded as hopeless cases, by prescribing a grape diet.

In 1927, determined to promote the remedy outside her own country, she set sail for the USA. Although initially prevented by medical red tape, the media publicised her work and within a year, the grape cure had received medical approval, not only for the treatment of cancer, but for complaints as varied as constipation, haemorrhoids, gastro-intestinal catarrh, duodenum and

This medieval illumination from Portugal shows the September grape harvest.

stomach ulcers, tuberculosis, diabetes, gum disease and obesity, as well as a general preventative against illness. According to Dr Brandt, when only grapes are eaten, their unique antiseptic and chemical content actually breaks down diseased tissue, which then enters the bloodstream and is subsequently excreted. At the same time, the grape's natural sugar and protein help build healthy new tissue.

THE GRAPE CLEAN-UP

The Grape Diet can be followed as an annual 'spring clean', to revitalise the body, to lose weight or for more serious or chronic

The first stage of the grape cure involves a pure diet of grapes, which is then supplemented with fresh fruits and cottage cheese in the second stage.

illnesses. It has been repeatedly proved that the grape diet can be safely followed for up to two months. But for periods longer that a few days you should seek the supervision of a sympathetic general practitioner or naturopath.

The cure is best begun on a empty stomach with a clean intestine. Ideally, this means a two or three day fast beforehand, during which plenty of water (preferably still mineral water) is drunk. A daily cleansing enema of 1 litre (2 pints) of water mixed with the strained juice of a lemon is also recommended. However, mild herbal laxatives may be taken to eliminate the system more rapidly if you prefer (see HERBAL LAXATIVES).

KIDNEY CURE

Having lost one kidney through a childhood illness, in 1957 – long before transplants became commonplace – Basil Shackleton, aged 53, discovered that his remaining kidney was diseased. Remembering a friend's casual remark that German clinics successfully treated patients with nothing but grapes, in desperation Shackleton embarked on the Grape Cure.

As he records in his book: 'I lived on grapes, and grapes alone for seven weeks, and on the 23rd day of the treatment, an abcess came away by the roots (later confirmed by a hospital biopsy) from my one and only kidney. My body had completely cured itself – after all orthodox medical treatments had failed over a period of 40 years'.

The complete Grape Cure comprises the following four stages:

Stage One – Grapes Only
Start the day with two glasses of hot or cold water, followed 30 minutes later by the first meal, up to 225 g (½lb) grapes. the grapes should always be thoroughly washed in hot water to remove all traces of pesticide. Chew the skin and seeds thoroughly, but it is not necessary to swallow more than a few. These however provide fibre and helps the elimination process. If treating a gastric ulcer, omit seeds and skin.

Since regular daily elimination is essential to the cure, unless the grapes act as a laxative, 1 litre (2½ pints) of lukewarm water should be drunk once or twice a day until there is a natural movement of the bowels. To effect total elimination of all toxins no other foods or medicines should be taken for the duration of the cure.

Seven grape meals a day should be eaten every two hours. Any ripe grapes are suitable, but as different varieties contain differing elements, it's advisable to eat as many different kinds as available, including seedless.

A minimum of 450 g (1 lb) and a maximum of 1.8 kg (4 lbs) of grapes should be eaten daily. A dislike of grapes may indicate excessive bodily toxins and possibly the need for another short fast. But unless the grapes are enjoyed, the person is probably better off seeking another cure. However, unsweetened, additive-free grape juice, widely available in health stores and supermarkets, can be used instead of, or as a supplement to, the grape diet.

Side Effects
During detoxification unpleasant symptoms may occur. These can include headaches, dizziness, vomiting, diarrhoea, sweating, joint pains, skin eruptions and weakness.

Dr Brandt advised patients to remain on the grape diet until they stopped losing weight. This signals the successful completion of the purifying process.

Stage Two
Other fresh fruits, tomatoes and sour milk or cottage cheese, may be added to the diet, though grapes alone should still form the first and last meal of the day.

Stage Three
This comprises any food which can be eaten raw, including vegetables, dried and

NUTRITIONAL NOTES

Grapes contain per 100g (4oz):
Calories – 62
Protein 0.7 g
Carbohydrate – 14.3 g
Calcium – 13 mg
Vitamin A – 30 international units
Vitamin C – 3 mg
There are also small amounts of fat, iron, other minerals, vitamins B1 and B2.

fresh fruits, sour milk, natural low-fat yogurt, buttermilk, honey and olive oil (see HONEY; OLIVE OIL).

With the gradual introduction of grated cheese and hard boiled eggs, the stage three diet may, if desired, become permanent. Alternatively, after a few weeks the person is ready for the final stage of the cure.

Stage Four – Mixed Diet
• A grape breakfast: one grape variety only
• A cooked dinner with steamed vegetables
• A salad supper

Should the original symptoms recur, it is advisable to return to a raw food diet for a few weeks longer.

All raw foods can be added in the third stage of the diet. It is possible to maintain this diet permanently if hard-boiled eggs or cheese are included.

EAT ORGANIC!

Before embarking on a grape-only diet, ensure that you have found a source of untreated organic grapes – most grapes for sale in larger stores are coated with pesticides.

GREEN LIPPED MUSSELS

A natural dietary supplement that offers new hope for arthritis sufferers

The extract of this New Zealand shellfish has allowed many arthritics to reduce and even stop taking the drugs they thought they could never live without

Shellfish are probably one of the oldest of Man's foods. They are palatable, readily digested and highly nutritious. Shrimps can be caught in the shallow waters of the sea at low tide, while crabs are found in rock pools.

Molluscs are abundant in coastal waters. They are soft-bodied, usually hard-shelled animals including snails, winkles, whelks, oysters, mussels, cockles and scallops, and are found on dry land and in both fresh and salt water. Cockles get stranded on beaches, and can be collected while the tide is

out. Winkles can be harvested simply by detaching them from the rocks to which they cling tenaciously.

Mussels – 'bi-valved' molluscs like oysters and scallops, with two hinged shell plates or valves – can be similarly removed from large stones, extracted from rocky crevices, and dug out from their hiding places in shallow mud or in the sand.

A fashionable food in the West today, especially when included in salads, stir-fry recipes and paella, or served as the French dish 'moules marinière', mussels

are also prized by the New Zealand Maoris, who eat the Green lipped variety daily in large quantities. They are rich in protein, minerals and other nutrients, and the Green lipped Mussel, *Perna canaliculus*, is also the source of a new, natural remedy for arthritis.

TESTING MUSSELS

Extract of Green lipped Mussel was used in cancer trials in the USA in the early 1970s, and those patients who also suffered from arthritis reported that their joint pain and stiffness were considerably reduced during the trial period. Many other trials have also been carried out and have shown the beneficial effects of this nutrient, time and again.

PURE MUSSEL

The purity of Green lipped Mussel extract produced commercially is ensured by deriving it from mussels cultivated in carefully controlled marine farms. They are grown on a matrix of ropes suspended in ocean water off the coastline of New Zealand, and the water is monitored daily for bacteriological, heavy metal or other pollution. They mussels are harvested after two years, cleaned, analysed for quality control, and subjected to freeze-drying before being packed into capsules.

Green lipped mussels are found only in the water off New Zealand.

A SIGNIFICANT TRIAL

Many clinical trials of the efficacy of Green lipped Mussel extract in treating arthritis have now been carried out. Of particular interest is the pilot study undertaken at the Glasgow Homoeopathic Hospital in 1971.

This trial was devised by consultant physicians Drs Robin and Sheila Gibson. Their interest in Green lipped Mussel extract was aroused by the considerable and sustained improvement in the condition of an 83-year-old osteoarthritis sufferer who was given the extract by a friend from New Zealand. Her condition had not responded positively either to orthodox or homoeopathic treatment and this sudden improvement led the doctors to organise a clinical trial to test the extract further.

Forty-six patients suffering from classical rheumatoid arthritis, in which membranes around the affected joints become inflamed; and ten patients suffering from osteoarthritis, where cartilage covering joint surfaces becomes thin (resulting in friction between the bone endings), were included as test subjects. All the patients in the trial had been treated with both conventional and homoeopathic remedies, but had failed to respond. The trial was backed up by laboratory tests performed at the outset and throughout its duration. Improvement was only considered to have occurred if both patient and doctor agreed, and if there was objective evidence – such as ease and speed of walking – to confirm this.

THE VERDICT

Green lipped Mussel extract was deemed beneficial to two thirds of the patients with rheumatoid arthritis and the improvement, which took 3 to 4 weeks to become noticeable, was independent of patients' age and the duration and severity of the disease. The extract, either alone or in combination with other 'first line' anti-inflammatory treatments, proved much more effective than salicylate (aspirin) given alone.

By contrast, only a third of the osteoarthritic patients – those suffering from the generalised form of the disease (affecting several joints) – gained relief. It was suggested that osteoarthritis affecting single joints only may result from a different disease process to the generalised form – a form which could have more in common with the rheumatoid variety.

ANTI-INFLAMMATORY

The active ingredient in Green lipped Mussel extract seems to be a large protein molecule which may attack the root cause of arthritis as well as reducing the inflammation itself. Its only side effects were mild nausea, flatulence and bowel looseness that disappeared after 2 to 3 weeks. It also seemed to protect the stomach from the irritating effects of other anti-arthritic drugs, including aspirin and the NSAIDs (non-steroidal anti-inflammatory drugs, for example piroxicams such as Feldene, or indomethacins such as Indocid).

In the UK alone, 22 million NSAID prescriptions are issued yearly. Their side effects account for one quarter of all the adverse drug reactions reported each year to the CSM (Committee on Safety of Medicines). The increasing popularity of Green lipped Mussel extract should help to relieve this problem too – the recommended dose is usually 350 mg three times daily, and some researchers have found it to be even more effective when combined with physiotherapy and a wheat-free diet.

LIVING WITH ARTHRITIS

A survey carried out recently indicated that more than 50 per cent of arthritis sufferers worry about the possible side-effects of the drugs they are prescribed and actively seek help for their conditions through dietary or other alternative therapies.

Of the arthritis sufferers who found relief from taking extract of Green lipped Mussel, 77 per cent noticed the improvement during the first three months, while 43 per cent felt better in the first month.

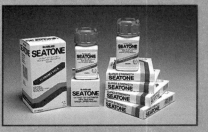

Green lipped mussel, in capsules.

NUTRIENT-ENRICHED BODIES

The mussels with which most people are familiar are about 2.5 to 5cm (1-2in) long. Like other bi-valved molluscs, they draw water in between their shell valves and extract food particles and oxygen through their inner surfaces and gills. 'Perna' Green lipped Mussels, by contrast, measure up to 15-20cm (6-8in), and have evolved a particularly efficient filter feeding system that has been termed 'a true marvel of nature'.

They filter up to 45 litres (ten gallons) of sea water daily, and their bodies become enriched with a unique blend of minerals, vitamins, trace elements, amino acids, mucopoly-saccarides and other nutrients.

GUARANA

Food of the gods and South American stress-reliever

Guarana (pronounced gwa-ra-na) has been used for centuries in its native areas – Brazil and the Amazon region of South America – but has only recently become known in other parts of the world as both a general tonic and an effective nerve-soother

Guarana (*Paullinia cupana*), a member of the soapberry family, is a woody, climbing shrub with a smooth, twining stem, tooth-edged leaves and clusters of short-stalked flowers. Its pear-shaped fruits are about the size of a hazelnut and turn red or orange when ripe. They contain tiny seeds, shaped like horse chestnuts, and it is these that are used in herbal medicine.

ENERGY ELIXIR
Among the Maués and other native Indian tribes of Brazil, the Amazonian guarana is a legendary herb, regarded as something of an elixir and believed to be a sacred plant sent by the gods to provide both food and medicine. The Maués made a tonic drink from guarana, either by mixing roasted, powdered guarana seeds with a little water and cassava root to make a paste which was stirred into water, or by infusing the seeds. They consumed this tonic in large amounts, to keep them going on their long treks through the forest in search of food. It helped them to overcome their exhaustion, and restored their energy.

A Jesuit priest, travelling in the Amazon region in the 17th century, described the fruit of the guarana and the way it was used by the indigenous Indians to allay hunger, and to cure fevers, pain and headaches. It has been traditional in Brazil to make the powdered seeds into a hard stick and to grate this – using the jaw-bone of a fish – into hot water to make a tea.

STIMULATING FINDINGS
In 1826, a German chemist, Von Martius, discovered that guarana contained a caffeine-like stimulant he called guaranine. But it was not until 1973 that significant modern research began into guarana. The centuries-old information on it was updated and checked for validity by the health department of the Brazilian government. Since then, guarana has been the subject of still further research and clinical trials, in Brazil and in other countries.

Research has produced evidence that guarana is a nervine (a nervine is something that helps the nervous system) and above all it has become valued as a tonic herb. Some sceptics have suggested that guarana's effect is like that of drinking several strong cups of coffee, because of its high quantities of guaranine. But, as with other plants, its effects are more complex. One South American authority on guarana says that

AGE-OLD REMEDY

Studies suggest guarana is an effective tonic for the elderly, and may help combat hardening of the arteries. A recipe said to improve energy and help combat signs of ageing is 5 ml (1tsp) each of guarana powder, brewer's yeast and wheat germ, combined with 15 ml (3 tsp) of pure honey and one glass of mineral water. Blend thoroughly and drink every morning before breakfast.

Guarana plantations have given an economic boost to communities in Brazil. The soil and climate there are ideal, while the environment is both well-balanced and relatively pollution-free.

Above: Seeds for supplements should be sun-dried rather than roasted for better body assimilation (so check the label for this). Left: Amazonian legends view the black and white shape emerging from the red, outer part of the guarana fruit as an 'all-seeing eye', looking out from the dark undergrowth. The black part is the seed that will eventually be ground up and used in remedies.

various parts of the world. Apart from its general tonic action, there is evidence that guarana may be positively beneficial for a variety of health problems, including:

- As a nervine, to relax the stomach, relieve migraine and other headaches, and ease the pain of neuralgia (pain caused by irritation of, or damage to, a nerve).
- As an efficient diuretic, to rid the body of excess fluid.
- Some users have found it effective for period pains and stomach upsets.
- As a febrifuge – to cool the body down when it is overheated.
- As an intestinal disinfectant, helpful in some cases of diarrhoea.
- As an anti-depressant, without becoming addictive.
- For weakness and debility. To help beat fatigue and exhaustion.

guaranine acts slowly on the body, unlike the caffeine in coffee, and also that it acts with the plant's other components in a natural, balanced way.

Apparently, guarana works as a gentle stimulant on the adrenal system (part of the hormone system), to prevent fatigue. It also appears to aid concentration and improve both intellectual activity and physical stamina. Some professional sports men and women claim that it improves their performance.

RANGE OF BENEFITS
Guarana is currently being used by individuals, and in herbal therapy, in

'SECRET EYES'
Guarana gets its name from a native word which means 'secret eyes' a name which is fitting because as you walk in the rain forests the split red pods of the plants with their black and white fruits look like millions of eyes watching your every more.

ADAPTING TO STRESS
Guarana is regarded as an 'adaptogen' and, because of this, may help build up our immune system and combat stress. An adaptogen is a remedy that literally improves the body's adaptability and the term is applied to remedies that help maintain a proper 'stress response'. When the body is heading for a stress overload, these remedies adjust various bodily functions to compensate, so that breakdown does not occur.

In his booklet, *Survival in the Concrete Jungle*, Brian Hildreth, a naturopath and herbalist, deals with the problem of stress. Based on research and his own clinical experience with patients, he advocates the use of guarana as part of a comprehensive anti-stress strategy.

Dr. Hildreth sees stress as a problem of misplaced energy, depleting our bodies. Certainly there are physiological changes when we are under stress, such as anxiety feelings, faster heart and breathing rates, and tightening of muscles. The adrenal hormones produce these 'fight or flight' responses, but at the same time suppress the body's immune system.

If the body is constantly subjected to stress, it follows that our immune system will not be able to work at its most efficient level. The body has to learn when 'emergency' responses are needed and when they are damaging. Brian Hildreth's anti-stress strategy involves a visualisation technique and a positive mental approach, combined with a course of guarana taken on a daily basis.

AVAILABILITY
Guarana capsules are available from some health food stockists, and some natural therapy clinics. They are made using selected guarana seeds, from plants organically grown in Brazil, which have been sun-dried and stone-ground. Each capsule provides 500 mg of guarana and the usual recommended dosage is two a day.

HAWTHORN

Wayside tonic

The hawthorn tree has long provided a natural, widely-available remedy for ailments of the heart and circulatory system

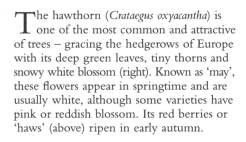

The hawthorn (*Crataegus oxyacantha*) is one of the most common and attractive of trees – gracing the hedgerows of Europe with its deep green leaves, tiny thorns and snowy white blossom (right). Known as 'may', these flowers appear in springtime and are usually white, although some varieties have pink or reddish blossom. Its red berries or 'haws' (above) ripen in early autumn.

SACRED TREE

Hawthorn is not only valued for its beauty but for centuries has been put to a variety of uses – as hedging, wood for stakes and small boxes, and as food and medicine. Hawthorn also features in many folklore traditions. In ancient Greece, for example, sprigs were given to wedding guests as a token of happiness for the bridal pair and it was often seen as a symbol of protection against evil – people would plant hawthorn trees next to houses to ward off evil or carry

Fresh, young hawthorn leaves, served here with beetroot, add a nutty flavour to salads.

NATURAL BEAUTY

In the Middle Ages, young girls would bathe their face in hawthorn dew on May morning to give themselves a beautiful complexion. As a beauty herb, hawthorn lotion, made by infusing berries or blossom is recommended for the skin, especially to clear facial blemishes. To make a hawthorn lotion soak two or more handfuls of dried flowers and berries in three cups of water. Leave overnight then bring to the boil and simmer for 10 minutes. Leave to cool before straining and pouring into a stoppered jar. Keep in the refrigerator and use within a week. Combined with other herbs such as rosemary and thyme, hawthorn lotion can make a mild facial astringent for use after cleansing.

sprigs to protect themselves against sickness.

Hawthorn has associations with Christian legends too. Its wood is reputed to have been used for Jesus' Crown of Thorns, while the first hawthorn bush was said to have grown from St Joseph's staff.

In the past, hawthorn was used in folk medicine as a general tonic and a heart stimulant, as well as for treating a number of other conditions, including gout, vertigo, and insomnia. Hawthorn berries were 'rediscovered' in the 19th century by an Irish general practitioner who used them as a heart medicine for his patients, while in 1899 an American physician wrote about their use as a heart tonic, for treating angina pectoris, oedema and other conditions. Hawthorn leaves and berries are still used today in both herbal and homoeopathic medicine.

HAWTHORN FOR A HEALTHY HEART

Hawthorn is a valued natural medicine, primarily as a heart tonic used especially for treating high blood pressure, and certain other heart troubles. Leaves, flowers, but most often the berries, may all be used medicinally, usually in the form of teas or liquid extracts and often in conjunction with other healing herbs.

It has a normalising effect, and can serve as either a cardiac depressant or stimulant depending on the problem. So, for example, it may be used to slow down and stabilise the action of the heart muscle when this is too rapid; to strengthen a weak heartbeat; or to

correct the heart's action when this is irregular. It may be prescribed in the treatment of angina pectoris, palpitations, and breathlessness related to ineffective action of the heart.

Good results have been reported for various heart conditions over the years. Numerous pharmacological studies have shown hawthorn to be an effective heart medicine, without side effects. One trial carried out in West Germany involved a hundred patients, all suffering from heart trouble. They were given regular doses of liquid extract of hawthorn over a period of

Renowned for its softening effect on the skin, hawthorn is often used in hand creams.

HAWTHORN TEA

Try this simple D!Y infusion:
1 Mix two parts of hawthorn leaves with one part each of lemon balm and sage.
2 Pour boiling water over the herbs and leave to infuse for at least five minutes.
3 Strain and drink sweetened with a little honey.
Alternatively, infuse two teaspoonfuls of hawthorn berries in a cup of boiling water for 20 minutes.

time and many showed a marked improvement in heart function. For some the hawthorn extract allowed them to reduce their intake of the drugs they had previously been prescribed while others were able to come off them completely.

BLOOD FLOW BENEFITS

Hawthorn has a vaso-dilatory action on the coronary blood supply. In other words, it increases the blood flow to the heart, with obvious beneficial results. Its general tonic action and its ability to dilate blood vessels means hawthorn is a useful remedy against hardening of the arteries, varicose veins and other circulatory disorders.

Hawthorn is also prescribed to normalise blood pressure, whether too high (hypertension) or too low (hypotension). High blood pressure brings with it a number of health risks, including strokes. Although there are a number of orthodox hypotensive and hypertensive drugs available, they do have a variety of unpleasant side-effects. Hawthorn and other herbs therefore offer a natural and safe alternative to controlling abnormal blood pressure, and avoiding its consequences. For the treatment of high blood pressure and the circulatory system, hawthorn may be used in combination with lime blossom, mistletoe and yarrow.

If it is taken in excessive amounts, hawthorn can cause dizziness, but used sensibly it is a gently acting, non-toxic remedy which is safe enough to take over long periods of time.

NATURAL SEDATIVE

Because of its action on the heart and central nervous system, hawthorn has been described as a classic remedy for the over-worked businessman or woman. It is one of the many herbal sedatives which have a

As well as being a herbal remedy, 'may' can also be used to flavour home-made wines.

calming and relaxing effect on the nervous system. It can help in cases of anxiety, for vertigo, nervous headaches and nervous spasms. An infusion of hawthorn flowers is recommended to calm the nerves, and as a bedtime drink can help combat insomnia.

Hawthorn berries for making your own infusion are available commercially from a number of herbal companies. An extract of the leaves of hawthorn and passionflower, together with arnica flowers and wild yeast, is used in a liquid remedy which is particularly recommended as a sedative for heart conditions and for vertigo. Hawthorn is amongst the ingredients in a number of other herbal tonics.

FOOD FROM THE HEDGEROWS

'Bread and cheese' is a traditional country name given to the young leaf shoots of hawthorn. Although they taste nothing like their name, they do have a pleasant nutty flavour. Leaf buds or very young leaves can also be eaten in salads, or used in sandwich fillings. Hawthorn blossom was traditionally used to make wine, while hawthorn liqueur is made by steeping the berries in brandy.

DID YOU KNOW?

The 'Mystical Thorn Tree' at Glastonbury, England, reputedly grown from Christ's crown of thorns, is a member of the hawthorn family which normally grows only on the hills around Jerusalem. The tree is thought to have been brought back to Britain by a returning Crusader. The tree is said to bloom on Christmas Day and creak in sympathy with Jesus every Good Friday between the hours of the Crucifixion.
Hawthorn was traditionally gather on Ascension Day and the branches of the tree were carefully preserved in medieval times, hung up indoors to keep the house and its inhabitants free from lightning, storms and calamities.

HERBAL LAXATIVES

The natural short-term solution

A healthy diet should ensure a healthy digestive system but if problems persist a number of plants offer natural relief from constipation

A properly-working digestive system is fundamental to good health, as it absorbs the nutrients we need and eliminates the waste matter we don't. Problems with this system lead to constipation – a failure of the body to expel its wastes quickly and efficiently. The poisons contained in the waste matter which remains in the bowel are then re-absorbed into the bloodstream and circulated through the body. Chronic constipation and lack of roughage are often contributory factors in various bowel disorders.

The best way to avoid such problems is through a healthy lifestyle and a healthy and varied diet, which should ensure the problem never arises, but if you do suffer from a bout of constipation, herbal laxatives can be of help in the short term.

ANTHRAQUINONES AND APERIENTS

Herbal laxatives are plants that actively promote bowel movements and which may be used for occasional,

Cascara

non-persistent constipation, or as a temporary measure while better habits are established.

Many herbal laxatives belong to a group known as anthraquinone laxatives, and this category includes senna, cascara and aloes. They stimulate contractions of the muscle walls of the large intestine, which happens about eight to 12 hours after ingestion, and so many cause griping pain in the abdomen. Such plants should not be taken over a long period of time or they may discourage natural bowel movement, resulting in a dependency on the use of laxatives. Milder laxatives, called aperients, are preferable as they act by encouraging natural bowel function. These include bulk laxatives based on seaweed gums, psyllium seeds and dietary fibre.

STRONG STUFF

Cascara sagrasa (*Rhamnus purshiana*) is a native tree of North America's West coast. It has dark green, serrated leaves, small green flowers, and reddish bark which has been used as a herbal laxative by generations of native American Indians. Once the bark has dried it forms quilled or curved pieces. Like senna it stimulates bowel action, and also appears to restore tone to a relaxed bowel. Recommended dosage is 1-3 grams (½ teaspoon) of well-dried bark taken before going to bed. You can make an infusion by steeping half to one teaspoon of bark in a cup of hot water for an hour.

Senna this shrub is the best known of all laxatives. Its fruit pods and leaves are where the active substances, called sonnosides, are found. It has a stimulant effect, working mainly on the lower bowel, but also tones and cleanses the digestive system. Senna can cause griping so care should be taken with dosage and it is best taken in combination. Like cascara it is better to combine it with carminative herbs such as dill, fennel and peppermint, or the spices ginger, cinnamon and cloves.

Two species of senna are used medicinally:

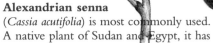

Senna

Alexandrian senna (*Cassia acutifolia*) is most commonly used. A native plant of Sudan and Egypt, it has lance-shaped, greyish-green leaves, and small yellow flowers.

Tinnevelly or **East Indian senna** (*Cassia angustifolia*) is a native plant of Arabia, and cultivated in Southern India. It has darker, narrower pods than Alexandrian, with leaves that are broader at the centre.

Dosage: half to two grams (¼–½ teaspoon) of dried pods or leaves or equivalent. Dried pods should be steeped in water for six to 12 hours. With Alexandrian senna pods use three to six pods per cup of water; with Tinnevelly senna use four to 12 pods.

THE GENTLE APPROACH

Dietary fibre which is not assimilated by the body increases the bulk of waste matter, so it is softer, and more quickly and easily passed out. Natural bulk-producing laxatives include linseed and psyllium seeds, which are useful mild remedies for constipation. They also have a gentle stimulating effect on the digestive process, primarily through the liver.

Linseed Linseeds (*linum usitatissimum*) are the small brownish seeds of the blue-flowered flax plant and are rich in oil. You can buy them as a supplement to sprinkle on foods such as breakfast cereals. Alternatively, soak a teaspoon of seeds in a cup of hot water for two hours, then strain and drink the liquid sweetened with honey and eat the seeds. They contain mucilage – a mixture of plant carbohydrates that becomes sticky in water, so that as well as combating constipation they are soothing and healing to the digestive tract.

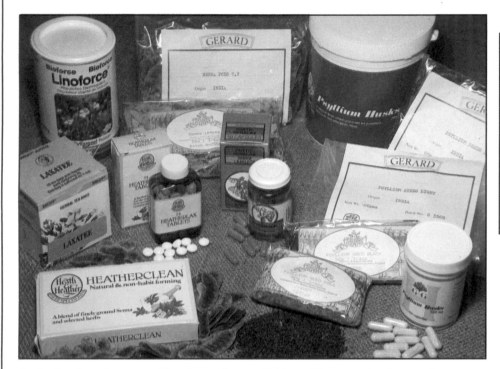

A selection from the range of laxative products available – tablets, capsules, bran, and even herbal tea bags or, if you prefer, dried seeds and leaves to make your own preparations.

Professional treatment should be sought for chronic constipation, bowel disorders, and for those whose constipation is caused by spastic colon or nervous spasms. In the latter case anthraquinone laxatives would only aggravate the condition.

Psyllium

Psyllium seeds work in much the same way as linseed. They are the seeds of two species of plantain:

Dark Psyllium (*Plantago psyllium*) Also known as fleaseed, this is a native of North Africa, Asia and Southern Europe. Its seeds are glossy, dark brown, and oblong in shape.

Pale or **Light Psyllium** (*Plantago ovata*) This species is a native of India and is also called Indian psyllium or ispaghula. Its smaller, boat-shaped seeds are pale greyish or pinkish brown in colour, and richer in mucilage than the dark variety.

In water, psyllium seeds form a gel which, like dietary fibre, is not assimilated so it produces more bulk in the bowels and speeds up the transit of waste material, encouraging a natural bowel action with no irritation or drastic stimulation. As it is also a lubricant, it does not cause griping pain and so provides a safe, effective laxative.

Psyllium has also been used to treat irritation of the bowel, and conditions such as colitis and diverticulitis, as its gentle action also has a local anti-inflammatory effect. Psyllium seeds can be mixed with a little hot water and left to stand for a few minutes until they form a tasteless gel. Taken two or three times a day for a limited period, this gel will give the colon a good 'spring clean'.

LAXATIVE LOW-DOWN

Dried senna leaves, pods, senna capsules and tablets; cascara bark; psyllium seeds and linseed, as well as psyllium capsules are available through health food stockists. There is also a wide range of combination herbal remedies, cleansing and laxative products on the market – including tablets, powders, liquid mixtures and teas. A typical formula might include aloes, cascara, or senna as laxatives; fennel to prevent griping;

dandelion as a tonic cleanser; antiseptic myrrh; and herbs such as lime and valerian to calm the system. One particular mild laxative tablet combines senna leaf with peppermint, aniseed, cloves and other spices. Some may include psyllium seeds for bulk, and elderflowers to break up any mucus.

THE DANGERS OF DIET

It has been estimated that half of the people living in affluent countries are constipated: the main cause of this is the typical Western diet – high in refined products and low in fibre. Refined foods can take up to three weeks to pass through the body, compared to one or two days for natural foods. the best remedy for constipation is therefore to switch to a wholefood diet – wholewheat grains and plenty of fresh fruit and vegetables. As well as being better for general health it provides the necessary roughage or fibre to ensure proper, natural bowel function. A good diet, plenty of exercise and regular bowel habits should prevent this problem.

Quite simple additions to diet can help constipation. One that is well-tried is good old-fashioned prunes. Soak them in water overnight and eat night and morning. A daily dose of mineral rich molasses can also help to combat cases of constipation.

SEEK PROFESSIONAL ADVICE

There are also a number of stronger forms of natural laxatives available, which are known as purgatives, cathartics and drastic hydrogogues. These are quite violent remedies and should be taken only under the careful instruction of a qualified practitioner.

HOMOEOPATHIC FIRST AID KIT

Nature's remedies . . . at your fingertips

Homoeopathy – one of the best known complementary therapies – is based on the principle of 'curing like with like'. Discover just how useful a handy homoeopathic first aid kit is in dealing with all kinds of problems

Homoeopathy uses natural remedies that produce similar symptoms to those of the illness being treated – 'curing like with like'. The aim of homoeopathic treatment is to stimulate the body's own natural powers of healing, taking into account the individual make-up of the whole person.

THE NATURAL SOLUTION
Many homoeopathic remedies derive from plants and minerals, others come from more unusual sources like snake venom. Homoeopathic medicines are prepared in a highly dilute form, so doses are minute; they are easy to take, safe for all the family and ideal for treating minor ailments and so for first aid in the home. You can buy homoeopathic first aid kits or build up your own, as a wide range of remedies is available from health food stockists.

Most of the preparations are taken as tablets, or granules – for home treatment the 6th potency (a specific degree of dilution) is recommended. For external use there are various liquids, creams and ointments.

CUTS AND BRUISES
No homoeopathic first aid kit is complete without Arnica – a marvellous remedy for shock, and for bruising after an injury. Several doses of Arnica tablets, at 15-minute to hourly intervals, help reduce pain and swelling and promote healing. Use Arnica lotion externally, but not if the skin is broken (see ARNICA).

For cleansing and dressing cuts and wounds, Calendula (marigold) can be used – 20 drops of tincture to 275 ml (½pt) of cooled, boiled water. This will help stop bleeding and, together with Calendula tablets, speed up the healing process and prevent infection (see MARIGOLD). For bruises, grazes and chapped skin, Calendula ointment is always a useful standby.

Hypercal tincture – a combination of Hypericum (St John's Wort) and Calendula – is excellent for cuts and grazes. Hypericum used on dressings is both pain-relieving and antiseptic and provides a good first aid remedy for painful cuts and puncture wounds, especially when there is damage to sensitive nerve-rich areas like the fingers. Preparations based on the herb Ledum (marsh tea), are useful treatments to have on hand for puncture wounds and splinters.

SPRAINS AND STRAINS
If you suffer from aching or strained muscles after too much physical activity, Arnica tablets and lotion will help relieve the pain and stiffness. Arnica is the choice for sprains when there is shock and severe bruising, whereas *Rhus*

toxicodendron (American poison ivy) provides ideal first aid for sprains or strains affecting joints, tendons, or ligaments, effectively relieving pain, stiffness and swelling. *Ruta graveolens* (rue) is recommended for tendon sprains, also for bruised bones and joints that worsen in the cold and damp, and improve with warmth and movement.

BURNS AND SCALDS

The stinging nettle, in the form of the remedy *Urtica urens*, will actually take the sting out of minor burns and scalds, as well as promoting healing. Apply the tincture or ointment, and take the potency tablets to reduce pain and redness (see STINGING NETTLE).

Calendula ointment, or another of the homoeopathic ointments for burns, will also soothe and heal. Cantharis (Spanish fly), taken by mouth or used externally, is another excellent remedy for burns, including sunburn. Use it, if possible, before blisters form.

BITS AND STINGS

Hypericum tincture or Hypercal are first aid remedies that relieve the pain and injury of minor animal bites and scratches, and are particularly effective for treating the nerves in damaged areas – two drops to one tablespoon of water can be used as a compress. Arnica is a remedy for stings that are painful to the touch and feel bruised – a drop of Arnica tincture on the sting should prevent swelling. If there is a stinging nettle type rash around it, then a compress of *Urtica urens* will bring relief, combined with 6th potency tablets. Pain and swelling from mosquito and other insect bites can be relieved by Hypericum or Hypercal tincture. As a protection against bites and stings, try Pyrethrum compound – another plant-based preparation.

DIGESTIVE UPSETS

A useful remedy to keep in the first aid box for minor digestive upsets is *Nux vomica*. It can help to relieve indigestion, including nervous indigestion, bilious attacks and nausea – a particularly soothing remedy for stomach ache and nausea when children have over-eaten. Persistent vomiting, which does nothing ultimately to relieve a general condition of nausea, may respond to Ipecac – prepared from a Brazilian shrub called Ipecacuanha – which is also a safe remedy for morning sickness.

COLDS AND 'FLU

Gelsemium (American jasmine) is useful to take at the onset of feverish colds or influenza. Aconite (monk's hood), besides being a first aid remedy for shock, can be used for the early stage of feverish colds, when symptoms include thirst, hot dry skin and restlessness. Aconite is also recommended for when a child catches cold after getting wet. For a streaming cold that feels worse indoors and better for being outdoors in the fresh air, the answer is an onion. *Allium cepa* is a classic homoeopathic cold remedy prepared from the red onion.

Some companies produce more comprehensive kits.

TAKING THE PILLS

Remedies taken by mouth should be dissolved on the tongue, allowing 20 minutes before eating or drinking. The remedies dissolve in the saliva and quickly pass into the very rich capillary supply near the tongue's surface. The blood supply here is also very rapidly renewed, making the tongue an excellent place for fast, efficient absorption of remedies.

The constituents of the remedies form such a delicate balance that, ideally, tablets and granules should be put directly on the tongue as quickly as possible, so that this balance remains undisturbed by contact with the air or with the hands.

SAMUEL HAHNEMANN

The founder and discoverer of the homoeopathic principle, Samuel Hahnemann (1755-1843) was a doctor who became dissatisfied with the medical practices of the time, which involved prescribing crude dosages of dangerous substances such as mercury and arsenic. Hahnemann began research on the basis of curing like with like, and discovered that higher dilutions gave more and more therapeutic results. As his reputation grew, opposition to his theories mounted and he was ridiculed by the orthodox medical profession.

NATURAL FIRST AID CHECKLIST

Here is a selection of homoeopathic remedies for your kit. Remember that remedies from other alternative disciplines can provide helpful additions to a strictly homoeopathic kit.

ACONITE: Particularly good for high temperatures, feverish colds, shock and fear

ARNICA: Effective for shock, as well as for sprains, bruises, injuries, boils, insect stings and exhaustion. Make sure you apply ointment only on unbroken skin

ARSENICUM: Excellent remedy to be included in the holiday first aid kit – helps non-persistent diarrhoea, mild food poisoning and vomiting

BELLADONNA: Good for high fevers, earaches and boils, nervous eczema and rashes

CALENDULA: Take for cuts and grazes, burns, scalds, dry cracked skin and cold sores

CANTHARIS: Good for burns, including sunburn, scalds and cystitis

GELSEMIUM: Take to counteract flu, flu-like colds and pre-examination nerves

HYPERICUM: Good remedy for burns, cuts, bites and sores

NUX VOMICA: Helps after-effects of over-eating or over-drinking and indigestion

PYRETHRUM: For bites and stings

RHUS TOXICONDRON: Take for sprins, rheumatism, chicken pox and shingles

WITCH HAZEL (Hamamelisu virginiana; used DISTILLED – keep in refrigerator). For insect bites and stings and mild sunburn

Remember that medicines are always better taken under qualified supervision, and any persistent condition must be seen by a practitioner

HONEY

A gift from the gods

Since ancient times, honey has been used to cure illness, increase vitality and provide health-giving properties.

Every medicine chest should contain a jar of fresh, unfiltered honey. Its most commonly recognised medicinal use is as a throat and bronchial remedy. Opera Singers and others who use their voices professionally find that honey soothes their vocal chords, and anyone with a sore throat or a husky voice should try nothing more complicated than a glass of hot milk and honey. Add a tot of brandy and you have an age-old remedy for influenza.

Taking a glass of hot water with one or two teaspoonfuls of new honey and the juice of half a lemon helps cure sleepless nights – but a spoonful of honey is also a good 'pick-me-up'.

FAST ACTING ENERGISER

Honey is of great value for digestive disorders: it excites the appetite, aids digestion and nourishes. Honey consists principally of simple sugars, readily assimilated by the body. As a result, it provides quick energy – especially important for athletes. Furthermore, there is much circumstantial evidence of the positive effects of honey on gastric and intestinal ulcers – the eminent Greek doctor Hippocrates was recommending honey as a means of curing ulcers as far back as 400 BC.

The sugars in the honey break down into products that create an unfavourable environment for bacteria; as a result it is of great value in healing minor scratches and cuts. Asthma and hay-fever sufferers claim that honey can greatly ease their symptoms.

There are many other illnesses that are said to be cured by honey, but even if these claims remain as yet scientifically unproven, consuming honey will not cause you any harm or have any after-effects – and it may well help to adjust your body chemistry, enabling you to get rid of any unhealthy condition.

EFFECTS OF POLLEN

Many of the beneficial effects of honey are thought to be due to the pollen it contains. It can be harvested from the

STORING HONEY

Honey should be stored in closed containers in a cool, dry place. Refrigeration hastens the crystallisation of liquid honey but, if granules do appear, they can be dissolved by standing the container in warm water. If hot water is used the enzymes may be destroyed and the flavour of the honey may be affected.

Strained honey contains all important vitamins and minerals and can be used to replace all or part of the refined white sugar in our diet.

hive using special traps that remove the pellets of pollen from the legs of the foraging bees, and if tiny amounts of pollen are consumed throughout the year, via honey, it is believed to provide an immunity against the allergy symptoms produced by the same pollen carried in the air. Honey consumed direct from the honeycomb is considered by many to be especially effective, as there are thought to be ingredients in the wax that enhance the effects of the pollen.

MASS-PRODUCED HONEY
As a natural food, honey needs little processing. Any treatment that heats or feeds the honey excessively will alter its flavour or texture. Large-scale honey process plants blend honey from many different countries in an attempt to produce a product of uniform colour and flavour. In a poor summer, honey production suffers and imports from other countries are required: because of this, honey bought directly from the beekeeper will usually be better than that bought in shops.

DIFFERENT HONEY FLAVOURS
Each floral source produces a nectar with a particular colour, aroma and flavour. Clover honey is light in colour and has a good flavour; the yellow flowers of oil-seed rape produce a fast-setting honey with a very mild taste; while honey from heather moors is highly prized for its strong flavour and aroma – but this, many feel, is an acquired taste.

Bees collecting nectar from clover (left) and heather (above) will produce honey with those flavours.

NCIENT BELIEFS

The use of honey as a remedy is older than the history of medicine itself. Many early civilisations believed it was the food of the gods and that it gave them their immortality. In antiquity and all through the Middle Ages honey was considered an important medicine. It was mixed with ointments and applied on plasters to treat boils, wounds, burns, ulcers and even eye cataracts. The Ancient Egyptians used it for surgical dressings and the Chinese for treating the scars caused by smallpox.

St Ambrose – patron saint of bees and advocate of honey.

The oldest mythologies are full of references that praise honey for its invigorating and health-giving properties. Honey is mentioned in the sacred writings of Persia, China and Egypt and is referred to in the Talmud and the Koran as well as in the Bible. The Song of Solomon recommends: 'Eat honey, my son, for it is good'.

St Ambrose is the patron saint of bees and he referred to honey as a gift from the gods. He tells us that: 'The fruit of the bees is desired of all and is equally sweet to kings and beggars and is not only pleasing but profitable and health giving, it sweetens their mouths, cures their wounds and carries remedies to inward ulcers.'

HOW HONEY IS MADE

Bees are attracted to flowers because of the bright colours they display, the perfume they give off and the nectar they know they will find there. Many flowers need bees to help transfer pollen (the male element in floral reproduction) from one blossom to another. Without bees many crops and wild flowers would fail to be pollinated and so would not reproduce.

The nectar from which honey is made lures the bees right into the centre of the flower where pollination must take place. The foraging bees carry the nectar back to the bee in a special 'honey stomach' which is separated from the bees' digestive system. The alchemy of the hive takes place as the foraging bees give their nectar to 'house bees', whose duty it is to transmute the base product into 'liquid gold' by passing the nectar back and forth between themselves several times.

Over 500 bees have to visit over 2.5 million flowers to produce 1lb of honey.

Each honey-bee contributes enzymes that split some of the larger sugar molecules in the honey into simpler ones. It is these simple sugars that are so easily absorbed by the human body. The original nectar (which is a dilute solution of sugars) is concentrated until the water content of the honey produced is less than 20 per cent. At this stage the honey is deposited in a beeswax cell and sealed in with a wax lid. These stores enable the bees to survive through the winter when there are few flowers about and it is too cold to forage. Honey sealed in a honeycomb is considered the best way to eat honey as it is completely natural and untouched or interfered with by man but, despite this, most honey sold is extracted from the comb. The wax cappings to the cells are first cut off with a knife and the honey is then removed by spinning the comb inside a drum. The liquid flows down the inside of the drum to the bottom where it can be drained off through a tap.

Products of the hive

Beeswax, honeycomb and honey extracted from the comb can all be gathered from a hive by an experienced beekeeper. The wax for the honeycomb is excreted from glands on the under-side of the bees' bodies. It is used in cosmetics, pharmaceuticals and in the making of candles and polishes.

Propolis is a sticky resin that bees gather from plants to seal and strengthen the honeycomb, and it has long been prized in varnishes. It is reputedly one of the ingredients of the varnish used by Stradivarius for his violins. It also has alleged medicinal properties.

Royal Jelly, claimed by its advocates to have wonderful rejuvenating powers, is the special food given by the worker bees to all the bees for the first three days after they hatch. The queen bee is fed on it for her entire life, hence the name Royal Jelly (see ROYAL JELLY).

Worker honey-bees filling the hexagonal chambers of their hive with honey.

COOKING WITH HONEY

Cooking with honey enriches and transforms cakes and pastry.

Many cooks have no idea of how beneficial an ingredient honey can be. The Ancient Egyptians, Greeks and Romans used honey for making cakes, sweets, beverages, wine and mead and to make salted meat more palatable. Honey has a special quality: it can enhance the individual taste of a dish – it is enrighing but not overpowering.

For baking, liquid honey is easier to mix with other ingredients if it is warmed slightly. Because honey has moisture-retaining properties it improves the keeping qualities of cakes and breads, and it will give a better texture to the bread's crust. Honey can also be used in cakes and biscuits: replace every 284g (10oz)

of white sugar with 227g (8oz) of honey, but reduce the liquid content in the recipe to allow for the extra liquid in the honey.

Honey is an excellent substitute for sugar in stewed fruits, and will add its own distinctive taste. When used to dress fish or meat, the honey penetrates deeper into the flesh than dry sugar. The delicate flavours of some honey are best appreciated in uncooked dishes: try sweetening fruit salads with honey, twirl it on to yogurt or pour it on to breakfast cereals – a recent survey indicates that more honey is consumed at breakfast than at any other meal. Honey can also be taken as a sugar substitute in tea and coffee.

SUGAR SUBSTITUTE

Honey can be used to replace all or part of the refined white sugar we use daily in our diet. According to the US Department of Agriculture's Food Composition Tables, 454g (1lb) of granulated white sugar, from sugar cane or sugar beet, contains nothing but carbohydrates and calories – all proteins, minerals and vitamins originally present in raw sugar are re-

moved in processing. In 454g (1lb) of white sugar there are 451 complex carbohydrates and 1748 calories.

Extracted and strained honey contains all important minerals and vitamins except for vitamin A. In 454g (1lb) of honey there are 1.4g of protein, 361 complex carbohydrates and 1333 calories. Try using honey instead of sugar in drinks and when baking.

To produce 454g (1lb) of honey, more than 550 bees have to visit more than 2.5 million flowers. If the bees are allowed to forage freely they will collect nectar from a variety of flowers during the season. The resulting multi-floral honey will be a subtle blend of flavours and aromas and the first taste of the season's blend is a thrill to every beekeeper. Single-taste honey, such as clover or orange blossom, is produced when the bees have nothing else available but large fields of these flowers.

WHY DOES HONEY CURE?

Modern scientific research into the constituents of honey has produced little that has convinced conventional medicine of its value as a curative substance. However, there are still elements in honey that have not been identified, and its use throughout the ages as a valued medicinal aid probably bears greter tribute to its healing abilities than any amount of incomplete scientific data.

BECOMING A BEEKEEPER

Beekeepers take a pride in the honey produced by their bees and it requires considerable skill to manage a colony of bees properly. You also need a stoical temperament to cope with the occasional sting!

If you are really interested in the quality of the honey you consume, try to find a beekeeper with their own hives in your locality who will supply you with honey in the comb of jars of honey that has simply been removed from the comb in a centrifuge without being treated in any way.

You could even start keeping your own bees. Part-time classes in beekeeping are available and there are many different societies that you could join to learn about beekeeping and setting up your own hives.

HORSETAIL

The silica storehouse

Horsetail is an unusual plant of which there are around 25 different species. It is the common or field horsetail (*Equisetum arvense*) that has been most generally used in herbal medicine. A native of Eruope, it also grows in other temperate areas, preferring a sandy, moist soil. Apart from invading our gardens, horsetail is widespread in fields, on moors and by the edges of streams and woodlands.

A PLANT WITH A DIFFERENCE

Unlike most of our familiar wild plants, the horsetail produces no flowers, or even leaves as such. It also has quite an unusual life cycle. Like the fern, it reproduces itself by means of spores. In spring it sends up thin, pale brown spore-bearing shoots. After releasing the spores, these shoots die down and are replaced by non-fertile, spiky green shoots, so the plant looks a bit like a miniature Christmas tree. The way the shoots grow gives the plant its name – in Latin, *equi* and *setum* literally mean 'horse' and 'tail', and it does bear a resemblance to a horse's tail. It is these green shoots – used fresh or dried – that are used in herbal medicine.

ANCIENT WISDOM

Fossil remains of huge *equisetum* type plants, millions of years old, have been discovered, showing just how ancient are horsetail's origins. It was certainly known and used by the Greeks and Romans – the Romans regarded horsetail as a general tonic, and as such ate the young shoots in salads, despite their very bitter taste. It was used medicinally for various ailments, as a lotion to stop bleeding or applied to wounds, for which the 2nd-century (AD) physician Galen called it a perfect cure.

In medieval times, it was employed as a medicine and even used in cooking, and the stems of some species were used to clean pewter, for which it was apparently very effective. Hence one of its names was pewterwort, or *Zinnkraut* in German-speaking countries, where it was used for this same purpose.

A NATURAL HEALTH STORE

Horsetail is a good source of the various minerals and trace elements that are so essential for our health, including

To many, the horsetail plant is just a troublesome garden weed, but to natural medicine it is a rich source of the valuable mineral silica, helpful to a wide range of health problems from gallstones to hair-loss

A GARDEN GIFT

Horsetail might be an unwelcome weed in your garden, but it seems tht it can actually be very good news for your garden plants. It is considered to be good for preventing mildew and deterring black spot. Spray leaves with a decoction made from 45g (1¾ oz) of horsetail to 3 litres (5 pints) of water.

potassium, magnesium, and calcium.

In addition, the tissue of the horsetail's stem is supported by a network of crystals of a natural chemical element called silica. The high silica content of horsetail is the most significant aspect of the plant, and it is this property that contributes to horsetail's wide range of beneficial and useful medicinal applications.

THE SILICA STORY

Silica is a mineral that is widely distributed over the Earth, even though we may not be aware of it. It strengthens plant stalks, giving them their ability to stand upright and resist winds. Silica is also present in our bodies, where it is involved in various processes.

Silica affects many of our tissues because it is needed to regulate metabolism. Amongst other things, it is involved in controlling the uptake of calcium, and its balance in the body. Calcium is of course most important in the formation of healthy, strong bones and teeth. It is of particular importance during childhood and in pregnancy.

Silica is also a re-mineralising agent, meaning that it helps to improve the body's own natural resistance, and aids the regeneration of healthy tissue. Another of its functions is to promote the elimination of waste matter. It can help break down abnormal tissue, such as localised accumulation of pus, caused by infection

SKIN-SAVER

For tired or problem skins, try an infusion of horsetail. Infuse 20g (¾ oz) of the dried herb in 100 ml (4 fl oz) of boiling water for 20 minutes and apply it to the skin. This will close the pores and tighten the skin, and is particularly good for greasy skins. Horsetail extract is used in some cleansing preparations, shampoos and hair rinses as well as in tonic foam baths.

SILICA SUM-UP

There are various sources of valuable silica, available for a wide range of health problems:

• **Dietary supplements** Some silica is present in the average diet, but it is not always readily absorbed. Silica obtained from plants such as horsetail is now available in the form of dietary supplements, in tablet or capsule form, on sale at health food stockists. These are designed to provide silica in a soluble, easily absorbed form.

Try ready-made remedies containing horsetail, or prepare your own.

Silica used in dietary supplements may come from various plant sources. Apart from horsetail, two plants rich in silica are hemp nettle and tropical bamboo. Silica is found, as a transparent sap called 'tabasheer', in the stalks of the female bamboo plant. This sap is said to contain 80 per cent organic silica, plus traces of te minerals copper and iron.

• **Herbal remedies** Horsetail is available as a dried medicinal herb from which infusions and lotions can be made. It is an ingredient in a number of herbal remedies too, including liquid tonics for both adults and children. One specific remedy for enlarged prostate gland and bladder discomfort has horsetail as the main ingredient, with other herbs including hydrangea. Another remedy, also available in tablet form, is for the relief of cystitis and it too contains *equisetum* as one of its components. Horsetail is also included in some herbal remedies specifically formulated to strengthen blood vessels.

• **Biochemic and homoeopathic silica** Silica is available as a single biochemic tissue salt and in various combination remedies for: minor skin ailments, brittle nails, hair-loss, nervous headaches and migraine.

You can also buy silica homoeopathic tablets in the medium strength potencies suitable for self-treatment of minor health problems. These tablets are recommended for chronic headeaches, sinus trouble, boils and abscesses. They should also help to improve the general condition of skin, hair and nails.

Among their many uses, silica preparations may help prevent hardened arteries.

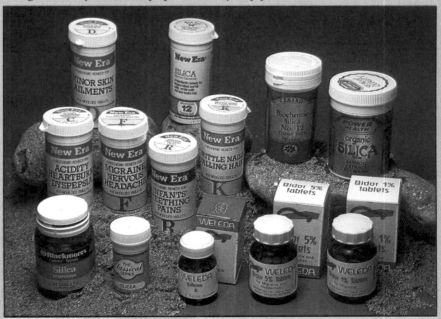

that are known as abscesses – getting rid of toxins and reducing inflammation.

Silica appears to play a part not just in keeping blood vessels healthy – helping to prevent hardening of the arteries by maintaining elasticity – but also in reducing degeneration of cartilage. A shortage of silica in the brain and nerve tissues is believed by many to contribute to poor memory, and lack of silica may also be responsible for the delayed healing of broken bones, particularly in older people.

SILICA AND SKIN

Silica is of particular importance for the skin, and is an element in tooth enamel and in the body's connective tissues (which support and connect the body's organs). The most common form of connective tissue is collagen. As we get older, our natural supply of collagen diminishes, with the result that our skin becomes less elastic, losing its smoothness and tone, while our nails may become brittle and our hair becomes coarser and loses something of its shine. Silica, in combination with vitamin C, protein and other substances, is needed to form and preserve this vital collagen tissue.

Silica thus helps to keep skin healthy and supple, at the same time as strengthening

Silica can be particularly effective in restoring healthy skin tone after an illness.

The body's uptake of calcium – important during pregnancy – is enhanced by silica.

hair, nails and bones. It has been used with good results to improve the complexion, brittle nails and over-dry hair.

HERBAL HORSETAIL

Horsetail has a wide range of applications and is used – for its silica content – in dietary supplements, as a medicine, and as a constituent in other medicinal herbal remedies.

As well as the applications already mentioned, horsetail's astringent properties provide effective relief from problems of the prostate gland in men and the genito-urinary tract in both men and women, reducing any bleeding and healing damaged tissues, thanks to its high silica content. Although a mild

diuretic, horsetail's astringency makes it beneficial in treating bed-wetting in children. For prostrate problems – inflammation or benign enlargement of the gland – horsetail is used alone or in some cases combined with hydrangea. Horsetail is also of value in treating cystitis – inflammation of the inner lining of the bladder, often recurrent, that particularly affects women, causing pain and considerable discomfort.

Silica is one of the 12 tissue salts that form the basis of the Biochemic System of medicinal therapy developed in the 19th century by Dr Wilhelm H Schuessler (see BIOCHEMIC TISSUE SALTS). Basically, Schuessler believed that the disease process was associated with a deficiency of one or more inorganic substances, which he called tissue salts. Prepared in a similar way and taken like homoeopathic remedies, tissue salts are available singly or in combination. The action of silica taken in this form is long-lasting and particularly effective on the bones, joints, glands and skin. It is used especially for boils, styes, brittle nails and scalp disorders.

HOT AND COLD

Do you suffer from sweat feet? If so, homoeopathic silica could be the answer to the problem, as silica can check excessive and offensive perspiration. On the other hand, people who always feel cold and shivery might benefit from taking silica for a couple of months, as it apparently improves the supply of oxygen to the body's tissues.

A HEALING CUP OF TEA

• Horsetail tea will help to heal and restore damaged tissue when there is internal inflammation, as in the case of ulcers. The tea is also recommended for chest complaints, including chronic bronchitis. The silica content of the plant enriches the blood and encourages the formation of blood corpuscles and so may be helpful for treating anaemia and loss of blood.

For mouth ulcers, it is recommended that the fresh juice or horsetail tea should be held in the mouth for a minute or two before swallowing. Gargling with the tea can also relieve inflamed tonsils.

Horsetail Tea:
1 Pour 1 cup of boiling water over 2 teaspoonfuls of the dried herb.
2 Infuse this mixture for approximately 15-20 minutes.

As a medicinal tea, this should be drunk three times a day.

• Due to its astringency, horsetail helps to sto bleeding from wounds and aids the healing of infected cuts, sores and external ulcers. A fairly strong decoction can be used as a compress or, in poultice form, horsetail can be applied externally to swellings and bruises.

BATH-TIME

Horsetail Bath Taking a bath to which a horsetail infusion has been added can ease the pain of rheumatism and chilblains. It is also good for skin troubles – try combining it with a soothing herb like marshmallow. For the bath, steep 100 g (4oz) of the herb in hot water for an hour or so and then add it to your bath-water.

Sitz Baths Horsetail can be used in sitz baths to help improve blood circulation in the abdominal region. This can be helpful for various conditions including bladder and menstrual problems. It is recommended that you use 100g (4oz) of horsetail to 5 litres (1 gallon) of cold water. Infuse for 12 hours, heat gently and add to a warm (not hot) bath.

Above: Microscope close-up of naturally occurring silica. Left: Ancient horsetail fossil.

A fertile, spore-bearing horsetail shoot.

Once the spores are released, these fertile shoots die down and are replaced by the familiar spiky green stems.

Silica preparations are also useful in helping to clear up or prevent suppuration, as in the case of boils.

HOMOEOPATHIC SILICA

In highly dilute homoeopathic form, silica has a long-lasting, deep-seated action on the body's tissues. This property means that silica is of great assistance in treating chronic conditions – conditions that are underlying and recurrent. Silica is particularly beneficial for the skin, for infections, and for chronic headaches, including headaches caused by migraine attacks.

As a homoeopathic first aid remedy, silica is useful for infected cuts and wounds, and for really stubborn splinters that have become deeply embedded in the skin – to help remove them and prevent the splinter area from going septic.

MIGRAINES

Silica and iron (in the form of ferrous sulphate) may seem an unlikely combination in the treatment of migraine and headaches, yet they are effective for many sufferers. They can help to reduce both the severity and frequency of migraine attacks. These two substances together, available as tablets, act in particular on the nervous and digestive systems to tackle the complex origins of the problems. They come in two strengths – a lower potency to take over a period of time, which helps to overcome a constitutional tendency to migraine, and a higher potency to take during actual attacks. Unlike conventional drugs used to treat migraine, they do not produce side-effects.

DID YOU KNOW?

In the days before Teflon-coated utensils, the high silica and soap content of horsetail gave it a practical use as pan scrubbers and pot scourers.

The nearest relatives to horsetail were giant plants which lived millions of years ago and formed much of the coal and anthracite we use today. The high silica content made the plants very fossilable.

HORSETAIL COMPRESS

A horsetail compress can help relieve rheumatic pain and chilblains and heal cuts and wounds. Leave 50g (2oz) of the herb to steep in 1 litre (2 pints) hot (not boiling) water for an hour, stirring occasionally. When tepid, pour onto a pad of cotton wool and bandage in place.

JOJOBA
A natural moisturiser from the desert

The marvellous lubricant qualities of the wax extracted from jojoba shrubs make it a 'natural' for skin and hair – its unusual degree of purity is an added bonus

The Apache Indians must be very amused by the so-called 'recent' discovery of jojoba (pronounced ho-ho-ba). For centuries they've been gathering the seeds and crushing them to extract their wax. They use this wax for almost every practical purpose: in cooking, as a lubricant, to dress their hair, as a natural sun-screen and even as a medicine. The 'civilised' world only uncovered the wonders of jojoba about 15 years ago, yet it is a truly remarkable substance.

DESERT DISCOVERY
Jojoba (*Simmondsia chinensis*) is a very long-living shrub that is native to the Sonoran Desert of Arizona, California and north-western Mexico. It is drought-resistant and thrives in marginally fertil, arid land. A young plant takes between three and five years to produce a seed, but the shrub can live for up to 200 years.

When the special properties of jojoba were first discovered, the seeds were gathered in the wild. The very first commercial crops were grown in Israel, but now that jojoba is big business, most plantations – are covering thousands of square kilometres (miles) – are concentrated in North America. Vast reaches of desert have been made green with these highly productive little bushes.

THE SOFT OPTION
What makes jojoba so special to the cosmetic industry is that it is one of nature's finest skin softeners. Until the early 1970s the industry had relied on two animal softeners – lanolin and sperm whale oil – to add to lotions and potions. It was the realisation that lanolin could cause allergies, along with the passing of the Endangered Species Conservation Act in 1972 (forbidding importation of sperm whale products into the USA), that began the search for a substitute. In the 1930s,

The seeds inside these leafy cases yield unusually high levels of a very pure, yellowish oil.

DEFEATING TECHNOLOGY

Even modern technology cannot improve much on the old Red Indian way of extracting the liquid wax from the jojoba seed.

The jojoba seeds are gathered and the outer leaves removed. These seeds are then pulverised and the pulp is firmly pressed, to allow the wax to run into vats. This wax is then put through a fine filter to remove any impurities. In some cases it is pasteurised (heat-treated), in order to purify it even further. Because jojoba wax is naturally odourless, colourless and very stable, it needs no further treatment.

As well as providing a valuable oil source, planting jojoba can stop land from becoming desert.

scientists had analysed jojoba and discovered that it was almost identical in chemical make-up to sperm whale oil. It therefore emerged as its very natural successor.

SUPPLY AND DEMAND

About 12 years ago, the cosmetic industry launched jojoba as the wonder discovery and it was included in practically every new product formulation. Picking crews were sent up into the mountains and deserts to locate and gather the seeds in order to meet the enormous demand. Eventually, the supply was unable to meet the demand, and the jojoba boom began to plateau. Now that it is commercially grown, you will see it starting to make a come-back.

PURE MAGIC

The wonderful thing about jojoba is that it is very pure. Although referred to as an oil, it's actually a liquid wax. Jojoba is extremely light, odourless and very stable. It simply doesn't go rancid so it needs no preservative added to it. This means that most products that include it in their formulation can be made without synthetic chemical additives.

Jojoba is so effective because as well as being very similar to sperm whale oil, it also closely resembles the skin's natural lubricant, sebum. It penetrates quickly and deeply into the skin, making it soft, but without leaving a greasy residue. Jojoba is primarily known as a superb hair conditioner, and in shampoos and hair conditioning products it acts just like the flow of sebum down the hair shaft, smoothing down the outer cuticle and adding a lustrous shine.

SKIN-DEEP

Jojoba's ability to penetrate the skin and hair has been carefully monitored in experiments at the University of Michigan, in the USA. Absorption is thought to occur through the pores of the skin and via hair follicles.

Jojoba does not cause the skin or hair to become greasy because absorption is so rapid that both pores and follicles remain open and unclogged, able to continue functioning freely. In fact, there is a very strong feeling that jojoba can actually help people with an oily skin. Research into why this should be so is still underway, but the theory is that, by behaving like sebum, it actually tricks the skin into stopping sebum production. Dermatologists studying this theory are interested to see if it will also yield a different approach to the treatment of acne, which is caused by the skin's over-production of sebum.

HOPE FOR BALDNESS?

Other claims for this unique liquid wax include its possible effectiveness in helping to prevent baldness. The theory is that certain types of baldness are caused by excess sebum blocking the hair follicles and literally suffocating them until they die. Regular application of jojoba is said to displace the hardened sebum and so keep the follicles unblocked, alive and thriving – able to produce healthy hair.

The baldness theory may sound a little far-fetched, but it does illustrate just how highly jojoba is thought of. Perhaps, now that supplies are becoming more readily available, we will once again see an increasing number of hair and skin care products using this very old, 'new' discovery.

Jojoba has been called 'a gift from the desert to the sea' because it provides an effective sperm whale oil substitute in cosmetics.

KELP EXTRACTS

Health on the shoreline

Seaweed has been used as a cure-all and folk remedy for centuries. It is only recently, however, that its high levels of essential nutrients have been fully appreciated and put to wider health uses

Kelp is a generic term applied to the larger types of seaweed. Over 800 species come under this category, and many of them are used in both domestic and industrial settings. Kelp has established itself as a valuable sea vegetable in cooking (either alone or in other dishes); it is also used in toiletries and cosmetics, as a gelling agent, as an addition to therapeutic baths, and in liquid fertiliser. Health-conscious shoppers will probably know kelp best as a food supplement, to be taken sprinkled on food or in tablet form.

AGE-OLD

Seaweed is one of the oldest cultivated crops. Pliny the Elder wrote about it in his *Natural History* in the first century AD, and the ancient Chinese offered it up in ceremonies to their ancestors. The Romans used seaweed as animal feed and crop manure, and the Greeks turned to it for treating gout and intestinal problems. During the Middle Ages the main method of processing seaweed was to burn it, and extract bromine, iodine and potash (crude potassium carbonate) from the resulting ash. This was particularly prevalent along coast lines and, in the British Scilly Isles, the practice continued until the 19th century. For a long time, the word 'kelp' meant the ash formed from the burned seaweed.

There was a revival of interest in kelp after 1880, when the process of making alginic acid from it was discovered. Alginates were first used for making transparent paper, but soon spread into many other industries. The greatest renewal of interest, however, has been during this century.

NUTRIENT-RICH

The varieties of kelp which are usually chosen to make supplements are the ones with the highest nutritional value. *Fucus vesiculosis, Ascophyllum nodsum* and *Macrocystes pyrifera* – all reddish brown in colour – are included in this category.

Although levels vary between varieties and the regions where it is grown, kelp is generally very high in the nutritional stakes, containing an impressive 13 vitamins, 20 amino acids and 24 trace elements. All edible seaweeds have an especially high iodine content, as they are capable of concentrating this element to an extraordinary extent. Some seaweeds contain 20,000 times more iodine that the water in which they grow.

Another important ingredient in kelp is chlorine. This chemical is necessary for the production of hydrochloric acid in the stomach – vital for the digestion of protein and fats, and the assimilation of potassium and sodium (which regulate the acid-alkaline balance within the body). Kelp feeds directly from sea water, and readily stores protein, carbohydrates, vitamins, and minerals in its leaves and stems. It is a good source of the vitamins A, C, D and B_{12}, thiamin, riboflavin, niacin and pantothenic

Five different forms in which to take kelp (clockwise from bottom left): arame, kombu, alaria, wakame and kelp tablets.

KELP VS RADIATION

Recently, kelp has attracted interest as a form of preventative treatment against damage from excess radiation in the atmosphere. Extensive tests at McGill University in Montreal, Canada, have shown that kelp harvested in the Pacific Ocean can reduce radioactivity absorbed through the intestines by up to 80 per cent. This research has been corroborated by the medical research radiological unit at Harwell, in the UK.

acid as well as the minerals calcium, iron and phosphorus. Its sugar content, mannitol, does not increase blood sugar, so kelp is a very useful food and a good dietary supplement for diabetics.

Kelp beds in the South Atlantic Ocean

HELP FROM KELP

You can take kelp for a whole variety of ailments. Problems related to thyroid function and general hormonal balance often respond well to regular and continued doses of kelp (see Box – *Iodine and the Thyroid*). Anything affecting the mucous membrane – a skin-like layer that lines many of the cavities and tubes in the body – will also be helped by kelp treatment. This includes respiratory ailments, especially where there is a lot of sneezing in an attempt to rid the body of excessive mucus, and bronchitis. If you have a tendency towards respiratory problems, it pays to take kelp on a continuous basis, not just when you are ill. The efficiency of kelp supplements will be enhanced by completely eliminating mucus-forming foods, such as dairy produce and possibly wheat, from your diet.

Mucous membranes also line the digestive tract. Indigestion and stomach acidity are common results of irritation in this area. Kelp can help to alleviate such problems by reducing acidity, since it is a highly alkaline food. Iodine deficiency can lead to a variety of digestive problems, and taking kelp on a regular basis will assist digestive tract function, from stomach to colon. Kelp can also prevent stones from forming in the gall-bladder and kidneys because of its alkaline action.

Kelp can help prevent, or heal, gastric and duodenal ulcers. Acidity contributes to ulcer formation and kelp guards against excessively acidic conditions. If the mucous membrane is attacked by acid and other irritants, and an ulcer forms, kelp can heal the inflammation. It also acts as a relaxant, reducing nervous tension – valuable for people prone to ulcers.

Irritation of the mucous membrane contributes to colitis – inflammation of the colon – with its chronic symptoms of constipation interspersed with diarrhoea, and abdominal pain. Kelp soothes the mucous membrane of the colon and also acts anti-septically, preventing chronic constipation from causing auto-intoxification (contamination of the blood by the faeces due to a break-down of the colon wall). Kelp is a cleansing agent for the whole lower intestine. Its high potassium content also helps replace amounts of this element lost in diarrhoea. Kelp can also help to correct constipation by encouraging peristaltic muscle movement.

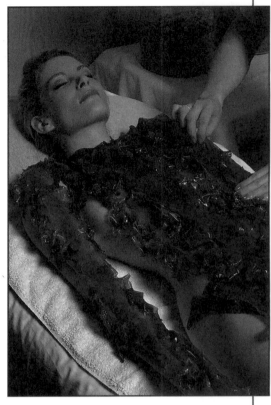

In this spa treatment, nutrients in kelp are absorbed by applying it directly to the skin.

IODINE AND THE THYROID

Iodine influences the balance of the hormone thyroxine within the body. Over 200 million people suffer from iodine deficiency diseases, the main sign of which is a swelling of the thyroid gland in the neck.

An adequate intake of iodine is essential to keep the body functioning, and kelp is one of the richest sources of organic iodine.

Obesity, resulting from an unbalanced metabolism, can also be helped by kelp. Increased iodine intake, regulates the thyroid, thus balancing the metabolism of food into energy. Other reported effects of kelp supplementation have been to increase brain function, and to reduce impotence.

TAKING THE MEDICINE

The powdered form of kelp has a distinctive flavour, and is best added to other foods which will disguise it. You can mix kelp with a wide variety of dishes – soups and sauces, salads, savouries and drinks. It will have a slightly thickening effect, which can be made use of for culinary purposes. In tablet form, kelp should be taken with meals – up to six tablets a day is the recommended dose.

UNDERWATER CROP

Japan is a world leader in kelp production. It is farmed underwater, and special teams of swimmers and skin divers are trained to cut it from off-shore seabeds. Seaweeds play an important part in the Japanese diet.

The second most influential country in world seaweed production is Norway, and good crops are also found in the UK – notably off the Welsh, Northumberland and Scottish coasts.

LEMON BALM

A time-honoured herbal remedy with many uses

Lemon balm is one of the easiest herbs to grow and a favourite with gardeners, herbalists and bees

There are few things more refreshing on a sunny day than a glass of lemon balm tea: a few sprigs of the plant infused in boiling water gives a delightful lemon-flavoured drink that is delicious either warm or chilled. It is also a tea that is certain to make you feel more relaxed and contented for, as Gerard, the 16th century herbalist and surgeon, wrote in 1597, lemon balm 'comforteth the hart and driveth away all melancholie and sadness'. It's also a plant that, through the ages, has been claimed as an 'elixir of life'. Today it still has an important place in the herbalists's repertoire.

Lemon balm is a member of the mint family and has the same pointed leaves and axillary flowers as its relatives. It is just as aromatic as well only, rather than a characteristic mint smell, balm emits a powerful lemon scent where the leaves are crushed. This is due to the essential oils in the plant, especially citral and citronellal. This oil is collected by steam distillation and is widely used in aromatherapy where it is generally considered to have a tonic and uplifting effect on the whole system.

BALM IN HERBALISM
Medicinally, balm (also known as *Melissa officinalis*) is mainly used as a carminative (curing flatulence), relaxant and anti-depressant – echoing Gerard's recommendations. The 17th century diarist, John Evelyn, was another balm enthusiast claiming that it 'is sovereign for the brain, strengthening the memory and powerfully chasing away melancholy'.

Paracelsus – a 16th-century physician – was also a fan of the herb. He concocted his own special recipe for an 'elixir of life', mainly from lemon balm and potassium carbonate, in a mixture known as *Primum Ens Melissae*. A couple of hundred years later one of Louis XIV's physicians recorded dosing an elderly chicken with Paracelsus's elixir, with the unexpected result that the creature grew new feathers and began laying eggs once again. A Dr Lesebure had also tried the same experiment on a couple of his elderly servants and he recorded the equally dramatic results in an early scientific paper (published in *Chemischer Handleiter* in 1685).

Like its close relative, mint, melissa gives off a pungent smell when crushed.

A DIGESTIVE REMEDY
Few herbalists would make such claims for lemon balm today. The plant is now used more prosaically as an ideal carminative for all sorts of spasms in the digestive tract, dyspepsia and flatulence.

Culpeper recommended that, 'a syrup made of the juice of it and sugar be kept in every gentlewoman's house, to relieve the weak stomachs and sick bodies of their poor sickly neighbours'.

A rather simpler solution is to make lemon balm tea using two teaspoons of the dried herb or a heaped tablespoon of the fresh plant to a cup of boiling water, infuse for 10 minutes and drink, repeating the dose three times a day.

As well as its relaxing effect on the digestive system, melissa is just as effective at calming the nervous system – so it's doubly ideal for stomach upsets that are due to anxiety and tension. This calming effect makes lemon balm just as useful as a relaxing tea at the end of a busy day or before going to bed.

A BALM FOR ALL ILLS

Lemon balm also has a diaphoretic action, promoting sweating and encouraging dilation of peripheral blood vessels. This makes it a useful remedy in feverish conditions, such as 'flu. As a vaso-dilator, melissa also has a hypotensive action and can help to

reduce high blood pressure. Combined with its calming properties it would therefore be a good remedy if the hypertension were related to tension and stress in general.

Although lemon balm is rarely used as a topical treatments for wounds and sores these days, it was a regular first-aid standby a few hundred years ago. The leaves were mixed with wine and used in poultices to bring boils to a head, the juice was used for fresh wounds and Pliny, the Roman writer, recommended balm for the bites of both scorpions and dogs as well as for 'scrofulous sores'.

Modern science provides support for some of these traditional applications – some of the aromatic oils contained in lemon balm have antiseptic properties so the fresh leaves could have made very effective wound dressings, helping to prevent infection.

An infusion of lemon balm is an ideal bed-time drink.

Melissa Blend Herb Tea

Net Weight 1.8 oz 50g · 25 Tea Bags – Caffeine Free!

THE LONDON HERB & SPICE CO.

BEE BALM

Lemon balm is also known as bee balm because of the way bees are attracted to the plant. Its botanical name *Melissa* comes from the Greek word for bee and in the ancient world the plant was also known as 'apiastrum' – this time from the Latin for bee.

The Roman writer, Pliny, records that 'if the (bee) hives are rubbed over with balm, the bees will not fly away, for no flower gives them greater pleasure. With brushes made of this plant swarms are controlled with the greatest ease.'

Some 1500 years later Gerard was noting that if balm is grown near to bee hives the bees will not stray and if they do they will 'find their way home again'. Indeed, honey from bees who have been feeding on balm is thought to be one of the finest. And just as bees are attracted by lemon balm, it has also been recommended through the ages as a remedy for bee and wasp stings and insect bites.

GROWING LEMON BALM

The fresh herb does taste rather better than the dried variety so it's worth growing a lemon balm plant in the garden if possible. However, it does tend to self-seed quite prolifically so it needs keeping in check. Variegated and

golden varieties are often available from herb nurseries, and have the same flavour and properties but usually do not grow quite as vigorously and look far more attractive in the garden.

The active principles of lemon balm are the essential oils found in the plant which can be lost when it is dried. For this reason it is important to dry balm quickly and away from direct sunlight. Many commercial specimens, for example, are completely lacking in any sort of lemon smell.

CARMELITE ELIXIR

Melissa once had a reputation as an 'elixir of life' and various long-lived medieval characters (including Llewelyn, Prince of Glamorgan, who survived until his 108th year) were reputed to have drunk an infusion of lemon balm daily.

The Emperor Charles V was an enthusiast for 'Carmelite water' which was largely made from balm. Dr Jean Valnet – a leading French herbalist and aromatherapist, gives this traditional recipe for 'eau de melisse des Carmes':

Spirits of wine (33°) 3 litres (5 pts)
Leaves and flowers of lemon balm 500g (1 lb)

Angelica root 16g (½ oz)
Lemon rind 125g (4 oz)
Cover the mixture and allow to stand for nine days stirring each day. Then strain the mixture through a fine cloth. Put the liquid into a jug and add:

Coriander 200g (7oz)
Grated nutmeat 40g (1½oz)
Powdered cinnamon 4g (½ teaspoon)
Cloves (whole 2g (½ teaspoon)

Cover and macerate for eight days, stirring each day. Then add 350g (12 oz) of water and leave for a further 24 hours. Filter and pour into bottles.

LEMON VERBENA

Sweet-smelling sedative

The aromatic leaves of lemon verbena make a relaxing herbal tea which can calm the stomach as well as the nerves

Lemon verbena (*Aloysia triphylla*) is native to Chile and Peru but was introduced into Europe by the Spaniards during the 18th century. In Spain it was known as *Yerba Louisa*, after Marie Louisa, the wife of King Charles IV of Spain, and in the UK too it was often referred to as Herb Louisa.

It is a deciduous shrub which, in ideal conditions, can reach the height of a small tree. Its pale green lance-shaped leaves, which are shiny on top and dull underneath, produce a volatile oil known as verbena and give off a strong lemon fragrance, hence the herb's name. Clusters of small mauve or white flowers grow on spikes at the end of the stems, and blossom in August.

SOOTHING INFUSIONS

Lemon verbena is mainly used a herbal tea and infusions of the leaves have long been popular in Spain and in France, where it is known as *tisane de verveine*. (It should not be confused with vervain (*Verbena officinalis*), however, which is a member of the same family and is mainly used as a herbal sedative.) Lemon verbena's lemon taste makes it a pleasant, refreshing drink at any time – either served hot or, in the summer, with ice. An infusion of lemon verbena offers a healthy alternative to drinks such as tea and coffee, whose high caffeine content stimulates the nervous system and also reduces vitamin and mineral absorption by

Grow your own lemon verbena – a useful herb and a fragrant addition to your garden.

the body. But it is not just a healthy refreshing drink. Lemon verbena has a gentle sedative effect on the system, soothing frayed nerves, and at night it can be taken as a relaxing aid to sleep, alone or blended with camomile.

To make lemon verbena tea infuse one teaspoonful of the dried herb, or three of fresh leaves in a cup of boiling water for five minutes. Strain and drink – adding a slice of lemon, or a little honey if you wish.

Like mint tea it is also good for the digestion and relieves minor but unpleasant problems such as indigestion, nausea, heartburn and flatulence. Lemon verbena tea helps settle the stomach and is also anti-spasmodic. To treat both digestive upsets and feverish colds it may be combined with mint. Lemon verbena is also recommended by herbalists to soothe and help relieve bronchial and nasal congestion.

ON THE SCENT

It first became popular in Europe for its lemon scent and flavour, and was often grown as an attractive, aromatic garden shrub. The leaves were used to scent the fingerbowls used at banquets and their oil was added to perfume, cosmetics and soaps. Although lemon grass is now often used as a less expensive substitute, lemon verbena is still added to some perfumes and soaps for its delightful fragrance. It retains its tangy scent well when dried – the leaves continue to give off their scent for two or three years – making it an ideal ingredient in the pot-pourri mixtures used in pomanders and herb pillows and sachets.

LEMON AID IN THE KITCHEN

Fresh lemon verbena leaves are better than dried ones for cooking, and can be used to give a refreshing lemon flavour to both sweet and savoury dishes.

Chopped leaves can be used in fish sauces, savoury stuffings, and salads. Include a few leaves when making ice-cream or apple

A relaxing tea can be made from the dried leaves or from handy individual tea bags.

jelly for a tangy, lemon flavour. Used sparingly, lemon verbena can also flavour fruit salads, custards, and other desserts, while steeping the leaves in drinks such as fruit or wine cups can add extra zest – use the leaves as an attractive garnish for the drinks.

HOW TO GROW IT

Lemon verbena is best suited to a warm climate, although it will withstand most cold winters provided it is planted in a sheltered place and it gets reasonable sunlight. May is a good time to plant and the soil should ideally be light, warm and well–drained. Lemon verbena can be grown as a pot plant too, or in a tub which can be moved outside in summer and inside in winter. If it is outside, cut it back in autumn and give it some protection against winter frosts. Propagation is by seed or cuttings.

Leaves for drying are best picked just before the flowers are fully open. Pick only

Lemon verbena lends its scent and flavour to a range of products, from soaps to herbal teas.

the perfect leaves, then lay them out flat and dry gently, allowing the air to circulate freely. They should have become brittle before being stored in a container, away from light.

Lemon verbena leaves also freeze well put in bags, whole or chopped, ready for use.

VERSATILE VERBENA

Lemon verbena is widely available from a number of companies, through health food stockists or by mail order. It is sold dried as a medicinal herb, or as loose herbal tea but is also marketed in handy packets of individual tea bags as lemon verbena tea. It can also be found as one of the ingredients in mixed herb teas where it may be blended with other lemon flavoured herbs such as lemon balm, or with mint. You can also buy dried lemon verbena leaves to add fragrance to your own pot-pourri or in ready made herbal products – such as herb sachets, and pot-pourri mixtures.

HOME-MADE COSMETICS

Mary Queen of Scots put wine in her bath; Cleopatra is supposed to have used ass's milk. Lemon verbena is perhaps a more practical

beauty aid which can be used on its own or blended with other herbs like mint, rosemary or camomile. Try the following treatments:

• Make an infusion of lemon verbena or other herbs as you would for tea, but leave it to infuse for about 30 minutes before adding half a litre to a warm bath.
• The same type of infusion can also be used as a final hair rinse, to leave your hair glossy and fragrant.
• A lotion made from lemon verbena is good for the complexion and keeps it clear of infection.
• To reduce puffiness around the eyes, soak cotton wool in an infusion and place over the eyes for 15 minutes.
• Macerate the leaves in almond oil for a fragrant massage lotion.
• An infusion of lemon verbena is also an effective mouthwash for freshening the breath.

LEMON SCENT

If you're feeling adventurous, you could make your own lemon verbena scented candles – infuse the leaves at 180°F, 82°C for 45 minutes in melted candle wax before pouring it into the mould. To decorate the outside of a candle with aromatic leaves, dip the candle into hot water for a few seconds, holding it by the wick, then roll it in the dried leaves, pressing gently.

RELIEF FROM HEARTBURN

Lemon verbena can be an effective remedy for heartburn – a common condition which can cause sleeplessness.

Make a refreshing drink from the fresh or dried leaves and drink three cups a day, the last before you go to bed. Ensure that you sit upright with a straight back and sip the infusion slowly for maximum effect.

LINSEED

As seeds or oil, a remedy that's worth its weight in gold

Most people still associate linseed, or flax seed, with an oil for cricket bats and wooden tables. Remarkable discoveries and cultivation techniques have brought linseed onto our tables in a new form — as a remedy for a multitude of digestive and chronic disorders.

Ordinary linseed is not suitable for human consumption – it is dark-coloured with a strong, unpleasantly bitter flavour. Edible linseed is organically cultivated from a particular, purpose-grown strain, under rigorously controlled conditions. As well as having an acceptable taste, the seed is carefully selected according to how how much it swells – the more it swells, the greater its digestive benefits. As a key source of essential fatty acids, linseed oil has also shown encouraging results in the treatment of a number of chronic conditions, from diabetes to multiple sclerosis.

DIGESTING THE FACTS

Many intestinal disorders respond well to a dose of the seeds – try them sprinkled on bread or over breakfast cereals. Their major action is in the prevention and correction of constipation. This is because linseed swells in the gut and so helps to speed the passage of waste products through the body. Conversely, the seeds can also help diarrhoea, as they bind excess water.

The seeds are specially prepared so that they swell gradually as they pass through the system. Each seed husk is partially split. This method was found to be necessary because fully-crushed linseed tended to swell too early (in the throat and stomach rather than the intestines), and whole seeds seemed to pass straight through the system, untouched. Their action is very gentle –

more so than some wholemeal and bran products, and certainly more than a great many commercial laxatives.

Linseed contains equal amounts of soluble and insoluble fibre, both of which have their own value in the diet. Soluble fibre – also found in whole grains – helps fill the stomach and is useful if you are on a diet or trying to reduce calorie intake. Insoluble fibre – contained in oats, fruit and vegetables – helps reduce absorption of both sugar and fat into the bloodstream, thus lowering cholesterol levels.

Oil from crushed linseed helps to freshen the skin, bringing relief from skin disorders.

Linseed also contains beneficial substances called mucins. These are sticky, gluey types of resin which coat the stomach walls and digestive tract, soothing the stomach and facilitating the contents to pass through easily. Linseed also has a considerable mineral content. Each kilogram (2lbs) of linseed contains: 9.5g ($\frac{1}{3}$ oz) magnesium, 2.4g ($\frac{1}{10}$ oz) calcium, 200mg sodium, 60mg iron, 30mg manganese, and 9.1mg copper.

MIRACULOUS OIL

Linseed oil has its own exceptional benefits. It is the richest natural source of omega-3 (also known as the n3 series) fatty acids, with almost twice the amount contained in the other main source, fish oils (see FISH OILS). This type of fatty acid has been called a 'miracle nutrient'. Essential for health it has numerous clinical applications, and is the fatty acid most likely to be lacking in the usual western diet.

High levels of omega-3 fatty acids relieve all sorts of disorders – and can also help to prevent many problems. Clinical trials have demonstrated that taking linseed oil regularly can help the following conditions:

• **Heart disease** Blood cholesterol levels have been reduced by up to 25 per cent. High intake of omega-3s also reduces the likelihood of blood clots forming where they can lead to strokes, heart attacks, pulmonary embolisms or gangrene. They also lower

DRESSING UP

Linseed oil can be taken in many different ways. You can take it straight from the spoon – when using it for specific therapies, up to eight tablespoons a day can be taken. A maintenance dose is one or two tablespoons a day. It can also be used like other oils in salad dressings, in mayonnaise or mixed with cottage cheese as a baked potato filling. When sweetened with fruit sugar, honey or maple syrup, the oil can be taken spread on bread or eaten with breakfast cereals.

high blood pressure.

• **Cancer** Linseed oil is an essential part of the work and treatment of alternative cancer specialist Dr Max Gerson. Dr Gerson has continued the research of German doctor and biochemist Dr Johanna Budwig, who achieved over a thousand cancer cures by prescribing high doses of omega-3s to cancer sufferers.

Dr Budwig's discoveries suggested that cancer patients often have very specific deficiencies of essential fatty acids in their blood. She prescribed such patients regular dosages of linseed oil, along with other nutritional changes. Tumours would swell initially, then disappear altogether, often within three months of Dr Budwig's treatment.

These results have been confirmed by the University of Chicago and other research, showing that omega-3s can kill breast, lung and prostrate cancer cells without destroying healthy tissue.

• **Diabetes** Dr Budwig has also shown that diabetes can be an omega-3 deficiency disease, compounded by a lack of other nutrients, such as vitamins and minerals.

• **Arthritis** Fish oils and linseed oils have been used in a number of successful arthritis treatments. Various trials carried out appear to show that a combination of omega-3

Seeds and oils: an effective cure for constipation or a first-class supply of the essential, alpha linolenic, fatty acid.

Linen is a traditional product of flax (*Linum usitatissimum*), from which linseed also originates. Linen fabrics have had a long history throughout Europe – their wide-scale manufacture occurring from the 1600s onwards.

and omega-6 fatty acids has enabled 60 per cent of rheumatoid arthritis patients to stop taking anti-inflammatory drugs, while a further 20 per cent have halved their drug intake.

• **Asthma** May respond to treatment with linseed oil within a matter days.

• **Allergies** Together with other nutritional supplements, linseed oil has helped decrease allergic responses to a variety of substances over a period of time.

• **Inflammatory conditions, including meningitis, bursitis, tonsillitis, gastritis, colitis, phlebitis, nephritis** All these conditions, which involve tissue inflammation, have responded well to treatment with linseed.

• **Skin conditions** Linseed oil is noted for its ability to keep the skin looking and feeling smooth, fresh and healthy, which it does by bringing essential oils to the skin cells via the bloodstream. Linseed oil can be particularly beneficial in cases of psoriasis, a common skin disease. The oil can be used directly on the hair, scalp and skin; it is also helpful for treating patches of dry, itchy skin.

• **Multiple sclerosis** Fatty acids are important to the health of nerve endings. Where nerve endings are damaged and unable to transmit messages efficiently to the brain, as in multiple sclerosis, linseed oil can be effective if included in a total dietary programme.

• **Stress, nervous tension, fatigue** People who take linseed oil regularly note improved all-round health and vitality. Sportspeople have noticed that muscles recover from wear and tear more quickly, and their stamina improves. Linseed oil also helps calm people under stress, reducing the absorption of excess toxins.

NOT FOR CRICKET BATS

Like linseed itself, the edible oil is produced under carefully controlled conditions – making it suitable for human consumption rather than for oiling cricket bats or thinning paint. Once bottled, the oil must be stored in a cool place, preferably away from direct sunlight, to avoid oxidisation: any oil not meant for immediate consumption can be frozen indefinitely. Unopened, the oil will keep for six months; opened, it should be used within four weeks.

486.—Flax-breaking.

The fibre for linen was obtained by subjecting flax stalks to several processes, including retting, drawing (top), drying, breaking (above), crushing and beating.

EXCEEDING THE DOSE

Very occasionally, linseed oil may cause allergies such as a skin rash, or slight nausea, which means the liver has exceeded its capacity for dealing with the oil.

A PAIN-RELIEVING INFUSION

An infusion of linseed can be a helpful and effective pain killer for those suffering from period pain and cramps. Steep 7g (¼ oz) of the seeds in 600ml (1 pint) of boiling water. Stand for five minutes and then strain carefully and drink 150ml (¼ pint) of the infusion every five hours. Regular drinks of this infusion can also help to soothe rasping dry and irritable coughs, and help to ease chest pains of a bronchitic origin.

MARIGOLD

The glorious healing herb from the Mediterranean

Not only is this hardy plant a joy to behold in the garden, it has been used as an effective, soothing remedy for centuries

Marigold ranks as one of the most useful of all herbs. It has been in service at least since the days of the Romans as a medicine, a cosmetic, a dye, and also as a colourful addition to a variety of foods.

Yet, like so many weeds that have been taken into cultivation and developed by horticulturalists, the marigold its so pleasing to look at that today it practical uses are largely overlooked.

There are nine species of marigold native to Europe, but it is the familiar single-flowered variety that is used for medicinal and culinary purposes.

THE HEALING HERB

Marigold contains several chemical constituents, each with its own unique healing ability. The most important of these is querticin 3-0-glucoside, which is believed to speed the healing of bruises, burns, cuts and scratches. Marigold also contains volatile oil, and it is this, combined with marigold's yellow resin calendulin, that is thought to be the source of the herb's antiseptic properties. Calendulin is also a styptic; this is a substance that stops bleeding by causing tissue to contract. The small levels of salicylic acid present in marigold are responsible for its anti-inflammatory action, and, when taken internally, the acid also helps to relieve headaches and nervous conditions.

Marigold contains many other chemical components, some of which may have healing powers, but their function is not, as yet, fully understood.

Marigold's botanical name *Calendula* is taken from the latin *Calends* – meaning the first day of every month – because, in its warm native climate, the marigold came into flower on every first day of every month throughout the year.

MARIGOLD MEDICINES OF THE PAST

The Romans used marigold as a remedy for a number of medical disorders, and not necessarily of the same type. For example, the juice of the crushed flowers and leaves was applied externally as a cure for warts, and taken internally to relieve fever.

During the nineteenth century, marigold continued in use as a medicine, but its devotees, instead of extracting the juice, used the leaves in food and drinks. Young marigold leaf salads were served to children suffering from scrofula (a common form of tuberculosis of the bones and lymph glands), and a quicker recovery rate than normal was observed in many cases. The petal tea, taken alone or with Indian tea, was thought to relieve various skin diseases, headaches, 'trembling of the heart', nervous conditions and delayed menstruation.

Marigold's much lauded anti-inflammatory properties and its reputation as a styptic led to its adoption by doctors of both sides during the American Civil War and later in World

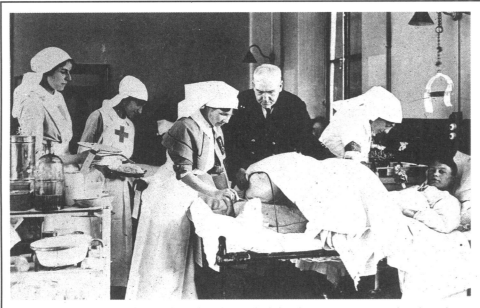

In World War I marigolds were bound up in surgical dressings to act as an antiseptic and to reduce the bleeding from wounds sustained on the battlefield.

War I. Gertrude Jekyll, a famous gardener of that time, sent bushels of marigolds grown on her Sussex estate to the field hospitals in France where they were used in dressings for the wounded.

MEDICINAL USES TODAY

Marigold can be used in several ways to treat a variety of complaints. Marigold tea, for instance, is reputed to be an effective remedy for mild digestive disorders. It is also taken to increase perspiration and so reduce the 'feverish' symptoms of illnesses such as 'flu. Other benefits believed to be derived from drinking marigold tea are relief from bad circulation and varicose veins, and the tea is even said to 'bring out' the spots in children who are suffering from measles.

The healing properties of marigold can be particularly beneficial in the treatment of skin complaints. Marigold

ointment applied to eczema patches, acne and common teenage spots has proved most effective in preventing the formation of scar tissue. Furthermore, the ointment helps to soothe minor scratches, cuts and grazes.

Sprains, bruises, burns and strained muscles can all be treated with marigold ointment: it should be applied to the area on a clean, soft lint pad. And a marigold poultice (see Marigold Medicines) can be effective in the treatment of chilblains.

MARIGOLD AS A BEAUTY AID

Marigold is a great favourite with cosmetics manufacturers: its soothing properties make it the ideal ingredient to use in non-allergenic skin preparations.

PLANT VARIETIES

Few plants grown on poor soil bloom as brilliantly as the marigold; once they are established they will spread without help.

The pot marigold or common marigold (shown above) originated somewhere in the broad band of the Mediterranean stretching from the Canary Islands to Iran, thriving in that region's full sun and tolerating its poor soils – characteristics that lent themselves well to the plant's later development as a great favourite of suburban and town gardens where similar conditions often prevailed. Today, there are dozens of improved varieties of pot marigold, from tall, double-flowered, erect-growing forms such as Golden Prince, Indian Prince and Orange Prince, through to the popular small bedding varieties – double-flowered, compact Gitana, Coronet and Gem, and older, single-flowered cultivars, namely 'Nova' and 'Hen and Chickens'.

M ARIGOLD COSMETICS

Marigold petal lotion: pour one cup of boiling distilled water onto a handful of dried petals. Leave to cool and then put in a sealed container. Apply with pieces of lint dipped in the lotion, carefully avoiding the eyes and mouth. Use the lotion with a few days of preparation.

Marigold tonic bath: in a bowl, add 450g (1lb) of dried petals to 4 litres (7 pints) of water. Allow the petals to soak in the water for at least 30 minutes. Strain and then add to a warm (but not hot) bath.

MYTHOLOGICAL ORIGINS

The French poet Rapin tells of the mythological origins of marigold. Of all the gods that dwelt on Mount Olympus Apollo was the most admired, and nymphs and shepherdesses vied with each other to gain his attention. Among the attendants of Apollo's sister Diana were four little wood nymphs. All were in love with the sun god. When Diana found them quarrelling she was so displeased that she turned them all into marigolds. Ever since, the colour yellow has represented jealousy.

IN BYGONE DAYS

Quite what marigold's first uses were we cannot be sure since all parts of the plant have value, though for different purposes.

Both the Romans and the Ancient Greeks used the dried petals as a substitute for the more expensive saffron in colouring soups, syrups and conserves, and it is probable that the bright yellow petals followed the same trade routes as saffron to the Far East.

In early Chinese records marigold is well documented as a dye. It is still used in many places around the world today, and is most effective in the dyeing of wool or silk. In India the Buddhists held the flower sacred to the goddess *Dwiga* whose emblem is adorned with the flowers and whose followers wore garlands of marigolds at her festivals. In India today marigolds still adorn funeral pyres before conflagration.

Marigolds are often seen adorning traditional Indian funeral pyres.

Marigold beauty products are widely available, but they can be made easily at home as well.

Marigold petal lotion, for example, is styptic and can therefore help to dry out oily skin. Marigold ointment (which is not so easy to make at home), acting as an emollient, can be massaged into chapped and rough skin. A marigold herbal bath is the ideal body tonic. It will soothe tired or aching limbs and stimulate the skin, leaving the bather feeling fresh and invigorated.

MARIGOLD IN THE KITCHEN

Marigold petals as food decoration proved very popular with wealthy Romans, since the colour yellow symbolised luxury and great riches.

Later cooks used the petals simply for their flavour, and marigold quickly gained a reputatio of being a versatile herb. Either fresh or dried, the petals were used in practically every course during stately sixteenth century

A HARDY ANNUAL

There is hardly a garden plant that thrives better in the poorest soils, grows as well under the worst possible conditions, or produces such brilliance of flowers with little or no attention after sowing. Indeed, once sown this hardy annual vigorously sets seed which produces self-sown plants year after year – a fact not overlooked by Charles Dickens in *Dombey and Son*, in which he mentions the small front gardens that had 'the unaccountable habit of producing nothing but marigolds'.

banquets. They were scattered over mutton soup, baked in buns, beef was garnished with marigold petals and the proper vegetable to accompany any feast was young marigold buds, boiled and eaten with butter. A salad would then follow made up of young marigold leaves and decorated with the petals.

Also popular for centuries were marigold custards, honey, wine, tarts and a splendid marigold farmhouse cheese – the French colour some of their cheeses with marigold petals.

The flavour of the petals is hard to define, but to the modern palate it would probably be described as exotic and somewhat acrid. As with most ingredients, however, it is not always to everyone's taste. Charles Lamb, the Victorian essayist, described the boiled beef prepared by Christ's Hospital where he was once a patient, as 'served with detestable marigolds floating in the pail to spoil the broth'.

The Dutch traditionally use marigolds discreetly to impart an unusual yet almost indiscernible flavour to soups and stews. And a special pudding is made using just one petal.

Marigolds certainly have a place in today's 'nouvelle cuisine', and not simply as a garnish; they are often added to the ingredients in fish, meat and dairy dishes, and even to drinks.

MARIGOLD CUSTARD

(To serve 6)

Infuse ½ oz (15 g) dried marigold petals in 600 ml (1 pint) milk. Beat 3 eggs with 50 g (2 oz) light muscovado sugar. Gradually strain in the milk. Pour into 6 individual ramekins; sprinkle a few crushed, dried petals over the top of each ramekin and bake in a bain marie (water bath) at 140°C (275°F) mark 1 for 1½ hours. Decorate with fresh marigold petals before serving.

MARIGOLD WINE

Put 2½ litres (4 pints) of marigold flowers, the juice and thinly pared rind of two oranges and one lemon into a large bowl. Add 1.4kg (3lb) of sugar to 4½ litres (8 pints) of water and bring to the boil. Pour into the bowl and allow to cool. Add 15g (½oz) of baker's yeast. Stir thoroughly, cover and leave in a warm place for one week. Strain into a fermentation jar, cover and leave in a warm place until gas bubbles no longer form. Leave in a cool place for three to four weeks before bottling. Store wine for six months before drinking.

W INTER MARIGOLDS

Marigold pot plants provide an excellent winter source of flowers and leaves. Sow the seed from July to September. When the seedlings are large enough to handle, prick off singly into 12cm (5in) pots and place in a cold frame until October. Then transfer the plants to a frost-free, well-ventilated and light position such as a conservatory or window and water sparingly through the winter.

MARIGOLD MEDICINES

Marigold tea: pour one cup of boiling water over four teaspoons of fresh marigold petals, or two teaspoons of dried petals, and leave to 'brew' for five minutes. Drink a small cupful as required.

Marigold ointment: melt white petroleum jelly in an enamel pan. Add an equal volume of crushed, dried marigold petals. Mix them together and press them well down. Bring the mixture to the boil and simmer gently for 20 minutes, or until the petals are crisp. Strain immediately into a container and cover when cold. Apply as required.

Marigold lotion: pour one cup of boiling water onto a generous handful of petals. Leave to cool and then strain into a sealed container. Soak pieces of lint in the lotion and cover the affected area. Replace and renew the lint as necessary.

Marigold poultice: crush dried petals into a pulp with a little milk or water. Spread the pulp onto a piece of cloth and heat between two plates over a pan of boiling water. Apply the poultice as hot as possible directly onto the chilblains.

MILK THISTLE

A weed that works wonders for the digestive system?

Used for centuries in European folk-medicine, the value of milk thistle has now been proved by up-to-date medical research

Many traditional, herbal folk-remedies have been proved, by modern research, to achieve spectacular curative effects. But, more importantly, these natural remedies rarely seem to bring on the side-effects, either on the body or the environment, that synthetic medicines often produce. This is certainly the case with milk thistle, which is now arousing great interest among health experts, because of its ability to protect the liver from poison damage, dietary abuse and a high alcohol consumption.

LIVER REVIVER

The milk thistle (*Silybum marianum*) is an annual or biennial weed with thistle-like characteristics, that belongs to the daisy family. Reaching a height of between 30-150cm (10-60in) when fully grown, it has smooth, white-veined leaves; the lower ones bearing wide, prickly lobes, and single, drooping purple flower-heads with prickly bracts. The plant's therapeutic factors, so beneficial to the liver, are concentrated mainly in the pale, brownish grey seeds, which measure about 7mm (¼in) in length, and should only be prescribed by a qualified herbal practitioner, although the whole herb is of value in stimulating the appetite and aiding digestion.

The plant is native to Southern and Western Europe and was introduced to North America, where it is found mainly in California. Its therapeutic properties have been recognised for centuries – it was used by the ancient Greeks to cure coughs, and was mentioned by Pliny in about AD 100 as a useful food source. Strange powers were attributed to it in the Middle Ages, possibly because it turned up so often growing in graveyards and cloister gardens, and superstitious people would avoid hanging it to dry above an oven, fearful that it would cause domestic strife.

Also known as 'Maria Thistle', 'Heal Thistle' and 'Christ's Crown', records of this plant's efficacy in treating liver disorders have appeared in European medical literature since the mid-16th century. Milk thistle was found to be especially beneficial in cases of chronic liver disease, including cirrhosis, hepatitis and jaundice, and for problems of the gall-bladder.

RESEARCH FINDINGS

The active ingredients in milk thistle include a digestive 'bitter' principle, flavonolignans, and a flavonoid, known as silymarin. The first of these partly accounts for its use in folk medicine in the treatment of appetite loss and digestive problems. The latter two – particularly silymarin – are associated with its benefits to an ailing liver.

Numerous trials have been carried out to determine the full scope of its therapeutic value. At present, it is known to prevent or greatly reduce the extent of liver damage caused by several potent toxins including carbon tetrachloride

Many plants with a 'bitter' taste contain a chemical that operates, via the nervous system, in promoting general good health. Milk thistle has a constituent that works along these lines (see BITTER HERBS).

A SPECTACULAR ANTIDOTE

Clinical use of milk thistle for poisoning from the Death Cap toadstool has proved especially interesting. When eaten, this fungus releases two potent liver-damaging substances that, on average, prove lethal in 30-40 per cent of cases, even when victims are treated with all the techniques modern medicine has at its disposal.

In a 1970s trial carried out in Germany by Dr Vogel, a leading researcher into silymarin, 60 patients suffering from severe Amanitine poisoning (poisoning by a certain species of fungus) were treated with milk thistle extract. All the patients survived, and Dr Vogel declared that the results ranged 'from amazing to spectacular'.

The aptly-named Death Cap toadstool.

Milk thistle joins half the plant world in containing flavonoids – good for the whole circulatory system as well as for the liver.

(used as a solvent in industry and in a number of specialist dry–cleaning processes), poison from *Amanita phalloides* (the Death Cap toadstool, see box above), thiocetamide (a substance that can cause cirrhosis-type damage to the liver), and various heavy metals.

THE WAY IT WORKS
When the active constituents of milk thistle are absorbed by the digestive system, the concentration in the bile exceeds that in the blood, suggesting that they selectively accumulate in the liver. Its beneficial effects on that organ seem to be threefold:
1. Stimulation of protein synthesis. This partly accounts for milk thistle's ability to regenerate damaged liver tissue.
2. Inhibition of leukotriene and inflammatory prostaglandin formation. Both classes of compound are released in response to chemical and other varieties of liver damage, and help to bring about the resultant inflammation which, itself, can lead to further damage.
3. The antioxidant activity of milk thistle has been shown to be considerably stronger even than that of vitamin E. Extracts from the plant are thought to be capable of counteracting the damaging effects of free radicals – supercharged fragments of molecules that are capable of harming living tissue and causing degenerative diseases and cancer.

THISTLE ON TRIAL
Hundreds of scientific studies now confirm the therapeutic value of milk thistle. No damaging side-effects have been recorded in its application over the years in Europe to treat a variety of liver conditions. Trials involving more than 2000 patients with some type of liver disorder have shown it to be useful in treating: alcohol- and chemical-induced fatty liver, cirrhosis, chronic hepatitis, cholangitis (inflammation of the bile ducts), pericholangitis (inflammation of the tissues around the bile ducts) and hepatic parenchymal changes (damage to the parenchymal tissues of the liver). All these benefits have been confirmed by clinical, laboratory and histological (tissue) studies. On a less crucial level, milk thistle can be used as a nutritional supplement to promote health by protecting the liver against the many adverse factors that can cause damage to this vital organ.

A SOLUTION FOR PSORIASIS?

True to its name, milk thistle extract has been found to enhance milk production in breastfeeding mothers.

Buy supplements or infuse a teaspoon of seeds in a cup of boiling water.

Interestingly, milk thistle has also proved a useful treatment for the skin disorder psoriasis. This is a common, chronic condition consisting of patches of inflamed skin, covered with silvery-white, dead skin scales usually found on the scalp, arms and legs.

Psoriasis has been found to be associated with high concentrations of circulating endotoxins, caused by the liver's inability to detoxify certain chemicals, and to the production of leukotrienes – both of which silymarin can help to counteract.

MINT

The warming herb

There's more to mint than simply using it in sauce with roast lamb. Varieties of mint have been used medicinally for centuries to treat just about everything – from the common cold to childbirth

Peppermint
(*Mentha piperita*).

Ask most people what you can use mint for and the answer is likely to be culinary – mint with new potatoes, after-dinner mints, mint ice cream, mint julep and so on. We all know the taste of mint, and most of us quite like it, but there's much more to mint than flavouring. The herb has been used medicinally since Roman times for an enormous variety of health problems.

MEDICINAL MINT
Although there are around 30 varieties of mint known world-wide, there are three main varieties used in herbal medicine:
- Peppermint (*Mentha piperita*)
- Spearmint (*Mentha viridis* or *Mentha spicata*)
- Pennyroyal (*Mentha pulegium*).

The garden mint used in mint sauce is generally either the ordinary spearmint, or the more exotic variety called Bowles or apple mint (*Mentha villosa*). Peppermint is itself a natural cross between spearmint and water mint (*M. aquatica*), while other common types of mint include eau de cologne mint (*M. citrata*), which is useful for making pot pourri, and field mint (*M. arvensis*), which is known in chinese medicine by the name *Bo He*.

All the mints share certain medicinal properties – they're warming, stimulating, anti-spasmodic and carminative (help flatulence) – but the actions do vary between types because the actual chemical constituents of the plants, especially the essential oils which give them their characteristic smell, are often quite different.

PEPPERMINT – TASTY AND THERAPEUTIC
Peppermint (*M. piperita*) is the main medicinal mint used today and may be given in teas, tinctures or used as an oil. Using peppermint's very warming properties – the 16th-century herbalist William Turner categorised the mints as 'hot in the third degree' – the herb can

A HISTORY OF MINT REMEDIES

Mint has been a familiar medicinal plant in western Europe for thousands of years:

- Pliny, a scholar of ancient Rome writing in the first century AD, tells us that if wild mint leaves are chewed and then used as a poultice, they will cure elephantiasis (extreme swelling of the limbs), the bites of serpents and the stings of scorpions. He also suggests steeping mint in vinegar and then pouring the liquid over the head while sitting in the sun as a cure for dandruff. Even more intriguingly, he tells us that:

'*A garland of pennyroyal is more suited to our bedrooms than one of roses for an application is said to relieve headache . . . nor do they suffer from the heat who carry when they are in the sun two sprays of pennyroyal behind their ears*'.

- However, more recently, the famous 17th-century herbalist and author of the *Complete Herbal*, Nicholas Culpeper warns that:

'*They say a wounded man that eats mint, his wound will never be cured, and that is a long day*'

be used to raise the body's internal temperature and encourage sweating. This makes it useful in treating colds, and a very tasty tea can be made by combining peppermint with elderflowers and yarrow (see Box).

Peppermint is a valuable digestive remedy. As well as acting as a carminative agent, it is also a bile stimulant and can help reduce vomiting and nausea. Peppermint tea – made by adding half a litre (one pint) of boiling water to 30g (1oz) of dried herb – is useful for indigestion, chills on the stomach, nausea, diarrhoea and nervous bowel (spastic colon). It can also be effective for morning sickness but, as with all herbs taken in early pregnancy you have to be very careful not to overdose, so never take it without professional advice.

Peppermint is also a useful relaxant and can be valuable for treating stress-related problems. An infusion of equal amounts of peppermint and a herb called wood betony (*Stachys betonica*) can be useful for relieving nervous disorders and insomnia.

SOME ESSENTIAL OILS – PEPPERMINT

Essence of peppermint in the form of oil is also used medicinally, and is made by distilling peppermint herb – passing steam through a quantity of the dried plant to extract the oils. Pure, undiluted peppermint oil is used in small amounts, due to its strength, by aromatherapists for treating nervous, digestive and respiratory problems. They may also use peppermint oil diluted in carrier oils to make massage oils for period pain and sinusitis.

Oil of peppermint has been traditionally used as a preventative measure for catarrh and head colds. Simply fill a glass tube – such as a small test-tube – with cotton wool and add a few drops of peppermint oil and eucalyptus oil. Cork the tube with an air-tight stopper and carry it around with you, regularly lifting the stopper to breathe in the fumes – rather like smelling salts. According to one elderly herbalist, this remedy had prevented him from catching any sort of common cold for 50 years. However, peppermint oil inhalants should not be used for long periods, and never for babies.

Pennyroyal mint (*Mentha pulegium*) – easily grown in garden or window box.

MILD SPEARMINT

The main ingredient in the essential oil from peppermint is menthol, whereas in spearmint – which is principally used in cooking – it is carvone, and pennyroyal consists mainly of an oil called pulegone. These different ingredients not only account for the markedly different smells of the three mints, but also for their medicinal properties.

Spearmint is a carminative and anti-spasmodic like peppermint, but it is much less powerful. Like many other culinary herbs, spearmint acts as a mild digestive tonic and it is traditionally used for children in preference to the much stronger peppermint. Garden mint, for example, can be used as a tea for childhood chills, nausea and colic.

POWERFUL PENNYROYAL

Pennyroyal mint, with 80 per cent of its essential oil made up of pulegone, is very much stronger than spearmint. In high doses, pennyroyal oil can cause convulsions and irritate the kidneys. The plant must never be taken during pregnancy, as it can damage the foetus.

Pennyroyal is less commonly used in herbal medicine today, although it has broadly similar properties to peppermint – easing flatulence and colic, relaxing spasmodic pain and reducing anxiety and tension. In France and Germany, pennyroyal is also used as an expectorant for coughs and is often used in remedies for bronchitis. Jean Valnet – a highly regarded French phytotherapist (therapist who uses plant remedies) – suggests combining liquid extract of pennyroyal with liquid essence of violet roots and a syrup made from maidenhair fern as an effective cough linctus.

GATHERING IN THE HERBS

All the mints should be gathered at or before flowering (June to August) and dried quickly to preserve the essential oils. They are all easy to grow, but it is important to keep the various species well separated in the garden, as cross-pollination is common. After a few years, the mint plants can be renewed by simply chopping up the roots with a sharp tool, watering well and covering generously with compost to encourage new growth.

MINT TEA – A REMEDY FOR COLDS

Like all herbal teas, mint tea lacks the caffeine found in 'conventional' tea.

At the first indications of a cold or 'flu, this tea mixture, drunk regularly, can considerably reduce cold symptoms, and in some cases can completely stop the cold developing. You will need:

- 30g (1oz) dried peppermint
- 30g (1oz) dried elderflowers
- 30g (1oz) dried yarrow

1 Mix the dried herbs together and store in an air-tight container, away from sunlight.
2 At the first hint of a cold, add two teaspoons of the dried mixture to one cup of boiling water.
3 Infuse for 5-10 minutes, strain and drink.
4 Repeat every few hours until the symptoms clear.

MISTLETOE

The common mistletoe plant (*Viscum albun*) is an evergreen semi-parasitic plant whose pale green, leathery leaves and sticky white berries are familiar to everyone. Found throughout Europe and northern Asia, it grows on deciduous trees, preferring soft-barked ones like the apple. It has a forked stem and pale yellow or green flowers – male and female. The female ones develop into the berries. The root penetrates the bark of the host tree, to tap into a ready-made food supply.

A HISTORY OF HEALING

Mistletoe has a fascinating history, steeped in legend, that goes back to Greek and Roman times. According to one legend, it was once a tree, condemned to be a parasite because it was the wood of the cross on which Jesus died. To the Druids, it was a sacred herb and 'heal-all', used in their rituals and traditionally cut with a golden sickle. Thought to protect against evil, it was used as Christmas greenery in feudal times. Kissing under the mistletoe is a custom that goes back to the 17th century.

For many centuries, mistletoe has been used to treat various ailments, including nervous debility, whooping cough, convulsive diseases, and heart complaints. It was particularly valued as a treatment for epilepsy and nervous disorders. The 17th-century herbalist Nicholas Culpeper noted mistletoe's medicinal uses, including that for 'falling sickness' (epilepsy), and belief in its effectiveness for epilepsy continued well into the 18th century. Today, mistletoe still has a part to play in both our Christmas and New Year festivities, and it is still used as a herbal remedy. It is not the 'magic' herb of legend and superstition – the medicinal

Mistletoe's pharmacology is very complex and its constituents depend on the host tree.

An evergreen remedy to calm the nerves

Mistletoe is associated with Christmas festivities, but it is also a useful natural medicine

properties of mistletoe are well recognised in healing and homoeopathic medicine.

Mistletoe is available as a dried herb, as well as being an ingredient in herbal remedies for a variety of disorders. Standard recommended dosage is 2-4g (1 teaspoon) of dried leaves and stems three times daily. An infusion is made by steeping a handful of the fresh herb or two to three tablespoons of the dried herb in cold water overnight.

CALMING THE NERVES

A natural sedative, mistletoe soothes and tones the nervous system. One of its main uses today is in herbal remedies for nerves and nervous tension. Usually it is combined with other herbal sedatives like valerian, skull-cap and hops. A well-tried nerve remedy is an infusion of equal amounts of mistletoe, valerian and vervain, taken cold, in two tablespoon doses, two or three times daily. Mistletoe's sedative and anti-spasmodic actions can help relieve nervous spasms and dull, throbbing headaches caused by tension and stress.

KEEPING THE FLOW GOING
Mistletoe can be helpful for a number of circulatory problems. It is a 'vaso-dilator', which means that it expands the blood vessels. This property of the plant means that it can also be of benefit in cases of migraine, when blood vessels become constricted. Mistletoe also strengthens the capillaries or smaller blood vessels in the body, and is listed in the *British Herbal*

Mistletoe, found as a bush on a branch of its host tree, is often seen high in the tree-tops.

Kissing under the mistletoe was once thought to lead inevitably to marriage.

Pharmacopoeia specifically for relieving hardening of the arteries. Swiss naturopath Dr Vogel describes 'fresh extract of mistletoe as one of the most wonderful cures for the loss of elasticity in the arteries'.

PRESSURE PROBLEMS
Research indicates that mistletoe has a regulating effect in balancing high and low blood pressure problems. Herbalists may

combine mistletoe with one or two other herbs, notably hawthorn berries and lime blossom, to bring down high blood pressure (hypertension).

HELPING THE HEART
Mistletoe is regarded as a heart tonic, and it acts directly on the vagus nerve, which is concerned with regulating the heart beat. So herbalists may use mistletoe to help steady a heart rate that is too rapid, as well as for conditions such as 'nervous tachycardia', a term that is used for a nervous quickening of the heart.

HOPE FOR CANCER?
Mistletoe has attracted the attention of cancer researchers, and there is some evidence to suggest that it may help inhibit the growth of tumours. Mistletoe is one of the herbs used in an alternative cancer treatment practised in Switzerland, based on the work of Rudolf Steiner, the founder of anthroposophy.

EXTERNAL APPLICATIONS
Externally, mistletoe is recommended as a poultice to relieve painful rheumatism and gout. Simmer a handful of mistletoe leaves and/or berries in milk or water for a few minutes, leave to cool for a few minutes, and then apply the mixture to the painful area. As a rub, pound a tablespoonful of the berries in a pestle and mortar and apply to reduce stiffness and swelling in joints.

MISTLETOE BEAUTY-CARE
Mistletoe is not a well-known beauty herb, but it is used with other herbal extracts in some skin-care products. It is very good for irritated and sensitive skins, as well as being antiseptic. Mistletoe is also an effective ingredient in anti-dandruff shampoos, and it can be found in some herbal and mineral toothpastes, too.

CAUTION
Mistletoe berries should NOT be taken internally. They can be prescribed under certain circumstances, but ONLY by a registered medical practitioner. Heart and circulatory problems for which mistletoe may be used should always be treated by a qualified practitioner. Remember, professional advice should always be sought for treatment of any condition – self-diagnosis can be dangerous.

MUD

Mud, glorious mud!

The great upsurge in interest in natural remedies such as herbs, plant oils and honey has left mud somewhat in the shade. However off-putting it may seem, mud has been valued for centuries for its healing powers, both in natural therapy and beauty treatment

Since ancient times, mud has been used as a therapy. The Greeks originally discovered mud therapy and gave this form of treatment the technical name pelotherapy (*pelos* means mud, or clay). More recently, Italy has been called the home of mud therapy as there are a large number of health resorts that specialise in the treatment. However, mud is also used in many other spas in France, Germany, Switzerland, Belgium, Hungary, Czechoslovakia and the Black Sea resort region, as well as further afield in countries such as Israel and Mexico. Spas generally are places where you can

unwind from stress and improve your overall health and fitness. The treatment is usually based on 'taking the waters' – that is drinking or bathing in mineral-rich waters or mud, in addition to eating a correct diet and taking some form of exercise, in a relaxed and stress-free environment.

WORKING THE MUD

Mud, or mud peat, is often used in conjunction with spa water in therapeutic baths. Alternatively it may be applied on its own in a poultice to specific areas of the body, such as knee or elbow joints. This can relieve pain and inflammation. The mud baths available at spas involve either lying in a tub of mud, or being completely covered. Having a mud bath has been compared to running a fast 1000-metre race. It increases the heart rate, dilates blood vessels, and raises levels of perspiration, thereby eliminating toxins. The result is a general invigorating and cleansing of the system. Mud baths expend so much energy that they need to be done under qualified supervision.

As mud is a low heat conductor, it can be used to apply heat to the body for a long period while the skin is able to absorb the

minerals contained in the mud. Naturally occurring mineral-rich spa waters and mud are used to relieve arthritic, rheumatic and skin disorders. Patients suffering from rheumatoid arthritis have an increased rate of erythrocyte sedimentation – this is the rate at which red blood cells settle out of

MUD FROM MOROCCO

Rhassoul mud comes from the Atlas Mountains in Morocco. Dried, and then mixed with water, it makes an excellent shampoo for greasy hair and dandruff. As a substitute, a mixture of Fuller's Earth and kaolin can be used. Mix to a paste with water, apply as a mud pack to the hair. Leave it on for ten minutes and then rinse off.

Therapeutic mud comes in many colours from green, brown and black to brick-red.

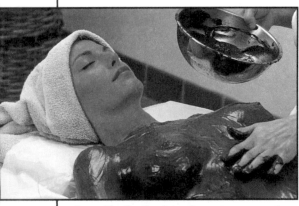

A mud both stimulates the system as much as running a fast 1000-metre race.

waters and mud are rich in essential minerals and trace elements such as calcium, iron, potassium and sodium, which vary in their proportions according to the area in which the mud or water is found. Volcanic mud is particularly therapeutic.

Some types of mud have bromine in them. Patients with the skin condition psoriasis have been shown to have lower than average amounts of bromine concentration in their bodies, so to them mud may be especially useful. Mud therapy can also be helpful in relieving nerve inflammation and is occasionally used in treatments to decongest the liver. In Austria, in particular, mud has been found to be successful in treating certain gynaecological problems as it contains substances that closely emulate the female hormone oestrogen.

PORE PENETRATION

Mud in the form of face packs and masks both nourishes and deep-cleanses the skin. The minerals in the mud gradually penetrate the pores: dead cells and skin impurities are removed, so the skin can breathe, and blood circulation is improved. Skin is left feeling fresher and smoother, and the natural ph

balance (the acid-alkaline balance) is maintained or restored. Mineral mud masks are especially good for problem skins and conditions including acne, oiliness, pimples and coarse, open pores. Mud-based shampoos and conditioners strengthen the hair's natural balance. Mud can also help to combat dandruff and itchy scalps.

FANGO PACKS

Fango, the Italian word for mud, occurs naturally as a greyish-black mud in the thermal lakes of volcanic regions, and in Italian thermal spas such as Abano, near Venice, and Battaglia. Fango packs have been used in therapeutic and beauty treatment for hundreds of years. Fango's qualities were described long ago by the Roman, Pliny, and the Greek physician, Galen. Roman emperors even built some of their spas beside the fango medicinal springs.

Fango mud and dried fango powder contains no less than 12 important minerals and trace elements. Two specialists at Padua University in Italy recently declared the mud of Abano to be an effective remedy for the relief of rheumatism. Dr Vogel, the respected

suspension in blood plasma. After taking mud or mud peat both these patients have reduced levels of erythrocyte sedimentation, which indicates a marked improvement.

MUD BREAKDOWN

Many patients have derived great benefits from mud, but quite how or why is not precisely known. The most likely solution is thought to be the combination of chemical and physical action. Both the spa

DEAD SEA MUD

The Dead Sea lies 394 metres beneath sea level, which makes it the lowest place on the earth's surface. The healing powers of the waters of this unique lake have been known since Biblical times when David, Solomon, and the Queen of Sheba all built curative bathing places on its shores. Dead Sea mud contains numerous minerals and trace elements and is especially rich in potassium and magnesium, as well as vegetable matter created by millions of years of sedimentation. Used in baths, or applied to specific areas of the body, mud can ease the pain of arthritis, strains and sprains.

The Dead Sea is a remarkable source of minerals and trace elements, many of which are used therapeutically. For centuries people have sought cures on its shores.

Fango products include a face mask, shampoos, hair conditioner and shower cream.

Swiss naturopath, advocated the fango cure for polyarthritis (pain and stiffening in a number of joints), combined with correct diet and other natural remedies, as it has proved extremely beneficial to patients severely affected by this crippling condition. Fango has also been used for its beneficial effects on the skin and scalp.

OBTAINING YOUR MUD

Many spas and some clinics include mud therapy in their range of treatments. Information is available from tourist offices and travel firms.

Crystals which provide the minerals found in the Dead Sea, along with 100 per cent natural 'peatmud' baths from Austria, are all available from health shops and beauty centres. In both cases they are just added to the bath water for relaxing and therapeutic home baths.

For skin and hair care there is a range of products containing Dead Sea minerals, including mud masks for all skin types, and mud for scalp problems. A soap containing sulphur from the Dead Sea is also available.

NATURAL CALMATIVES

Providing a rest from stress

Research is uncovering more and more natural ways to tackle a general, underlying state of anxiety and tension, while for those going through a particularly stressful period in their lives, there are also a number of different – and natural – alternatives to conventional tranquillising drugs. Various nutritional supplements and herbal remedies can be extremely effective as natural tranquillisers and nerve tonics, reinforcing the body's anti-stress mechanisms without producing the unpleasant (and, even more worrying, occasionally unknown) side-effects of so many orthodox tranquillising drugs.

Many of these natural remedies are described in much more detail under their individual headings, but in this article, remedies are brought together to provide a handy summary of all those with specifically calmative properties.

NUTRITION FOR NERVES

Nutritional therapy is a fairly modern idea for dealing with nervous problems, but research suggests that a lack of certain nutrients in the body undoubtedly impairs the nervous system. Eating a healthy and balanced diet provides maximum nutrition for both mind and body. The ability to cope with physical and mental stress is greatly reduced if our diet is lacking in vitamins and minerals, and certain naturally occurring substances can have a marked positive effect on nervous disorders.

People are finding increasingly that natural, holisitic approaches offer positive, long-term solutions to stress, anxiety and nervous problems

VITAMIN B COMPLEX

B complex vitamins (some 13 vitamins, the more important of which are described below) are essential for mental health, and for the nervous system to function properly. A deficiency of any one of the B complex vitamins can contribute to a wide range of nerve problems.

VITAMIN B_1 (THIAMIN)

Perhaps the most important of the 'nerve' vitamins, it has been described by one nutritional expert as an emotional 'normaliser' – tranquillising those who are agitated and lifting those who are depressed. B is vital to the functioning of the nervous system and if the body has insufficient it cannot break

down carbohydrates properly. This can lead to the build-up of a substance called lactate, which is linked to anxiety. Lactate is a salt of lactic acid – a constituent of fermented milk products such as cheese – and is found in the blood; it is associated with processing sugars in the body. Research studies have shown an improvement in moods and nervous symptoms when B_1 is taken. Many foods are fortified with added vitamin B_1.

VITAMIN B_3 (NIACINAMIDE)

Niacinamide is a modified form of niacin or nicotinic acid – other names for vitamin B_3.

Studies suggest that it has similar properties to the tranquilliser Valium. It relaxes muscles, and has a sedative influence, especially when combined with magnesium. Symptoms of niacin deficiency include tension, depression and nervousness.

VITAMIN B_6 (PYRIDOXINE)

Vitamin B_2 is needed by the body to produce a tranquilising chemical known as GABA. In this way it acts as a natural tranquillising agent, and fatigue and various other nervous symptoms result from its deficiency.

VITAMIN B₁₂

Low levels of B_{12} in the body can contribute to a build-up of lactate, which in turn has a bad effect on the nervous system. Vitamin B_{12} can improve energy, mood and quality of sleep, while good results have been achieved in elderly people with mild confusion or poor memory. Vegans may be short of this vitamin as it is found almost entirely in animal foods.

INOSITOL

Sometimes classed as a B vitamin, inositol is concentrated in the nerves. Research suggests that it has a tranquillising effect on patients with nervous disorders. It is usually present in B complex supplements, and in lecithin (a dietary fat) products.

VITAMIN C

A leading orthomolecular psychiatrist, Dr Abram Hoffer, has said that ascorbic acid (vitamin C) can be as effective as major tranquillisers. Vitamin C acts as a dopamine receptor blocker. Dopamines are neurotransmitters – chemical messengers essential for brain function – which influence mood and behaviour. High brain levels of dopamine have been associated with aggression, irritability, and a number of severe mental disorders. By  inhibiting the effects of dopamines, vitamin C can have a natural, tranquillising effect on the body.

MINERALS AND TRACE ELEMENTS

CALCIUM

Apart from its importance for strong bones and teeth, calcium can help to calm nervousness, to relieve insomnia, and to ease muscle-nerve symptoms such as cramps.

MAGNESIUM

Magnesium has a sedative action on the peripheral nervous system. Supplementary doses of this element can help to relieve tremors, nerve spasms, and muscular tension (although mega-doses may actually cause nerve disorder symptoms). Several different trials carried out in the USA suggest that magnesium is effective as a natural tranquilliser.

MANGANESE

Manganese deficiency can cause various defects of the nervous system. This trace element can help calm nervous irritability and nervous tremors. Some practitioners use it in the treatment of 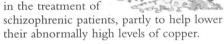 schizophrenic patients, partly to help lower their abnormally high levels of copper.

ZINC

Zinc is vitally important, involved as it is in so many physiological processes. A deficiency can adversely affect mental functions and could be implicated in hyper-activity in children. Zinc also acts as an 'antagonist' of copper, working against copper's tendency to

excite the nerves. In the United States, zinc has been used in nutritional therapy, and it has also been prescribed in combination with various other minerals and vitamins, as an alternative treatment of depression and schizophrenia.

AMINO ACIDS

The building blocks of protein, amino acids provide the raw material of our cells and so they are vital to life. Amino acids are also required by our bodies in order that substances called neuro-transmitters – the brain's chemical messengers – can be produced.

PHENYLALANINE

DLPA is a combination of two forms of the amino acid phenylalanine which, according to research, increases and extends the production of the body's own pain-killing substances, endorphins. By increasing endorphin levels, DLPA also works as an anti-depressant (see DLPA).

TRYPTOPHAN

This amino acid (as well as vitamin B_6) is used by the body to produce serotonin, a substance concerned with sleep, mood and sensory perceptions. When not enough serotonin is produced, depression and sleep disturbances may result. Because of this function, tryptophan has a sedative effect, calming nervous tension and aiding sleep. For those suffering from insomnia, a dose of

A WOMAN'S VIEW

Women have special stress problems – the tension associated with pre-menstrual syndrome (PMS), postnatal depression and menopausal stress. An holistic approach, dealing with emotions and physical symptoms, is needed.

Nutritional and herbal therapy can also help. For instance, vitamin B_6 can often relieve the tension, irritability and depression, as well as the physical symptoms, of PMS. Recommended dosage is one 50mg tablet twice a day (this can be increased to 150-200mg) from three days before pre-menstrual symptoms start to the third day of the period.

Additional magnesium can also be of great benefit, along with the vitamin B_6. Sedative herbs like skull cap and valerian, or herbal and nutritional supplements specifically for PMS may also help considerably.

The oral contraceptive pill increases the body's need for certain nutrients, notably vitamin B_6, folic acid, vitamins C and E, and zinc. Trials indicate that women who become depressed while taking the Pill may be suffering from a lack of B_6; giving B_6 supplements has been found to put this right, relieving depression and anxiety symptoms.

If you suffer from these problems, seek the advice of a naturopath – you will be amazed at the various treatments available to you.

Women's stress problems respond particularly well to natural calmatives.

500-1000 mg, taken at bedtime, is usually recommended. Note: higher doses administered for depression should always be medicinally supervised.

CALMATIVE CHOICE

Vitamin and mineral supplements are widely available – singly and in various different combinations, as tablets, pleasantly tasting 'chewable' tablets, capsules and liquid. Having the correct vitamin and mineral balance within the body is vital; for example, it is recommended that individual B vitamins should not be taken – B complex is more effective. However, many single B vitamin supplements do include brewer's yeast, which is rich in B complex vitamins (although some sufferers of thrush (*candida albicans*) may need to avoid yeast in supplements).

Natural vitamins and minerals are to be preferred – look for 'chelated' supplements, as these are in the most readily absorbed form. Amino acid capsules and tablets are also available and the prefix 'L' indicates that they are in the natural form.

NATURAL HERB RELAXANTS

Herbs, as part of an holistic approach, can be helpful to the nerves. A correctly prescribed herb can tone up the whole nervous system and have a tranquillising effect on the body. It is the nervine relaxants such as valerian that act as natural alternatives to tranquillisers.

CAMOMILE (*Matricaria chamomilla*)
Camomile tea, made from the fresh or  dried daisy-like flowers of the plant, is an excellent gentle sedative for both adults and children. An effective relaxant it both calms the body and soothes frayed nerves; taken at bedtime, it aids refreshing sleep.

HOPS (*Humulus Lupulus*)
The ripe female fruits of hop plants are a well-tried remedy for easing nervous tension and insomnia because of their sleep-inducing properties – you can be wafted off to sleep by their hypnotic scent in a traditional hop pillow. Dried hops can be drunk as an infusion or used in a bedtime bath, and they are included in some herbal remedies.

Anti-insomnia Jamaican dogwood.

JAMAICAN DOGWOOD (*Piscidia erythrina*)
In its native West Indies, the bark of this tree is used as a fish poison. It is a strong sedative, and an effective remedy for neuralgia, but is mainly used, with other herbs, in remedies for insomnia and related nervous tension.

PASSIONFLOWER (*Passiflora incarnata*)
This tropical American plant is highly valued for its narcotic properties, and is one of the best herbs for inducing natural, relaxing sleep. Passionflower leaves contain various active principles that together produce the sedative action. It can also help tension-related problems such as headaches and various nervous disorders, and it can also help to relieve some of the problems associated with the menopause.

SKULLCAP (*Scutellaria laterifolia*)
The North American herb skullcap is beneficial for nervous exhaustion and debility. It is a relaxant, with a tonic effect on the central nervous system. (A species of the *Teucrium* group of plants is often used as a substitute for skullcap today.)

VALERIAN (*Valeriana officinalis*)
Valerian is the classic herbal medicine for nervous disorders. Sometimes described as nature's Valium, its roots is included in almost all herbal nerve remedies. It has been used for centuries to reduce nervous tension, anxiety and hysteria. Studies show that it cuts down the time taken to fall asleep and improves the quality of sleep, without

producing a 'hangover' effect the next morning. Valerian's sedative, anti-spasmodic and pain-relieving actions make it useful for pain associated with tension. Recommended dosage is 1-4 g (1-2 teaspoons) of dried root, infused and drunk three times a day – a little honey, lemon balm or peppermint will improve the taste.

WILD LETTUCE (*Lactuca virosa*)
The milky juice of this plant was once sold as 'lettuce opium'. Its dried leaves are a valuable remedy for insomnia, nervous excitability, and restlessness. It is often an ingredient in combination remedies for nervous problems.

OTHER HERBS FOR THE NERVES

Asafoetida – the circulation booster.

ASAFOETIDA (*Ferula asafoetida*)
A medicinal gum that stimulates blood circulation. Traditionally used for nervous tension, insomnia and to calm hysteria.

GENTIAN (*Gentiana lutea*)
Yellow gentian root provides a nerve tonic and is useful for general debility and anorexia (general poor appetite – not the specific clinical condition called anorexia nervosa).

LADY'S SLIPPER (*Cypripedium pubescens*)
The root is a sedative and nerve tonic. May be used for emotional tension and anxiety.

LEMON BALM (*Melissa officinalis*)
LIME BLOSSOM (Linden – *Tilia europaea*)
LEMON VERBENA (*Aloysia triphylla*)
Infusions made from any one of these plants (or a combination) make pleasant herbal teas that are gently relaxing for the nerves. Use approximately 1–4g (1-2 teaspoons) of dried herb per cup.

The excellent heart tonic – motherwort.

MOTHERWORT (*Leonurus cardiaca*)
A natural tranquilliser, especially useful for nervous palpitations. Also beneficial for menstrual irregularities caused by stress.

VERVAIN (*Verbena officinalis*)
Strengthens and sedates the nervous system. Can help ease depression and melancholia.

AVAILABILITY

Herbs are widely available from health food stockists, as dried herbs and tea, and in capsule, tablet and liquid forms. There are also many combination remedies for nervous problems, which can be used as alternatives to tranquillising drugs and sleeping tablets. Various combinations are used, with valerian as one of the most common ingredients. Some also contain B vitamins, or other natural ingredients, such as mineral-rich kelp (seaweed) or amino acids, to reinforce the herbal action.

RELAXING AROMATHERAPY
Massage with essential oils is one of the best remedies for reducing stress and tension. Dilute eight drops of essential oil in 15ml (3 teaspoons) of a carrier oil such as sweet almond oil and ask a friend or your partner to massage the oil into your back and shoulders. Alternatively, try using a vaporiser in your bedroom at night-time. Oils of bergamot, camomile, lavender and geranium are all particularly calming with a sedative effect.

STRESS-CONTROL CEREAL

Believe it or not, oats are one of the finest natural 'nerve foods' available. Highly nutritious, and a source of protein, they are especially rich in B vitamins and minerals – all good reasons for having porridge for breakfast. Oats (*Avena sativa*) are also used as a homoeopathic nerve remedy. One compound available combines oats with hops, passionflower, and valerian as an aid to relaxation and natural stress-control.

Nutritious oats are well-known for their 'thymoleptic' effect. Thymoleptic remedies are those that raise the mood and lift depression.

UNWIND . . . NATURALLY

Herb teas can help you to unwind and get rid of nervous tension after a hard day. Gentle tranquillising ones include camomile, lime blossom and lemon balm. Or take a relaxing bath with the addition of a herbal infusion, essential oils, or one of the herbal bath oils on sale. In the case of essential oils, add 5-10 drops (never any more) to the bath-water when drawn, mixing well – the oil will be inhaled and absorbed through the skin. Some essential oils act as 'pick-me-ups', others, such as camomile, clary sage and hyssop, have a more tranquillising effect; rose and jasmine oils have anti-depressant properties.

Calming camomile tea is easy to make yourself. Some ready-made teas come in special combinations, with words such as 'sunset' in the name, indicating their soothing 'bedtime' properties.

OLIVE OIL

Oiling the wheels of good health

Throughout history, olive oil has been cherished for its versatility – in ancient times, athletes massaged it into their bodies to give their muscles greater elasticity and the women of Ancient Rome found it helped them to stay healthy and young looking. Long appreciated for its culinary contribution, the full nutritional value of good quality olive oil is increasingly coming to the fore

Olives are believed to have been growing since man first appeared on the Earth. Mythology speaks of the olive branch as the symbol chosen by the god Zeus precisely because it represented so many qualities vital to life.

Cultivation of olives is thought to have begun in earnest in some Mediterranean countries around 6000 years ago and it is estimated that the Phoenicians first brought olive trees to Spain (the world's main exporter of olive oil), although the exact date of this is unknown.

AN EVERGREEN REMEDY
The olive tree – often praised for its beauty over the centuries – is a sub-tropical, broad-leaved evergreen, usually ranging in height from 3 to 12 metres (3 to 13 yards). It has many branches and distinctive leaves with dark green uppers and silver undersides.

Olives ripening on the branch, showing that green and black olives are just different stages (unripe and ripe respectively) of the same fruit.

OIL EXTRACTION

The olive tree flowers between April and June, depending on the country, and the fruit reaches full maturity during winter. Olives are traditionally hand-picked, which preserves the quality of the fruit.

For top-quality 'virgin' olive oil, the oil is immediately extracted during the week following the collection of the fruit and extraction of the oil is carried out exclusively by mechanical means and without the use of any chemical solvents. Whole olives are first of all crushed and mixed to obtain a paste; this paste is then pressed – while cold in the best 'cold-pressed' virgin types – and yields a liquid made up of oil and water. Finally, the oil is separated off by a process of centrifugation (placing the oil and water mix in a vessel that is made to revolve very rapidly, causing the water and oil to separate out). A full 5kg (11lb) of olives are need to produce just one litre (1¾ pints) of oil.

Hand-harvesting olives in Italy. Careful hand-picking is an important part of ensuring top-quality olives and oil.

Putting crushed olives into filters before placing in a press. Pressing produces a liquid from which oil can be extracted.

The trees bloom in late spring, when loose clusters of small, whitish flowers appear. There are two kinds of flowers: those with both male and female parts – which develop into olive fruits – and male flowers, which contain only pollen-producing parts. The olive tree is wind-pollinated.

PRESSING CONCERNS
Olive oil is made solely from pressing olives and there are two basic categories:

1 Virgin Olive Oil
This is the juice extracted from the olives by simple pressing methods and, as such, it contains the full flavour, aroma and nutritional value of the original fruit.

Virgin olive oil is graded according to its degree of acidity into two types, 'extra' and 'fino'. Of these, the extra has the least acidity and is generally considered by gourmets to be the superior of the two. The degrees of acidity are firmly set by European Community law and are as follows: extra – less than one per cent acidity; fino – less than two per cent acidity. However, the distinct aroma and flavour – not to mention the price – of virgin olive oil leads some people to recommend it for use as a dressing, rather than as a cooking oil.

2 Olive Oil
Virgin oil that does not meet these grading standards is refined and then blended with premier quality oil to create a product that is cheaper than virgin oil and is thought by some to be more suitable for cooking, although it can also be used in salad dressings. The use of this kind of olive oil in Spain, for example, accounts for 90 per cent of Spanish olive oil consumption.

Both virgin and non-virgin olive oils are fats rather than oils – they are called oils because they are liquid at average temperatures.

GOOD HEALTH
Although highly regarded for its qualities as a cosmetic, olive oil has, throughout the ages, been most valued for its culinary uses – used either for frying, or as a salad dressing it can help create all kinds of superb dishes.

Nutritionally, olive oil is superior to other fats, with the virgin types containing significant amounts of vitamin E, the essential nutrient for healthy cells in the body. Olives also contain good quantities of vitamin A, and the minerals potassium magnesium, calsium and phosphorus. Contrary to popular belief, olives have a relatively low calorific value – containing around 80 Calories per 100g (4oz) portion of unpitted fruit.

Olive oils is also high in monounsaturated fatty acids, while most oils, such as vegetable oil, contain mostly polyunsaturated fatty acids. Although polyunsaturated fatty acids are generally less harmful to our health than the saturated kind and have some positive benefits, monounsaturated fatty acids are thought to be better still. Both play a role in lowering blood cholesterol – but the monounsaturated kind is believed to help our bodies retain more of the nutrients essential for a healthy life.

THE HEART OF THE MATTER

The beneficial effect of monounsaturated fats is thought to be one of the reasons why people in Mediterranean countries (where olive oil is widely consumed in large quantities) are far less prone to heart disease than northern Europeans and Americans. Due to its high proportion of monounsaturated fatty acids, olive oil appears – after rigorous scientific studies – to be an essential element in the prevention of cardiovascular disease (diseases affecting the heart and blood vessels).

Understanding olive oil's chemical composition gives some idea of why it is valuable to good health. It consists of no more than 15 per cent saturated fatty acids (mainly palmitic acid), about 76 per cent monounsaturated fatty acids (principally oleic acid) and up to 10 per cent polyunsaturated fatty acids (mostly linoleic acid).

This fatty acid balance ties in exactly with the latest nutritional ideas, which

Above: Olive oil as a regulr part of the diet has been said to ease conditions as diverse as gallstones, rheumatism, depression and colds. Below: A Spanish olive orchard. Like wine, olive oil has 'good' years, and varies in quality from one region to another.

recommend reducing fat consumption in industrialised countries to 30 per cent of total Calorie intake. Nutritionists are also suggesting that people should aim for a better distribution of the three types of fatty acid in their diet. Ideal fat intake should be split into one quarter saturated fatty acids; one quarter polyunsaturated fatty acids and one half monounsaturated fatty acids.

THE CASE FOR MONOUNSATURATES

Recent research has uncovered the fact that, although Italians and Greeks consume as

THE HEAT IS ON

Oxidation of fats – when they react with oxygen – raises the risk of atherosclerosis (diseased arteries). This oxidation increases with high temperature, but the less saturated the individual fatty acid concerned, the lower the degree of oxidation. Olive oil resists oxidation well, and is heat-stable even at very high temperatures. Therefore at normal cooking temperatures – around 180°C (350°F) – olive oil does not produce harmful side-effects.

much as fat as the Finns and the Americans, and much more than the Japanese, they had a level of cardiovascular disease and mortality close to that of the Japanese – and much less than American and Finnish levels.

Knowing Mediterranean countries were the principal consumers of olive oil, it was suggested that oleic acid – and monounsaturated fats in general – affected the fat content of the blood and helped to protect the heart.

During the research the following could be observed:
• In health volunteers, the effects of three diets rich in:
1 linoleic acid (polyunsaturated)
2 oleic acid (monounsaturated)
3 saturated fatty acids
on fat levels were closely monitored. Results showed that the first two diets brought about a significant decrease – about 10–15 per cent

COSMETIC APPLICATIONS

Ordinary 'refined' olive oil that is not quite good enough to earn the label 'virgin' oil, can also be used as a very effective base for soaps and creams, helping to nourish and moisturise the skin and replace lost natural oils.

– in both the 'bad' cholesterol (LDL cholesterol) and 'good' cholesterol (HDL cholesterol) types that exist in the body. However, one important difference emerged during the research: linoleic acid produced a fall of around 10 per cent in HDL cholesterol, while oleic acid produced a selective fall in LDL, without altering levels of HDL.
• This short-term (1 month) trial was followed by a study of monks who stuck rigidly to a diet in which fats made up 30 per cent of their total Calorie intake. When various vegetable oils (sunflower, soya, and peanut oil) and olive oil were compared, the latter produced much higher levels of HDL.

PROOF FOR POLYUNSATURATES
It is now recognised that, while olive oil supplies a lot of monounsaturated fatty acids, it also contains valuable amounts of polyunsaturated fatty acids. Polyunsaturated fatty acids are essential for the maintenance of many physiological functions, such as cell membrane permeability and prostaglandin synthesis. Prostaglandins are substances produced in the body that affect the nervous system and blood flow in the kidneys, as well as stimulating the contraction of uterine muscle – in childbirth for example.

However, excessive consumption of polyunsaturated fatty acids should be avoided. These fatty acids easily become oxidised (combine with oxygen) and

Green olives are usually preserved in brine and black ones in salt. Olives destined to be pressed for oil must be picked at exactly the right point betwen green and black stages.

therefore generate chemical substances called free radicals, which leads to an increased risk of atherosclerosis – arterial disease where fat deposits build up on the artery wall lining.

THE SUCCESS STORY CONTINUES
Olive oil's main health plus point is its role in cardiovascular protection. However, other benefits should not be forgotten; these include:
• Healthy functioning and protection of the gall-bladder and
• Bone growth and mineralisation.

BEARING FRUIT
Moving on to the fruit from which the oil is extracted, there is now a wide selection of olives available, varying in both types and size. Green, black, with or without stones, stuffed with pimento, almonds, onions or anchovies – people with very different tastes can enjoy the goodness offered by olives. However, few people realise that although the green and black olives look like completely different varieties, they are, in actual fact, exactly the same. This is because green olives turn black naturally if left to ripen on the trees.

Nature's peelable purifier

THE ONION

The humble onion is found in every kitchen, but its curative powers, well-known to the ancients, make it an important medicinal plant too

There can be no doubting the power of the juices contained in onions – anyone who has ever sliced one is only too aware of that. But the uses onions can and have been put to are more varied than most people might expect.

For an easily cultivated bulbous herb, grown in most parts of Europe and other moderate climates, the onion has had a rather exciting past. Deified in ancient Egypt, it was used in many medicines both there and in Babylon; later on it was taken as a preventive medicine during epidemics of cholera and plague. It was apparently eaten by the Roman emperor Nero as a cure for colds, and its reputation, both as an aphrodisiac and a bestower of longevity, has made it popular in the diets of many countries.

Quite apart from its real medicinal properties onion is, quite simply, delicious. It forms the basis of so many dishes, whether raw, sauteed, baked, steamed or boiled, that it would be difficult to imagine the cuisine of any country without it.

RECENT DISCOVERIES

The uses of onions in folk medicine and various complementary forms of treatment have been known for many years. Onions have been used in particular for the relief of coughs, colds and catarrh – but more recently, some of their curative properties have been isolated by scientific research. Research suggests that onions contain a compound called diphenyl thiosulphate, which can have a soothing action on certain types of cough – especially those associated with asthma.

Scientists now also recognise that onions can protect against heart attacks. This is because they can reduce the likelihood of clots forming in the blood and causing cardiac arrest or thrombosis. To back this up, evidence suggests that in the areas of Hungary and Bulgaria where onions are widely grown and form a large part of the staple diet, inhabitants are far less likely to suffer from heart attacks than their Balkan neighbours with a substantially smaller onion intake.

Another effect of onion is to stabilise blood-sugar levels. Experiments carried out as long ago as the 1920s revealed that onion has a similar effect in this respect to insulin. Onion is slower to take effect than insulin, but on the other hand its effects are longer lasting. This does not mean, however, than onion can be used as a substitute for insulin therapy; but it can be of help to those who suffer from unstable blood-sugar levels (hypoglycaemia).

ONION POWER

Obviously, then, the onion is more than just a tasty, romantic culinary plant. It contains sugar, vitamins A, B, C and E, and minerals such as sodium, potassium and iron. Among its many uses, it stimulates the digestive and nervous systems, acts as a diuretic, anti-rheumatic, expectorant (a cough remedy that encourages the coughing up of phlegm), and vermifuge (for expelling worms from the body). It has a distinct antibiotic effect, for example, and so can kill bacteria – the fresh juice kills both the diphtheria and tuberculosis bacilli.

Onion lowers blood cholesterol, particularly if eaten raw. Raw onion is also highly recommended in the treatment of sinusitis.

The reason that onion is so much more active in its raw state than when cooked, is that its active principles are contained in a highly volatile oil, which is partly destroyed by heat. When eaten raw, however, its juice acts as an irritant and some people find it difficult to digest. Those who can eat it in its raw state should do so as often as they can – chopped in salads, for example. But for those who are not tempted by the idea of eating raw onions, there follow various simple methods of preparation that may make them more palatable.

THE ONION'S REVENGE

The smell of onions can be a problem, both on the hands and on the breath.

• After chopping onions, try rinsing the hands with cold water, rubbing them with salt, rinsing again and then washing them with soap and warm water.
• To remove the smell of onion from the breath, eat a few sprigs of parsley or an apple, or chew a coffee bean to conceal the odour.

Onion wine, a pleasant drink and effective remedy, made from onion, honey and white wine.

Feature onion regularly in your diet.

Feature onion regularly in your diet.

recommended for anaemia, arthritis, rheumatism, colds, influenza, dropsy or oedema (excess fluid collecting in body tissues), general water retention problems, and cystitis.

When cooked, onion can be very soothing to both the digestive and respiratory systems. For people with sensitive stomachs, this is a far more suitable way to enjoy the healthy benefits of onions:
• Take 3 onions, cut into chunks, and boil them in half a litre (about 1 pint) of water for 5-10 minutes.
• Sweeten the resulting liquid with honey, as wished, and drink throughout the day at regular intervals.

Onions baked in their skins, in a similar way to baked potatoes, are also delicious. This method of cooking keeps all the goodness inside, but the resulting flavour is milder and more aromatic than that of raw onions.

KNOW YOUR ONIONS – INSIDE . . .

Onions can be used therapeutically both internally and externally. For taking internally, onion wine is an easily made preparation, still using raw onion, but in a more digestible form:
• Take 3 parts (in weight) of finely chopped raw onion, 1 of honey and 6 of white wine. Mix together in a covered container and leave to stand for about 48 hours, stirring thoroughly from time to time.
• Strain the mixture and take between 2 and 4 tablespoons of the resulting liquid each day.

For those who prefer a preparation made without alcohol:
• Take 4 medium onions, sliced, and add 1 litre (about 2 pints) of hot water.
• Leave to stand for 2-3 hours and take a glassful 2-3 times each day.

These mixtures are particularly

. . . AND OUT

There are many ways onions can be used externally. They are sometimes made into poultices, for rheumatism or arthritis, or applied to the forehead as a cure for migraine. A piece of freshly-cut onion rubbed over wasp, bee or other insect bites brings speedy relief, and red onion can be rubbed on warts and verrucas to encourage them to disappear. The delicate membrane that separates the layers of an onion can be used as an antiseptic dressing for cuts, sores or burns, then covered with gauze for further protection.

The stimulant effect of onion on the skin was harnessed by Arab doctors hundreds of years ago in a remedy for hair loss: onion mixed with salt and pepper and applied to the scalp.

There is always the possibility, however, that no one will get close enough to see that you are losing your hair, because the smell of raw onion is not known for its allure. But it is clear that onions have far more uses than most of us imagine and, even without making them into syrups, infusions or poultices, we can enjoy some of their many health-giving properties simply by incorporating them into our daily diet.

THE HOMOEOPATHIC ONION

Allium cepa is the homoeopathic remedy made from onion. An invaluable cure in winter, it is recommended for use when colds and sore throats start during cold, damp weather; if the nose is constantly running and making the upper lip and nostrils sore; and for hoarseness or coughs brought on by cold air.

Allium cepa can also be used as a treatment for headaches, particularly in the forehead; for neuralgia, and, in minute dosages, for treating colicky babies with stomach pains.

Allium cepa *in homoeopathic tablet form.*

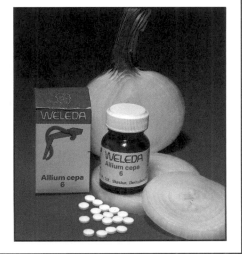

PARSLEY

Parsley has long been renowned as a versatile herb – both culinary and medicinal – from seasoning fish to reducing flatulence

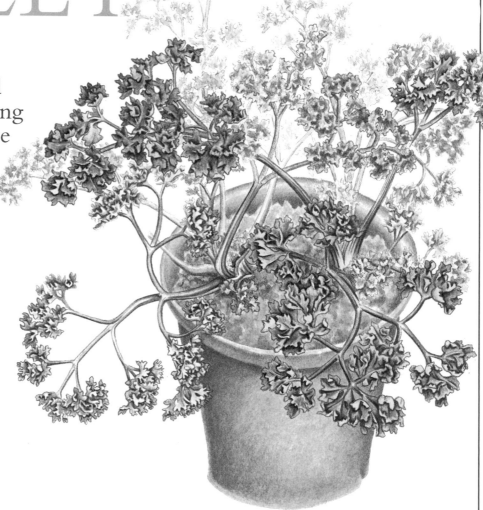

Parsley, (*Petroselinum Crispum*) is a member of the Umbelliferae family which also includes other well-known herbs such as aniseed, dill, fennel and caraway. The name Petroselinum can be traced back to two Greek words: Petra meaning rock or stone, and Selinon which means celery, thus Petroselinum means Rock or Mountain Celery. It is from this origin the common name parsley was derived.

GROWING PARSLEY

Parsley is a bi-annual plant that will grow to between 30 and 70cm (12 and 28in). The distinctive leaves are triangular in general outline, and the flowers are congregated in umbels (flower-clusters forming a curved surface), which are between 2 and 5cm (1 and 2in) in diameter, and have a yellowish-green colour.

The flowers bloom between June and August and the seeds and leaves can be harvested at this time. The root can also

Removing flower heads from parsley will encourage growth of the leaves – for both culinary and medicinal purposes.

PARSLEY TEA

To use parsley medicinally, make a tea from the fresh or dried leaves. If using fresh leaves remember to increase the amount of herb as plants have a high water content. The normal recipe is 28g (1oz) of dried leaves to 500ml (1 pint) of boiling water. If, however, you wish to make a smaller amount, use just 1 teaspoon of leaves to a cupful of boiling water per person. Parsley tea is a helpful digestive aid after a meal.

The seeds can be steeped in cold water and then drunk; alternatively crush them and sprinkle the resulting powder over your food.

The root has a tough external cell wall, so it has to be decocted (simmered) for about 20 minutes, again using 28g (1oz) to 500 ml (1 pint) of boiling water. Strain and drink a cupful three times a day.

be used but this is best collected in the autumn from 2 year-old plants. The dried leaves can be used throughout the winter when supplies of the fresh herb obviously dwindle. The stems can also be dried and used for dyes and food colouring.

Parsley's natural habitat is Southern Europe, from Sardinia through to Greece and Turkey. Now it is cultivated in all temperate areas. The first record of cultivation in Britain dates from 1548.

MEDICINAL USES

A volatile oil, made up of apiol and parsley camphor, is found throughout the plant in varying quantities which range from 2.7 per cent in the seed, 0.3 per cent in the leaf, to only 0.1 per cent in the root. The plant also contains Vitamin C, starch, mucilage, sugar and a glycoside, apiin. The volatile oil is considered to be parsley's active constituent.

Parsley, like other plants of the Umbelliferae family, has carminative properties (reducing wind) – although carrum carvi (caraway) seeds are probably the best for this – and is very comforting to the stomach. Parsley is used for complaints such as flatulence, colic, dyspepsia and any generalised inflammation of the digestive system. Parsley is also a useful diuretic (diuretics increase the functioning of the kidneys and are used to increase urination). A tea made from the fresh leaves will help to reduce swollen ankles and water retention before periods. The fresh leaf also has a bitter taste which helps to

stimulate appetite and digestive activity in the stomach. The herb also acts as an emmenogogue (stimulating the menstrual cycle) and as such is useful for painful and late periods, but should not be taken in medicinal amounts during pregnancy.

Externally, an extract of parsley has been used for conjunctivitis (inflammation of the eyes), and as a remedy for arthritic conditions and complaints such as gout. Due to its toning effect on the liver, it has been used for skin conditions, in particular childhood eczema and dermatitis, and any liver ailment such as jaundice (a symptom of liver disease).

In the U.S.S.R. parsley is valued for its anti-spasmodic action and is also used in treating hypertention (high blood-pressure).

F RENCH USES FOR PARSLEY

The French use parsley as a 'drawing ointment' in swellings and boils. It is recommended that the parsley should be pounded with snails, then applied to the swelling! The crushed leaves have been used in a similar fashion to comfrey for bruising.

The French also use parsley in treating kidney stones and gravel in the urine. In French folk medicine parsley developed a reputation as a blood cleanser and aphrodisiac. Presumably, this was because of its ability to increase the vitality of the whole individual, rather than working directly on the reproductive glands.

P ARSLEY AS A FOOD

Eating parsley as a food is a pleasant and effective way of utilising its medicinal properties, and the roots, cooked in the same way as turnips, make a change from run of the mill vegetables. Parsley is used extensively as a garnish or seasoning herb in soups, stews, stuffings and fish dishes. It should be added to food towards the end of a dish's preparation in order to preserve the vitamin and mineral content.

Parsley is the main ingredient of dried mixed herbs and its stalks are always part of a bouquet garni.

Chewing fresh parsley leaves also helps destroy the smell of garlic and spicy foods on the breath.

PARSLEY TINCTURE

Parsley can be extracted in alcohol by placing 112g (4oz) of the chopped herb in half a litre (1 pint) of alcohol (preferably an alcohol that is 40 per cent proof, such as whisky or vodka). Store this mixture for 2 weeks in a place away from direct sunlight, turning it daily. Then press as much alcohol as possible from the herb, through a sieve or press, and bottle the tincture. The medicinal dose is to take between 3 and 5ml (½-1 teaspoon) in water three times a day with meals.

The parsley tincture will keep through winter when fresh herbs are no longer available.

PARSLEY AND HISTORY

In Greek mythology parsley was dedicated to Persephone and to funeral rites; tombs would be festooned with wreaths of parsley. The superstitious considered it unlucky to transplant parsley, possibly because of its connection with funerals.

Culpeper, the famous 17th century herbalist, cites numerous uses for parsley, most of which are still in use today. He also suggested that parsley, fried in butter, made a useful external application for hardened breasts and for reducing bruising.

The flavour of white fish, such as cod, is greatly enhanced by a parsley sauce.

PARSLEY PIERT

Natural stone–breaker

Since medieval times parsley piert has been used a remedy for kidney and bladder stones and urinary infections

If you do not feed and cut your lawn regularly, you may find it being invaded by parsley piert. This wild plant is seen by gardeners as a troublesome weed, especially on lawns. Yet, as with other so-called weeds such as nettles and dandelions, it has properties which can be useful for treating illness and infection (see NETTLE, STINGING; DANDELION).

Parsley piert (*Aphanes arvensis*) is an annual wild plant, closely related to another valuable herb, lady's mantle. In fact, it is sometimes referred to as field lady's mantle. Parsley piert gets its name from its superficial resemblance to parsley, and from the old

French term *perce-pierre* which literally means pierce stone or a plant that grows in stony ground (see PARSLEY).

Parsley piert grows throughout Europe and in North Africa. It thrives in fields, gravel pits and wastelands it particularly likes sandy soil. A low-growing herb, it has a thin, branched stem with lobed, fan-shaped leaves. The whole plant is downy with slender, scattered hairs. It has tiny, green flowers that cluster at the base of the leaves.

OLD REMEDY

Parsley piert has been used for centuries as a natural treatment for kidney and bladder problems, and was certainly known in medieval Europe. The Flemish botanist, De

L'Obel, writing in the late 16th century, recorded that it was widely used by the poor to 'break' stones in the kidney and bladder.

The famous English herbalist Nicholas Culpeper describes parsley piert as a common herb, and as being plentiful about Hyde Park and Hampstead Heath. He thought parsley piert to be a very good salad herb, which should be picked so it could be eaten throughout the winter. Medicinally, he recorded it as being able 'to provoke urine, and to break stone'. He recommended a strong infusion for gravel or kidney stones and believed it to be good for jaundice. He also advocated it as a cleaner for the kidneys and urinary passages.

MEDICINAL PROPERTIES

Parsley piert is an astringent, demulcent and diuretic all rolled into one. Astringents have a binding action on mucous membranes and exposed tissues. It helps to soothe inflammation by coating irritated surfaces and creating a barrier against bacteria and toxins.

Demulcent herbs have a soothing effect on inflamed surfaces, enhancing the

CURING BY COMBINATION

Parsley piert is often prescribed as part of a combination of herbal remedies which combine diuretic, antiseptic and soothing qualities to tackle an illness from all angles. The herbs most commonly used in such a collection include buchu (a urinary antiseptic particularly useful in cases of cystitis and urethritis), bearberry (a general antiseptic), couch grass (a urinary antiseptic), clivers (which reduces body temperatures and blood pressure) and juniper (which is both an antiseptic and a diuretic). Marshmallow and dandelion may also be included in this list. The latter is a particularly effective tonic for the bladder, liver and kidney.

Parsley piert should be collected when it is in flower. It is most effective when fresh.

astringent action. They are particularly helpful for areas such as the digestive and urinary tracts. Two other well-known demulcents are slippery elm and marshmallow (see SLIPPERY ELM).

Parsley piert is also a diuretic, which means that it helps to stimulate an increase in the flow of urine. Urination is one of the ways in which the body rids itself of excess fluid and waste products, and in doing this can reduce the problems associated with urinary infections.

BLADDER AND KIDNEYS
Parsley piert's medicinal properties make it an ideal remedy for bladder complaints and a number of different kidney problems. Herbalists prescribe parsley piert, often in conjunction with other herbs such as gravel

root, for kidney stones and bladder infections such as cystitis. Its diuretic action helps to flush out infections and unwanted deposits in the urinary tract. The symptoms associated with bladder infections, such as difficulty and pain in passing water, are also relieved by parsley piert.

COUNTERACTING CYSTITIS
Cystitis is a recurring complaint that mainly affects women, and which can be treated naturally. Herbalists have a range of useful herbs available to them, including parsley piert, or urinary disinfectants such as bearberry and buchu. The soothing effects of marshmallow may give some immediate relief from discomfort. However, it is unwise to rely solely on the healing properties of herbs to cure cystitis. The condition frequently recurs (so common, in fact, that it is sometimes called 'a cold in the bladder'), so it is important to take other preventative actions. These may include practical measures such as scrupulous hygiene, avoiding synthetic underwear and any chemical irritation, drinking plenty of liquid, and adhering to a healthy diet. It is also wise to avoid sugar, because sugary urine provides the perfect breeding environment for infectious bacteria.

OTHER MEDICINAL USES
Nicholas Culpeper wrote that parsley piert

TEA OR TABLETS

Although it is generally considered most effective when freshly collected, parsley piert is available as a dried herb for making medicinal tea, or in capsule form. The tea can be made by infusing one teaspoon of the dried herb in one cup of boiling water for 15 minutes. Parsley piert is also an ingredient in many diuretics and herbal remedies prescribed for cystitis, backache and lumbago, either in tablet or liquid form. The recommended dosage is 2-4g (½ teaspoon) of the dried herb equivalent, three times a day.

'is likewise good in jaundice, and other complaints arising from obstructions of the liver . . .' He also recommended it as being helpful 'for the stranguary'. It is also an ingredient in some diuretic formulae designed to help get rid of excess fluid which may build up in the body's cells or tissues.

THE PROBLEM DISSOLVED
Parsley piert has been prescribed for centuries as a remedy for gravel or kidney stones. To be sure of getting rid of these problems, it is a good idea to increase your intake of other stone-removers, too. Clinical trials suggest Vitamin B_6 and magnesium could offer a nutritional approach to prevention and treatment of kidney stones. Stones are most commonly composed of calcium oxalate. Vitamin B_6 appears to help control the body's production of oxalates and limits the amount getting into the kidneys. Magnesium helps urine dissolve more oxalates, so reducing the risk of further kidney stones forming. The recommended daily amounts for those prone to this problem are 10mg of vitamin B_6, and 300–350mg of magnesium.

A CULINARY TREAT
Parsley piert thrives on very stony, unproductive steep ground. On the rugged island of Colonsay, which is off the west coast of Scotland, parsley piert was consumed raw in summer in salads or cooked as a vegetable. In the autumn, the islanders traditionally collected and then pickled large quantities of the plant for consumption in winter.

Containing tannins, sugars and minerals, the plant formed an important part of the islanders' diet.

Parsley piert products are widely available in dried herb and capsule form. The herb has many effects, including reducing water retention in the body.

PFAFFIA

Brazilian Ginseng

The ancient Amazonian answer to good health and a life-style free of stress

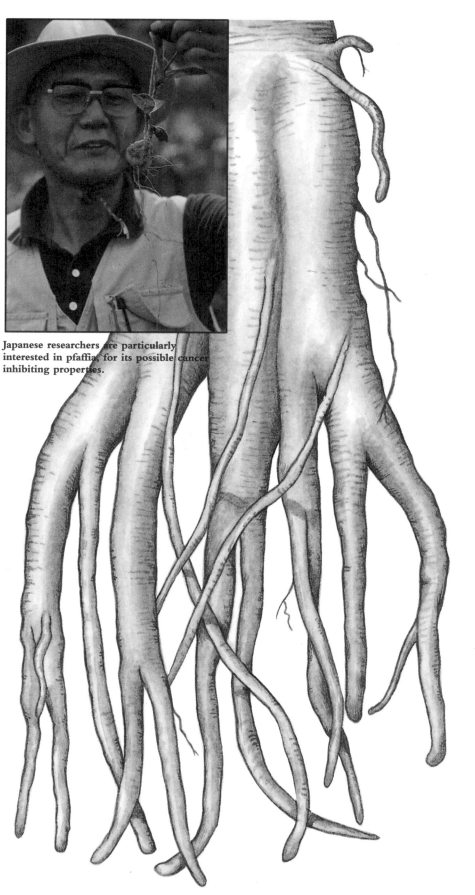

The rain forest of Brazil are a wonderfully rich source of medicinal plants. Pfaffia, a lush green flowering plant, is one of these, growing along cliffside and in ravines. Also known as 'Suma' and 'Brazilian Ginseng', this herb is not to be confused with Asiatic ginseng, to which it is not related (see GINSENG). There are more than 20 varieties of pfaffia, but it is the *Pfaffia paniculata Martius Kuntze* that possesses medicinal properties. Like the Eastern ginsengs, it has a thick root that, if left for seven years, may be harvested to provide a source of medicine.

TRADITIONAL HERB

Pfaffia has been known to the Amazon Indians for thousands of years, mainly in the Matto Grosso area of Central Brazil, where it serves both as a food plant and herbal remedy. In folk medicine, the native Amazonians use it as a tonic, an aphrodisiac, a wound herb, and for other illnesses. When Europeans settled in the region later, the plant's benefits became more widely known and it was adopted by physicians as well as folk healers.

Japanese researchers are particularly interested in pfaffia, for its possible cancer inhibiting properties.

Pfaffia paniculata (above right) and another pfaffia variety, with the roots both crushed and flaked.

Pfaffia's native Portuguese name is Para Tudo which means 'for all things', a reflection of the belief in its all-healing powers. Over the last 40 years this belief has been vindicated by various studies conducted by herbalists and pharmacologists into pfaffia's active ingredients. The root is currently being investigated in clinics and laboratories across the world, notably in Japan, where research has been extensive.

The herb is rich in nutrients – vitamins A, some B, and C; amino acids; iron, calcium, potassium and other minerals and trace elements. Scientists have also discovered the presence of hormones and pfaffosides (see Suma Surveys, overleaf). Some of the vegetable hormones it contains appear to parallel the body's own

hormones, and may help stimulate and harmonise hormonal balance:
• Beta-ecdysone helps rejuvenate cell growth, enabling new and healthy cells to be produced
• Sitosterol controls blood cholesterol levels
• Stigmasterol is a vegetable hormone similar to oestrogen.

TONIC HERB

According to research, pfaffia has a regulating effect on a number of activities in the body. Regarded as a tonic herb, it seems able to combat both physical and mental stress. Although it has not yet been scientifically proven, there have been consistent reports from various countries that people taking pfaffia on a regular basis experience an improvement in their feeling of well-being. Stamina levels go up, mental alertness increases, and people feel calmer, stronger, and more able to cope with life in general.

As an adaptogen, pfaffia is a plant whose properties help the body to adapt to stress, whether physical or emotional in origin. Adaptogens are believed to act on the hormonal (or endocrine) system, particularly the adrenal glands that produce anti-stress hormones. They are able to balance the hormones, thereby improving the body's functions. Pfaffia also appear to improve general resistance to infections so a regular dosage – particularly in the winter months – could help to maintain good health.

ANTI-TOXIN ACTION

Brazilian physiologists have revealed pfaffia's ability to increase oxygenation between cells, and to prevent enzyme blockages. These can cause a build-up of toxins that prevent nutrients from being utilised properly, which in turn results in the degeneration of cells. The herb

appears to regulate the body's acid–alkaline balance, which is important in toxin neutralisation.

SUMA SURVEYS

The head of the Department of Pharmacy at the University of Sao Paulo, Dr Milton Brazzach, conducted extensive research into pfaffia. In order to demonstrate its healing powers, he treated over three thousand patients with the herb. Dr Brazzach saw encouraging results in the treatment of a variety of diseases and conditions ranging from osteomyelitis, high blood cholesterol, and joint problems, to diabetes and cancer. He reported a success rate of between 50 and 66 per cent in the treatment of certain malignant tumours if

The ancient cure pfaffia is helping to relieve a modern problem – stress.

the administration of pfaffia was started early. Leukaemia, too, appeared to respond to use of the herb.

Japanese research has since reinforced Dr Brazzach's findings and confirms that pfaffia may be able to inhibit cancerous cells and arrest the growth of tumours. The active ingredients which work in this way are

Pfaffia is well tolerated and there are no toxic symptoms.

compounds called pfaffosides which have been discovered in the herb.

HELPING DIABETICS

Pfaffia seems to have potential as a natural means of treating diabetes. It is able to normalise the insulin-producing cells of the pancreas, and, if taken regularly, pfaffia can additionally stabilise blood sugar levels. Dr Brazzach discovered that after six to eight months' treatment with pfaffia, some of his diabetic patients no longer needed daily supplies of insulin.

Pfaffia has been used with some success in the treatment of ulcers, hypertension (high blood pressure) and nervous disorders, and it has helped to heal wounds and alleviate degenerative conditions such as rheumatoid arthritis.

AVAILABILITY AND DOSAGE

Capsules containing powdered pfaffia are available from some health food shops. The recommended prophylactic dose is one to two 500 mg capsules per day. However, doctors may recommend far higher dosages for particular problems.

PROPOLIS AND POLLEN

Be healthier with remedies suited to everyone, from workers to queens

*Propolis and pollen are essential to the daily life and
survival of honey bees, and for centuries man has shared in the
bounty of these unique, natural foods*

Propolis is a resinous material used in beehives as a cement and disinfectatnt. The word comes from the Greek 'pro' meaning before, and 'polis' meaning city, and the material is used by bees to maintain their hive as a fortified city, free from infection. The bees collect this resin from the bark and buds of trees, favouring the hottest time of day during the months of June to October.

The composition of propolis works out at about 50 to 55 per cent resins and balsams, 30 per cent beeswax, 10 to 15 per cent essential oils, and approximately 5 per cent pollen. The most active ingredients of propolis are compounds called flavinoids, substances which have a remarkable capacity to control micro-organisms and to stimulate the immune system of humans and animals alike.

FIGHTING DISEASE AND IMPROVING HEALTH

Propolis was used by the ancient Egyptians, the Romans and the Greeks for healing, and its use is illustrated in paintings of those times. Nowadays, there is a wealth of scientific literature about the uses of propolis to treat medical disorders. The majority of the research has been carried out in the Soviet Union and Eastern Europe, where propolis has been used by doctors for years.

Propolis sprang to the attention of western Europeans during the Boer War, when wounds treated with dressings of propolis and petroleum jelly were found to heal quickly, without infection setting in. Propolis helps to heal wounds, ulcers and burns by destroying invasive micro-organisms, creating a sterile environment and encouraging the re-growth of blood capillaries and surrounding tissue.

A BOOST TO THE IMMUNE SYSTEM

There is currently great interest in the possibility of boosting the body's natural ability to fight disease. The idea is to stimulate the immune system, and it seems that propolis can do just that. Research carried out on mice has shown that those mice that received propolis produced twice as many defensive blood cells (the ones that fight infection) as another control group, which received none. Similar effects have been observed in humans.

Gargling with a few drops of propolis in water rapidly destroys the bacteria that cause sore throats. And while most anti-bacterial drugs tend to destroy friendly micro-organisms of the digestive tract along with the invasive ones, propolis is safe and gentle. However, a very small minority of people (about one in two thousand) may show an allergic response to propolis in the form of a skin rash.

Because it stimulates the immune system, propolis has been found of value in viral and fungal infections. It also acts as a mild anaesthetic: as it fights sore-throat bacteria, for example, it will also numb the pain. It has been found to be particularly useful in the treatment of ear, nose and throat infections,

Bees are the most resistant of all members of the animal kingdom to diseases caused by micro-organisms – living proof of the efficacy of propolis.

and is used extensively in the treatment of painful teeth and gums.

POLLEN – A HARVEST OF HEALTH

The food value of pollen has long been recognised. It was used by the Apache and Pueblo Indians in their fertility rites, and the Navaho Indians valued it in their 'search for peace'. The exceptional nutritional value of pollen has only become clear this century, although the Maoris of New Zealand have eaten it for centuries, made into cakes.

Our ancestors must have unwittingly eaten a lot of pollen along with their honey, because it is only recently that honey has been strained, with much of the pollen being removed. Many cheap brands of blended honeys nowadays are not only finely filtered, but also heat-treated so that the vital, natural enzymes are destroyed. Honey treated in this way has little nutritional advantage over sugar.

In its original state, pollen is a granular or powdery substance produced by the anther of a flower. Its purpose is to fertilise the ovules of the same or similar plants. Pollen grains vary enormously in size, but even the largest are very tiny: a single male cone of one kind of conifer can produce a thousand million grains.

Pollen is extremely rich in protein– indeed it is the main source of this nutrient for growing bees. Pollen also contains carbohydrates, fats, fibre and a varied assortment of vitamins, minerals and trace elements. It is these micro-nutrients that are believed to give pollen its power, even in small amounts, to benefit human health. Many authorities think that it is much more important to have a balanced and widely-spread supplement of vitamins and minerals than to take large quantities of a single one (except in cases of specific deficiency), and pollen provides just that. The Soviets have given it to their athletes and astronauts for years and now pollen is being used similarly in the West.

BUZZING WITH GOODNESS

Studies have shown that people who felt nervy and irritable noticed a marked improvement after an eight-day course of pollen. It has also been found to improve the appetite, reduce pre-menstrual tension and some menopausal symptoms, and aid recovery from disorders of the prostrate gland, such as prostatic hypertrophy. Other conditions that have been helped by pollen include anxiety states, stress, depression, arthritis and rheumatism, and hair and skin problems.

IMMUNITY AGAINST HAY FEVER?

Surprisingly, pollen has also been found to be successful in the treatment of hay fever. What makes this surprising is that hay fever sufferers are allergic to inhaled pollen, but some doctors believe that the body can be trained to ignore the irritation caused by clouds of flower or grass pollen by giving carefully-measured doses of the substance prior to the hay-fever season. The time may come when pollen tablets are made with different mixtures of pollens, to treat the individual allergies that cause hay fever.

POLLEN PREPARATIONS

Pollen can be found in many forms in health stores, and it is a matter of trial and error to find out which is best for you and your condition.

A leading manufacturer based in Belgium, for example, supplies pure, bee-collected pollen. The bees, when they enter the hive, go across the special pollen trap which is harvested one or more times a day during the season. The pollen is gently dried and packed in drums. Pollen grains in this form have not had their outer coat (exine) removed, so quite a lot – between 50 and 60 grams (two to three ounces) – has to be taken each day.

Over 14,000 pollen grains are needed to weigh just 1 gram.

Another technique is used by a Scandinavian producer. Plants which are considered to yield good pollens are cultivated but, instead of relying on bees, the pollen is harvested using a sort of giant vacuum-cleaner.

Yet another, more expensive, type of pollen is first gathered by the bees then painstakingly removed from the combs by hand. This type comes mainly from Yugoslavia, and the hives are located in remote areas so that the pollen will be untainted by insecticide or industrial pollution.

PROPOLIS AND POLLUTION

It is most important that propolis for human use should be harvested in unpolluted areas. If bees are in a place where resin-rich buds or barks are not available, they will look for any alternative, and the propolis that results may, accordingly, be of lower quality. In Greece, bees have even been filmed harvesting resin from melted tar on the roads.

THE CONTENT OF POLLEN

Pollen is so complex that it has so far defied complete analysis. About 15 vitamins have been identified in the substance, however, and numerous minerals including sodium, potassium, calcium, aluminium, iron, magnesium, copper, zinc, manganese and sulphur. A large number of enzymes have also been isolated. Pure pollen of good quality should be rich and diverse in colour, with granules ranging from deep blue to yellow and orange. This shows it comes from a wide variety of flowers.

ROSEMARY

A mild antiseptic and natural stimulant

A daily cup of rosemary tea eases digestion, stimulates circulation and de-toxifies the liver, giving your whole body a 'spring clean'

Lamb is not the same without a sprinkle of rosemary. In fact, within the kitchen, this strong scented herb enhances the flavour of many dishes – both sweet and savoury. But while its culinary uses are widely known, its value as a medicinal herb is often totally overlooked.

GATHERING AND STORING ROSEMARY

Rosemary, *Rosmarinus officinalis*, grows wild on the coastlines and mountains of southern Europe, and all over the UK. It usually prefers sheltered spots with light, dry soil.

The pale, lilac flowers and the needle-like, greenish silver leaves are the parts which are used medicinally. Rosemary flowers are among the first spring blossoms to appear, usually at the end of March, and this is the best ime to pick them. If the leaves are to be used, they should be removed from the stems before the flowers appear.

ROSEMARY TEA OR TISANE

Rosemary is a strong herb, best taken in the form of a tea or tisane (see CHOICE – HERBAL TEAS). Use one teaspoon of the herb to one cup of boiling water. Be sure to cover the cup and allow it to stand for at least 10 minutes, as this give the water time enough to extract the active principles from the plant. It is important to cover the cup, as the active principles dissolve into the steam and will escape unless covered. The tea can be slightly sweetened with a drop of honey. Never mix it with milk. Take rosemary tea, twice daily, before meals for 10-14 days, and feel the difference.

Storage should be somewhere away from direct sunlight in a cool, dark place; sunlight will reduce the active properties of the herb. A darkened glass jar in a cellar, or outhouse, is ideal. Once dried, rosemary will remain active for at least a year – maybe longer. To tell whether it is still active, smell or taste the herb; if it has a strong flavour or fragrance then it is still usable.

EASING DIGESTION

Rosemary has been analysed and found to contain a volatile oil called borneol, a substance similar in structure to camphor. Borneol stimulates the

R OSEMARY SHAMPOO

Rosemary stimulates the hair bulbs to start growing and to prevent premature baldness. Many shampoos these days incorporate rosemary for this reason. An infusion of the dried herb massaged into the scalp, or used as a *final rinse after washing will strenthen the hair and prevent dandruff and dull, lank hair. Alternatively, add a few rosemary leaves to a bottle of ordinary shampoo and leave it to 'infuse' for a few weeks.*

All sorts of products containing rosemary are available – mainly from health-food shops. As well as delicately-scented shampoos, soaps and moisturising creams, the range incorporates essential oil of rosemary.

secretion of digestive juices and saliva. It also stimulates the action of the whole of the digestive tract, moving food and waste matter through more efficiently. It can therefore be used to stimulate a sluggish digestion, to help the body process foods more efficiently, to aid the absorption of nutrients, and allow you to obtain maximum benefit from the food that you eat. It also helps to relieve the bloated feeling after meals and to reduce any wind, indigestion or nausea associated with eating.

A LIVER TONIC
A substance known as bitter is also present in rosemary. This stimulates the action of the liver, therefore helping any

Rosemary is a strong herb, and as such should be used sparingly in cooking.

liverish conditions. Being 'liverish' is best described as that 'monday morning feeling' that we all know so well; the general feeling of being unwell, lethargic, clogged-up and under the weather. A bitter stimulates the liver to work even harder to clear the back-log of toxins present in the blood – especially if you drink alcohol or smoke to excess – allowing the body to be flushed out and cleansed. In effect, it purifies and refreshes the whole system.

INCREASE YOUR BRAIN POWER
Rosemary also works on the nervous system. It is a gentle, non-addictive stimulant which is much used by herbalists in the treatment of depression and general lethargy. It stimulates the brain and heightens concentration by increasing blood flow to the brain. In ancient times, students wore wreaths of rosemary around their heads to improve their memories.
Because rosemary affects the

BREATH FRESHENER

'the flowers of rosemary being drunke at morning and evening first and last, taketh away the stench of the mouth and the breath, and make it very sweet, if there be added thereto, to steep or infuse for certaine daies, a few cloves, mace, cinamon and a little anise seed.'

(Gerard 1597)

As it is a sweet smelling antiseptic, rosemary will help to freshen the breath and to combat any infections of the teeth and gums. If you grow rosemary, take a few of the topmost leaves and chew them slowly. Alternatively, make up a tea and use it as a mouthwash after brushing the teeth. Because rosemary is a remedy for the digestive system, it will alleviate bad breath due to a fermenting stomach.

circulation of blood to the brain, it is also used in the treatment of migraine. Migraines can be caused by a number of factors, such as allergies, stress, hormonal imbalances, bad circulation and liver upsets. When the attack occurs, the blood vessels in the skull go into spasm, and then dilate, causing the intense throbbing pain felt at the temples and feelings of nausea and vomiting. Rosemary will not cure an attack of migraine, but used regularly it will reduce the severity and frequency of attacks. Taken over a period of time, it can help to balance the circulation of blood to the head. The blood vessel spasms are then reduced or disappear entirely, and all the resulting symptoms are relieved.

IMPROVED CIRCULATION

Rosemary also stimulates the circulation of blood to the rest of the body and can be used where there is poor circulation causing cold hands and feet, chilblains, excessive bruising, arteriosclerosis and varicose veins. It is one of the few herbal remedies which will actually raise low blood pressure.

It is not known why, but women are more prone to low blood pressure (hypotension) than men. Theories include hormonal imbalances, anaemia, poor nutrition and poor muscle tone. Heavy bleeding in the monthly periods or 'flooding' at puberty or the menopause is a common cause of anaemia and low blood pressure.

The symptoms of hypotension are fairly vague and include fatigue, depression, dizziness, palpitations, sensitivity to the cold and irritability, but your GP can easily check your blood pressure if you are unsure. Although

hypotension is not as life threatening as hypertension (high blood pressure), it can still make life a great effort for a large number of women who often feel exhausted. Rosemary acts to raise blood pressure by making the heart beat more efficiently. It will not increase your blood pressure unless it is below the normal level.

For those people with generalised circulatory problems, a good everyday remedy is a mixture of equal parts rosemary, yarrow and mint, taken as a tea twice daily before meals.

ROSEMARY FACIAL STEAM

As a facial steam, rosemary deep cleanses the skin by opening the pores and ridding the skin of its impurities. The steam cleans the surface of the skin, removing everyday grime, stimulates the tissues of the skin and encourages perspiration and the circulation of blood. This clears the skin of toxins and helps to prevent the build-up of pus which leads to pimples and acne. Those people with sensitive skins, or who suffer from broken veins should not steam their faces.

To make a steam facial, put a handful of dried or fresh rosemary into a bowl of boiling water. With a towel over your head, allow the steam to work on your face for ten or more minutes. Splash with cold water afterwards to close the pores. Do not go out for an hour after a steam bath.

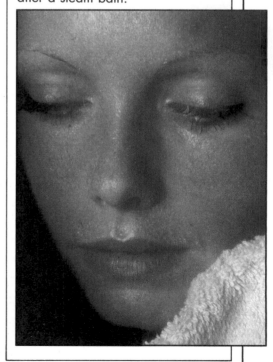

The name 'Rosemary' is derived from the Latin Rosmarinus which, literally translated, means 'dew of the sea'. This refers not only to its sea-side habitat, but to the dew-like appearance of its flowers when viewed from a distance.

HUNGARY WATER

Rosemary was the main ingredient of 'Hungary water', a cosmetic distillation invented for the Queen of Hungary in the thirteenth century. The queen was said to have been completely cured of paralysis by its use. It was also used as a remedy for gout, and washing in it was said to have rejuvenating powers, by removing wrinkles.

It was prepared by putting ¾kg (1½lbs) of rosemary tops into 4 litres (a gallon) of spirits of wine and allowing it to stand for four days and then distilled.

ESSENTIAL OIL OF ROSEMARY

Nowadays, Hungary water is no longer in use, but essential oil of rosemary can be used as an external stimulant in much the same way. Added to linaments, essential oil of rosemary invigorates the affected area by encouraging blood flow to the skin surface, and thus aiding repair. A mixture of 100 drops of the essential oil and 150ml (¼pt) of sunflower oil, massaged into paralysed limbs can have a beneficial effect. Used on a daily basis, for at least six months, it is said to help stimulate damaged muscles and bring some power back into them.

The essential oil is a very potent extract of the plant and should always be diluted before use, in a carrier oil such as unflower, safflower, almond and olive oil. Avoid synthetic oils as these cannot penetrate into the skin, and can irritate sensitive skins. Always buy pure essential oils, as synthetic ones, although cheaper, will not work as well. Do not take essential oils internally, unless advised by the manufacturer.

ROSEMARY BATH

A rosemary bath makes a marvellous 'pick me up' for when you are feeling sleepy or just lazy. Run a warm bath and as the water is running, drop 10 drops of essential oil of rosemary into the water. Keep the steam in the bathroom, as it will contain dissolved particles of the essential oil. When the bath is drawn, simply lie in it for as long as you like, breathing in the invigorating vapour and allowing it to penetrate the pores of your skin and gently energise those tired blood cells. Don't use soap or any other kind of detergent while lying in the bath, as this will destroy the essential oil, just lie back and soak it up. You will be amazed at how refreshed this makes you feel afterwards.

If you cannot get hold of the essential oil, make yourself a pouchette into which you can put your herbs. A small muslin bag with a drawstring top will do. Hang this underneath the hot tap to enable the water to extract the active parts of the herb. Or, if it is more convenient, you can use one of those oval, stainless steel hinged tea containers – for making individual cups of tea – and hang it under the hot tap.

MYTHS AND TRADITIONS

Rosemary was a herb well known to the ancient Romans for its medicinal purposes. Throughout history, its use has been well documented at weddings and funerals, for decorating churches and banqueting halls on feast days, as incense in religious ceremonies, and for spells in witchcraft. It was traditionally known to strengthen the memory and was a symbol of love and loyalty.

For this reason, it became a symbol for lovers, and in weddings the bride would often carry rosemary within her bridal posy – Anne of Cleves, Henry the VIIIth's fourth wife, was said to have worn a wreath of rosemary at her ill fated wedding – unfortunately, Henry VIII was not impressed. The guests at the wedding were also often presented with a rosemary branch which was gilded and wound with ribbands of all colours.

Because of its association with remembrance, rosemary was given to mourners at a funeral for them to put springs of the herb into the coffin before it was lowered to the ground – a custom which continued in parts of Wales until fairly recently. Known for its antiseptic qualities, rosemary was also believed to protect anyone who touched it from pestilence.

ROYAL JELLY

The 'milk' of the honey-bee

A natural energy source from the beehive could prove to be an essential ingredient of tomorrow's fast-moving society

The Chinese have been investigating royal jelly, the food of the queen bee, for centuries. It has unique properties as a natural catalyst, working on the body and nervous system to increase energy and improve resistance to disease. The British Royal Family are well known for their interest in royal jelly and alternative medicine as a whole. Reports in the daily newspapers proclaim Prince Philip to be a keen advocate: the Duchess of York and Princess Diana are said to take it, and Diana took royal jelly during both of her pregnancies.

The key quality of royal jelly, mentioned by everyone who takes it over a period of time, is its ability to release bursts of energy. Many other properties are also attributed to this unusual substance: it has been hailed as a remedy for disorders as diverse as depression and dermatitis, anorexia and arthritic pain.

WHY IS ROYAL JELLY SO SPECIAL?

Royal jelly contains 22 amino acids, many of the B vitamins, vitamin C and six minerals. There is also a percentage of the jelly (four per cent) that has, so far, defied scientific definition – and that is probably why all attempts at manufacturing a synthetic substitute have failed.

Amino acids are chemical elements that, when combined, form proteins and play an important role in producing energy for physical activity and vital bodily functions. They also assist in the body's resistance against disease. However, amino acids function mainly as body-building nutrients, and they are responsible for growth and replacement of tissues. Eight of the 30 amino acids that occur in nature are 'essential' (which means the body cannot produce them itself from foods). For those of us who eat meat, animal protein is the main nutritional source of these 'essential'

F IT FOR A QUEEN

Royal jelly is a milky, whitish solution secreted by worker bees from glands in their heads. The queen is fed exclusively on it, both as a larva and as an adult. The bees hold the jelly on their tongues and lick her wherever she goes in the hive. She absorbs the jelly, and this amazing food supports her throughout her six-year life, helping her to produce millions of eggs for the beehive.

The queen bee laying her eggs.

amino acids. But royal jelly contains all eight and could, therefore, be of great value to vegetarians.

VITAMINS AND MINERALS

Vitamins are organic substances that help to form enzymes which convert food into energy and play an important role in the body's defence mechanism. Vitamins B_1, B_2, B_3, B_5, B_6, B_7, B_8, B_9, B_{12} and vitamin C have been traced in royal jelly. The B vitamins are generally considered vital for a healthy metabolism (which involves chemical reactions occurring within cells) and blood composition. B_6 and a complex of B vitamins are often recommended to help alleviate pre-menstrual syndrome (PMS), and B_{12} is regarded by many as an indispensable dietary supplement for vegetarians. The importance of vitamin C in the diet is recognised by most people: it is not, however, a vitamin that the body can store so any extra sources are helpful.

Six minerals have been discovered in royal jelly. These are: sodium (required for the regulation of the water balance within the body); potassium (which works with sodium in fluid control); iron (which is vital for the production of haemoglobin, and therefore oxygen distribution throughout the body); as well as traces of chromium, manganese and nickel.

FRESH OR FREEZE-DRIED?

Many manufacturers freeze-dry royal jelly once it has been extracted from the hive, making it easier for them to handle and put into capsules. But does freezing also remove some of its goodness?

In the early 1970s, Irene Stein, a health and beauty specialist and managing director of a leading royal jelly manufacturer, developed a method of producing and marketing fresh royal jelly. She believes that the process of freeze-drying removes too many of its special properties.

Research at Bologna University in Italy has shown that changes to the protein structure of royal jelly do occur during freeze-drying (lyophilisation), but these changes do not necessarily mean a reduction in its potency. Use of freeze-dried royal jelly has given rise to some remarkable stories of recovery or increased well-being. Fresh royal jelly is also more expensive, and Irene Stein believes that it is up to the individual to decide whether the increased potency of fresh royal jelly is worth the extra expense incurred.

DID YOU KNOW?

Bee larvae fed royal jelly become twice as large and live 30 times longer than other larvae.

BUYING ROYAL JELLY

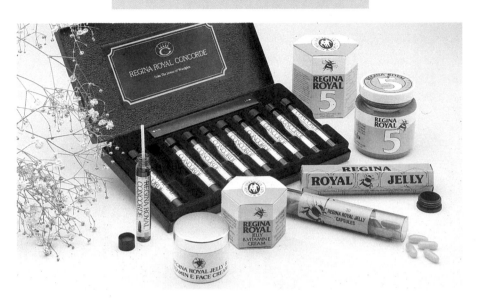

Royal jelly comes in many shapes and sizes. Bought fresh by the jar it comes as a yellowish-white liquid that looks unappetizing, smells odd and tastes rather peculiar – it is taken daily by the spoonful. To make it more palatable, some manufacturers blend it with honey, adding other ingredients such as herbs, pollen or natural vitamins. The most favoured way of taking it is in capsule form – freeze-dried, or fresh, royal jelly in a gelatine coat. The usual content of these capsules is 100-150mg and it is in capsule form, taken regularly every day for a period of a few months, that royal jelly has produced the most dramatic results.

Recently royal jelly products for external application have been introduced on to the market. These come as a cream to be applied to the skin and have been hailed as effective remedies for skin complaints such as bad spots, acne and stretch marks.

Pet products containing royal jelly have also appeared on the market and are said to work on a variety of complaints, including poor coat condition, pining, and arthritis.

A LONGER, HEALTHIER LIFE

Professor Lim Zhibin, chairman of the Department of Pharmacology at Beijing University, China, has investigated royal jelly in a number of controlled experiments. These showed that royal jelly boosts the immune system by making the body healthier and, therefore, better equipped to fight infection and disease. He also found indications that royal jelly slows down the ageing of the immune system; the professor concluded that royal jelly could be particularly valuable for older patients.

Royal jelly has a 'two-way normaliser action', which means an ability to relieve conditions with opposing symptoms, such as hypertension (high blood-pressure) and hypotension (low blood-pressure). Users of royal jelly report wide-ranging and varied effects: they claim that it accelerates the metabolism; the metabolism; stimulates the appetite and digestion; acts as an anti-depressant; speeds up recovery from illnesses and operations; relieves stomach cramps and tension associated with PMS; helps with insomnia; reduces asthma attacks; slows hair loss and lessens morning sickness during pregnancy.

SAGE

A powerful remedy – handle with care

The strong flavour of sage is an indication of its fortifying and stimulating properties when used as a healer

There are many varieties of sage, but it is the leaves of ordinary garden sage, *Salvia officinalis*, that have been so highly prized by herbalists over the centuries. Sage leaves are still widely used today, for medicinal and cosmetic purposes as well as for cooking. The botanic name for sage comes from the Latin word 'salvere', which means to be in good health.

HEALTHY HERBAL REMEDIES

Sage contains essential oils and tannins which make it a good antiseptic when used internally or externally.

It also acts as an astringent, which means that it draws together and tightens slack tissue. This makes it ideal for treating bleeding gums, mouth ulcers and diarrhoea, as well as helping to stop itching in the genital and anal areas when applied as a compress.
•Its bitter content stimulates the digestive juices, so it is good for stomach, liver and gall-bladder problems, dyspepsia and flatulence.
• Sage is very soothing for nervous troubles of all kinds – nervous excitement, depression, trembling and dizziness – and, drunk as tea, is said to improve the memory.
• As a tea or tincture, it lessens menopausal flushing and sweats, and this is perhaps the most widespread use that modern herbalists have for it. The beneficial effects begin about two hours after taking it, and can last for up to two days. It can be used in the same way for the night sweats of tuberculosis, and to dry up excess mucus, especially in the respiratory tract and stomach.
• Sage covered in boiling water and used as an inhalation is excellent for congestion of the nose and head. The same property of drying up secretions is used to dry up the milk of women who want to stop breast-feeding.

SAGE TEA

Sage tea can be used as a herbal remedy for any of the conditions mentioned above, and also as a wash for fresh wounds or old ones that are not healing properly. As the taste is very strong, one to two teaspoonfuls to 275ml (½pt) of water is sufficient when taken as a drink.

Pour boiling water over the dried leaves and let the liquid stand for 20 to 30 minutes, then strain. It is important not to use aluminium containers to soak herbs. Three to four cupfuls can be drunk throughout the day. In summer it can also be infused in cold water in sunlight to make a pleasant tonic drink.

SAGE TOOTHPOWDER

To prevent or treat bleeding gums and to remove yellow stains, grind some fresh sage leaves together in a mortar with sea salt. Dry the mixture in a slow oven until it is hard and then pound it to a powder. Rub or brush this over the teeth, both morning and evening. The Arabs use fresh leaves in the same way.

S AGE IN HISTORY AND FOLKLORE

To the ancient Greeks sage was a cure-all, and even today sage tea is served in cafes throughout Greece. An old British saying is, "He that would live for aye, should eat sage in May', and another, from the Middle Ages, runs, 'Why should a man die who has sage in his garden?' It was thought that it could restore failing virility, as well as curb unnatural sexual desires.
Folklore has it that as the sage in the garden thrived or withered, so would the owner's business prosper or fail. As with parsley, it is said that where sage grows vigorously, the wife is the one who wears the trousers.
If you are concerned about toads in the garden, one traditional method of keeping them away is to plant rue and sage close together.

SAGE POULTICES

These are very warming and comforting for cold joints. Make up some sage tea as described and while it is still hot, mix with some instant potato flakes to form a thick paste. Apply to the affected areas and leave on until cooled.

SAGE GARGLE

This is excellent for mouth and throat ulcers, sore throats and bleeding gums. Ordinary sage tea can be used, or diluted half and half with vinegar – raspberry vinegar is especially good – and sweetened with honey. Use some to gargle and some to drink.

FIRST AID FOR INSECT STINGS

Because sage leaves are antiseptic and astringent, they can be used for stings and bites. Simply crush a leaf and rub it over the affected area.

SAGE HAIR TONIC

Sage infusion is used to darken greying hair. It also improves the texture and the growth of hair, as well as helping to remove dandruff. Pour 600ml (1pint) of boiling water over 30gms (1ox) of dried sage, infuse for half an hour and strain. Brush this regularly through the hair.

This infusion can also be used as a final rinse after washing the hair, and this way it has the added bonus of acting as a setting lotion.

WHEN NOT TO USE SAGE

Taken in the doses suggested, sage, true to its name, is a safe and health-giving herb, but there are certain situations where it should not be given:
• during pregnancy, because it contains thujone, an essential oil which can cause the uterus to contract and induce labour.
• for nursing mothers, as it dries up milk production.
• in kidney disease, or for people suffering from kidney problems.
  As sage is a powerful herb it should not be taken in high doses over a long period of time.

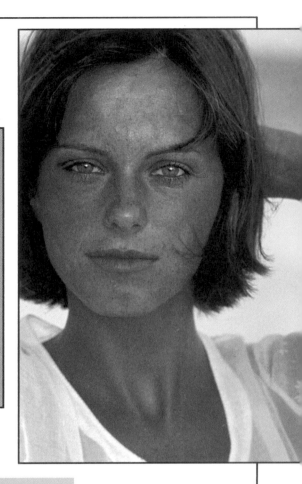

Darken grey hair by brushing regularly with an infusion of sage. This will also improve the hair's texture.

COLLECTING AND CULTIVATING

Sage is gathered in June or July, just before it flowers, and spread out in a single layer on newspaper in the dark until dry. Like all herbs, it should be stored in a non-plastic airtight container in a cool, dry place.

Cuttings can simply be taken from an old plant, after it has rained, and planted. Another way to grow sage is to peg down branches of old plants in spring or autumn and cover with 1.5cm (¾in) of soil. These will produce roots just by being in contact with the earth. When the young off-shoots are big enough, they can be cut away from the parent plant and transplanted.

SCHISANDRA

A 'superior' healing herb

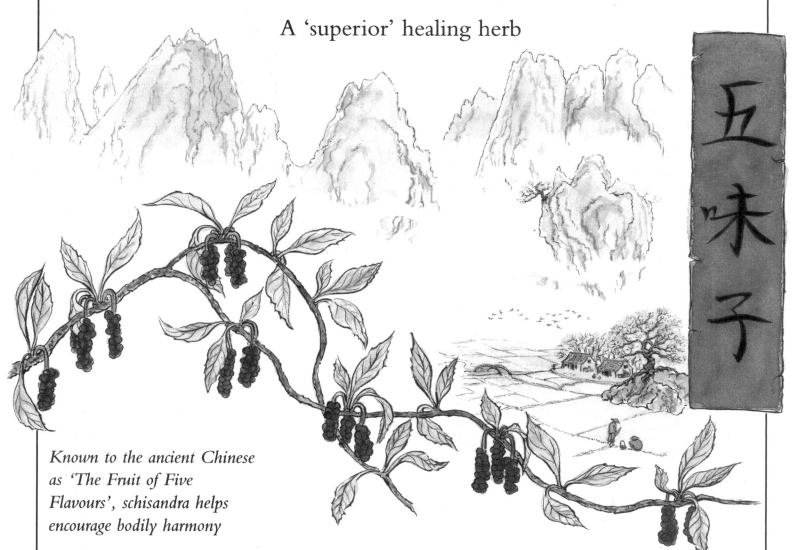

Known to the ancient Chinese as 'The Fruit of Five Flavours', schisandra helps encourage bodily harmony

New nutrients and herbs are discovered – or rediscovered – with great frequency. In addition to the familiar and time-honoured remedies such as comfrey, ginseng, garlic and propolis, we can all benefit from interesting new dietary supplements. Schisandra, *Schisandra chinensis*, also known as Chinese Magnolia vine, is an aromatic woody vine used as a healing herb and well known to ancient Chinese physicians for its health-giving qualities. Through the centuries it has been, and continues to be, used to treat a wide variety of ailments in Far Eastern countries, particularly China, Japan and Korea. It is also a popular remedy in the USSR, while more recently it has been 'rediscovered' in Scandinavia and northern Europe. In Sweden, research at the Swedish Herbal Medical Institute has provided scientific explanations of its many qualities.

A CHINESE LEGACY

Other recent nutritional discoveries include germanium, a natural trace element found in nearly all living plants and which is derived commercially from coal. Natural beta-carotene, the precursor of retinal pro-vitamin A, is another recent discovery which has been found to protect the skin from damage caused by sunburn. It can also nullify some of the destructive effects of free radicals (chemical substances generated when polyunsaturated acids are oxidised by the body, which lead to an increased risk of arterial disease) and certain types of cancer. Recent research has also revealed that many people are deficient in Co-enzyme Q-10 (CoQ), a hitherto unknown body chemical vital to the proper functioning of the heart.

Schisandra was discovered centuries ago, growing in the mountainous regions of Tibet, China and the eastern Siberian plains. The berries were dried before being eaten. In 2697 BC, the Chinese writer and physician, Pen Tsao, included the small bush with pale pink blossoms in an encyclopaedia of healing plants later known as *The Yellow Emperor's Study of Inner Medicine*. Pen Tsao classified schisandra as one of 50 'superior' plants with overall restorative and healing powers (See Box – The Fruit of Five Flavours).

ANCIENT ADAPTOGENIC

Schisandra is an adaptogen. The term adaptogen was coined by scientists to describe biologically-active substances which help to control homoeostasis. This is the name given to the means by which the body's many interdependent and interrelated physiological processes are maintained in balance by the nervous system and glands. Homoeostasis

Schisandra is a small, thorny bush with pale pink blossoms and reddish-brown berries. The Chinese recognised its extraordinary qualities over 4000 years ago.

orchestrates and harmonises the action of body cells and various biological processes such as digestion, respiration, waste excretion, blood circulation and the synthesis of hormones, enzymes, nerve and brain neurotransmitters. First discovered and described by the French Professor of Physiology and Medicine Claude Bernard (1813–78), homoeostasis is vital to the healthy function of every organ in the body. It can be disturbed by many different factors, particularly those associated with diet, environment and lifestyle. Physical and emotional stress, fatigue, smoke and other atmospheric pollutants, high consumption of alcohol and unhealthy foodstuffs can all combine to disturb our inner harmony.

ENCOURAGING OXYGEN ASBORPTION

Schisandra promotes bodily harmony by encouraging the body to absorb, transport and use oxygen more efficiently. Improved oxygen intake regenerates cell tissues and helps to restore lost energy. It is this overall effect on the cells that gives schisandra such a wide variety of beneficial properties.

Oxygen is needed by every cell of each of the body's organs and the harder a particular organ works, the more oxygen it requires. Oxygen is absorbed into the body through tiny, thin-walled blood vessels in the lungs. It attaches itself to haemoglobin, a pigment in red blood cells, and is transported throughout the body by the arterial system. Minute arterioles deliver the oxygenerated blood to muscles and

organs. Schisandra increases oxygen intake on the surface of the lungs by dilating the blood vessels in the alveoli (tiny air sacs in the lungs where the oxygen is absorbed).

Any impediment to the absorption of oxygen in the lungs or its transportation within the body has a damaging effect on its overall biological operation. A regular supply of oxygen is particularly important to the brain and the heart. The uplifting effects of schisandra's adaptogenic properties largely result from

its encouragement of oxygen absorption.

ACTIVITY IN THE BODY

Further research into schisandra's adaptogenic properties has revealed that it safely balances and stimulates electrical activity in the central nervous system, particularly in the spinal cord and brain which control all of our movements, emotions, thoughts and intellectual faculties.

Schisandra pleasantly stimulates nervous tissue in a non-toxic and apparently non-addictive manner. It enhances electrical cellular function and energy capacity which, in turn, have been shown to improve the powers of logical thought and concentration, to increase work capacity, and to improve the physical endurance and fine co-ordination of muscle tissue. By contrast, other brain and body stimulants, such as amphetamines, are highly toxic and harmful to many of the body's systems, and furthermore they may be addictive.

SPORTSMAN'S STIMULANT

Schisandra has commonly been used in the past to improve physical and mental performance. In ancient China, hunters ate the berries to give them energy. During the Second World War, Russian fighter pilots took schisandra to keep them mentally alert and to aid oxygen intake at high altitudes. In recent years, the successes of the Swedish skiing team have in part been attributed to the herb.

Schisandra extracts are frequently

Present-day herb gatherers follow in the footsteps of ancient Chinese hunting tribes who collected schisandra berries for their energy-giving qualities.

given to professional sportsmen and women to increase the intake of oxygen during exercise. It also had a rapid effect upon thirst and muscular fatigue and pain. Research has shown that schisandra actually improves performance more effectively than other well-known stimulants such as caffeine and amphetamines.

OTHER ADAPTOGENIC ACTIONS

Schisandra has adaptogenic properties other than as a stimulant. It is used as a treatment for chest infections because it helps the sufferer absorb oxygen more easily and helps to dry up and disperse mucus in the lungs. Schisandra helps to maintain blood pressure within safe limits because it stimulates the heart muscles which, in turn, improves the flow of blood through the coronary arteries. It reduces the body's cholesterol level and helps to prevent the build up of fat deposits in the arteries.

The herb also helps to maintain stable blood sugar levels, restoring both high levels (hyperglycaemia) and low levels (hypoglycaemia) to normal. Because of this, schisandra may be useful as a treatment for diabetics. People affected by gastric ulcers may also benefit from this ubiquitous herb. Laboratory tests have shown that it reduces both the production of hydrochloric digestive acid by the cells lining the stomach, and the squeezing motions of the stomach wall, both of which can cause severe upper abdominal pain. Schisandra can also alleviate the effects of heartburn if the abdomen is inflamed, and laboratory tests have shown that it lowers the raised liver enzyme SGPT (serum glutamic pyruvic transaminase) in patients with hepatitis.

Herb traders have been part of the fabric of Chinese society for centuries. Here, traditional medicines are sold on a holy mountain in Sichuan Province.

THE FRUIT OF FIVE FLAVOURS

In 2697 BC, the Chinese physician and writer, Pen Tsao, classified schisandra as a 'superior' plant, one of 50 highly effective remedial herbs.

Ancient Chinese physicians categorised their traditional drugs according to their 'energy' (of which there were four types – cold, cool, warm and hot) and their taste. They would then use these classifications to ascertain the properties of potentially remedial herbs.

The energies were judged by the body's reaction to and the effect of the drug – generally speaking, those used to treat fevers fall into the 'cold' or 'cool' categories, while chills and colds were treated with 'warm' herbs such as ginger. In addition there were five different tastes used as a means of identification, each one corresponded to a different part of the body: sweet (the spleen), sour (the liver), bitter (the heart), salty (the kidneys) and pungent (the lungs).

The characteristic taste of the plants indicated to the taster the medicinal qualities of the plants under investigation and the part of the body on which they would be most effective. The energy and taste also warned against certain uses, for example bitter and cooling drugs were considered harmful to the stomach and spleen. Schisandra was known as 'The Fruit of the Five Flavours' because it incorporated all the tastes recognised in association with healing plants.

After tasting, the herbs were further categorised under three headings – inferior, common, and superior. 'Inferior' plants had limited uses. They were usually highly potent and were only used to treat serious afflictions. Everyday, traditional herbs were classed as 'common', and were usually related to specific organs or bodily functions. 'Superior' plants, the classification given to schisandra, were extremely rare – only one in a thousand plants investigated in The Yellow Emperor's Study of Inner Medicine turned out to have the healing and restorative powers needed to merit this type of classification.

SCHISANDRA AND SELF HELP

Take schisandra tablets twice daily.

Today, schisandra is avaialble as a dietary supplement in tablet form. The tablets consist of 600 mg of herb extract derived from the reddish-brown berries and their clove-flavoured seeds. The usual recommended dose is one or two tablets daily. Used as a dietary supplement, schisandra enhances general health by:

• Improving our powers of concentration, manual dexterity and mental alertness when we are tense, stressed or fatigued.
• Providing extra energy, vitality and stamina when we are mentally or physically tired.
• Increasing our resistance to viral infections and the effects of stress.
• Maintaining the health of our immune defence systems.
• Functioning as a natural, non-addictive stimulant during vigorous sports and games and taking aerobic exercise.

Schisandra can be used with other medicines because tests have failed to reveal any incompatibility with other drugs. The tablets have few side effects, although they can cause transient nausea.

Our immune defence system benefits from schisandra's adaptogenic qualities. The immune system consists of millions of cells arranged in groups throughout the body. It produces the white cells (leukocytes) which constitute our body's main defence against infection and helps to inhibit the production of malignant cancer cells. Schisandra has also proved successful in treating viral infections and the indications are that it could be an effective treatment of bacterial infections as well.

TURNING BACK THE YEARS
It seems remarkable, given its multifarious remedial and medicinal qualities, that schisandra is not more widely used. However, its role in helping the body replace its old and dying cells with new ones may change that. The herb enhances cellular regeneration throughout the body by stimulating the production of the genetic protein molecules RNA (ribonucleic acid) and DNA (deoxyribonucleic acid). As we grow older, our cells grow less efficient at producing these proteins.

When this happens they cannot do their work properly. By helping to replace the proteins, schisandra holds out exciting possibilities for combating the ageing process.

DEPRESSION RELIEF
Further research studies have shown schisandra to improve many other conditions including depression, Ménière's disease (a condition that affects hearing and balance), motion sickness and depressive forms of schizophrenia. In Russia, it is a prescription-only drug used to treat vision difficulties such as short-sightedness and astigmatism.

Schisandra is often called 'the herb of the future' because of its healing qualities.

SLIPPERY ELM

Red Indian remedy with world–wide applications

This gentle, woody, herb makes a useful and soothing addition to your first aid kit

Slippery elm (*Ulmus fulva*) is a North American tree with dark green leaves and clusters of small flowers. It is not as large as the common British elm, but it is related. A native of the North American continent, it is found in forests and woodlands, from Florida in the south right up to the Canadian provinces bordering the USA. The slippery elm gets its name from its moistened inner bark which the North American Indians called *oohooska*, meaning 'to slip'. The inner bark is collected in spring, dried and processed into a powder that is used as a medicinal remedy. Other names by which the Slippery elm is known are Red elm and Moose elm.

INDIAN MEDICINE

The North American Indians were the first people to make use of Slippery elm for practical and medicinal purposes. They dried the inner bark, ground it to a powder and mixed it with liquid to make a nourishing food. They also used the bark as a natural preservative to stop animal fats going rancid. A piece of bark was added to melted fat, which was then heated for a short time before the fat was strained off. Once the fat had coagulated, it was ready for storage.

Slippery elm was also known to the North American Indians as a medicine, and it was later adopted by European

SLIPPERY ELM POULTICE

A poultice can easily be made by mixing Slippery elm powder to a paste with hot water. Spread this on a clean piece of gauze, and bandage it on to the affected area. This should be renewed every few hours. A slippery elm poultice is a particularly good first aid remedy for drawing out splinters or thorns which are deeply embedded.

settlers in the New World. The inner bark was powdered to make drinks for the sick and used to make soothing skin lotion and poultices. Early 19th-century American books list Slippery elm as a remedy for dysentery. It also appears to have been used for the treatment of other internal complaints, as well as in lozenge form, for sore throats, especially irritation for the pharynx. Today it is still a significant part of the American pharmacopoeia.

BARK BENEFITS

The inner bark of the Slippery elm contains its medicinal properties. Regarded as one of nature's finest demulcents, it has a soothing effect on the body's mucous membranes. It is rich in mucilage, a sticky mixture of carbohydrates which is

A variety of Slippery elm products, from tablets to powdered food.

found in plants. Slippery elm soothes and heals, forming a coating in the digestive tract. It relieves internal inflammation, and neutralises stomach acids. It also aids the digestion of milk.

Traditionally, Amer-Indians have used Slippery elm bark as a laxative. As they also used the bark as a mechanical abortive, the remedy is now only available commercially in the powdered and hence the harmless form.

It has been considered as an essential part of the herbal pharmacopoeia in Northern Europe for centuries and is rich in nutrients containing a similar amount to that found in oatmeal.

AIDING CONVALESCENCE
Slippery elm is best known as an invalid food. It is ideal for people with weak digestion, for babies, the elderly, and those who are recovering from illness. It is generally therapeutic as well as being helpful for specific problems affecting

DIGESTIVE DRINK

For digestive upsets, a hot or cold infusion is recommended, using 7 g (¼ oz) of Slippery elm powder to 20 fl oz (1 pt) of boiling water. To make a soothing drink for an upset stomach or internal irritation, mix a teaspoonful of Slippery elm powder to a paste with cold water, gradually stirring in a cupful of boiling water or milk. The taste is bland so you could add cinnamon which is warming, and sweeten it with a little honey.

the digestion. It is particularly beneficial for people who secrete too much acid, like those who suffer from nervous indigestion or peptic ulcers, for instance. It can be very soothing and helpful for mucous inflammation, whether of the bowels, stomach, kidneys or bladder. It has also been used to relieve diarrhoea, bronchial inflammation and catarrh. For chest problems of this kind, it may be combined with herbs like liquorice and marshmallow.

BREAKING DOWN THE MILK PROBLEM
Some people – and particularly newborn babies – have difficulty in assimilating cow's milk because their digestive juices cannot break down the protein particles efficiently. These particles can form into solid, indigestible curds. Slippery elm, with its mucilage and cereal starch, separates the protein particles making them easier to digest. Consequently the stomach needs to produce less acid. This is not an artificial means of digestion, so there is no danger of weakening the system – it simply helps the process along.

TOPICAL TREATMENTS
Slippery elm's soothing, healing qualities can be put to very good use in external treatment, to bring relief and heal wounds, burns and scalds. It is useful for drawing out splinters, infection from boils, ulcers and infected cuts. As well as easing localised pain, it helps to get rid of inflammation and promotes natural healing. As a lotion it can also be used for badly discharging eye inflammations. Slippery elm is often blended with other natural healers, such as marshmallow, in ointments available from health food stockists.

Marshmallow was also mixed with Slippery elm to make poultices: another

combination was with brewer's yeast and milk for treatment of severely infected wounds. A traditional remedy for painful rheumatic joints is to bind them with a poultice made with mashed wheat bran and Slippery elm mixed with hot vinegar.

SLIPPERLY ELM PRODUCTS
Slippery elm is available from health food stores in tablets, capsules and ointments, as well as in a pale pinkish-brown powder. Slippery elm food also comes in powdered form, and milk or water is added for a quick, nourishing drink.

Slippery elm food drinks are often blended with wheatmeal, barley flour, or oatmeal for extra nourishment. The fat is usually removed or reduced so there is no strain on the digestion, providing an ideal invalid food.

One 'nerve food' that is available from health food stores contains Slippery elm combined with other

Slippery elm has long been taken as a nourishing drink.

selected ingredients; among them homeopathic minerals, and herbal extracts of marshmallow and camomile. Marshmallow is a very soothing herb, whilst camomile is used for its relaxing and calming properties (see CAMOMILE). This particular nerve food is recommended for those suffering from nervous indigestion, mucous colitis and inflamed digestive conditions.

PRESERVE THE TREES
Commercial preparation of slippery elm involves stripping off large parts of the tree bark to obtain the inner bark, often resulting in the tree dying. So check slippery elm products to ensure they were obtained as naturally as possible.

STINGING NETTLE

A source of iron and Vitamin C

A walk in the countryside may be marred by an unwelcome brush with a stinging nettle, but this much-maligned weed is a medicinal asset

and is best gathered in May and July, just before or when it is about to flower. The whole herb is used for medicinal purposes, and the young plants are preferable.

SKIN HEALER

As well as serving as a general all-over tonic for the body, nettle is excellent in the treatment of skin complaints – especially eczema, and in particular the nervous eczema that is experienced by young children.

Surprisingly perhaps, nettle is also used to help relieve nettle rash. The

Latin word for the rash is *Urticaria*, which is derived from the Latin name for the stinging nettle. It is so called because the skin of someone suffering from urticaria looks and reacts (it itches and burns) as if it has been stung by nettles.

A NATURAL ASTRINGENT

Another of nettle's most valued attributes is its naturally astringent quality. Taken in the form of a tea or a tincture, it has been known to help staunch bleeding, whether externally, for example, from the nose or the

Stinging nettle (*Urtica dioica*) has served many purposes throughout history; once it was even used in the manufacture of cloth. Today, however, thanks to its high content of iron, vitamins and minerals, nettle is generally taken as a tonic in the form of a tea or an alcoholic tincture.

NETTLE HAUNTS

Nettle is widespread and grows on wasteland, especially damp, nutrient-rich soils. The plant is instantly recognisable by its heart-shaped leaves with their finely-toothed edges tapering to a point. It usually grows to a height of 16-25cm (6½ -10in), but if cultivated and cared for, it can grow to over 50cm (20in). Nettle's most notable feature is, of course, its fine covering of stinging hairs. The reaction they cause is due to the plant's formic acid content.

Nettle flowers from June to September

N ETTLE TEA

Nettle tea, usually taken as a tonic, has a beneficial action that stimulates the liver to excrete excessive accumulated toxic waste. At the same time it cleanses the skin and helps to ease the discomfort of rheumatism.

The tea can also be used as an after-shampoo rinse to improve the lustre and general condition of the hair.

Nettle tea is simple to make. Ideally, fresh nettles should be used, as much of the valuable formic acid is lost after only a few hours. This is why dried nettle is less than satisfactory. However, even dried nettle has a high iron content and contains valuable amounts of mineral trace elements.

To make nettle tea, use about 40g (1½ oz) fresh, washed nettle leaves to 20 fl oz (1 pint) boiling water. Using kitchen scissors cut the leaves into 2.5 cm (1 inch) lengths. Put them into a pot or jug and pour over

the boiling water, then cover the pot. Drink a cupful of tea three times a day.

Nettle tea is also available ready-made (usually in filter bags) at health food shops. Leave the tea to infuse for two or four minutes so that the full flavour has time to develop.

For variety, add a slice of lemon or a teaspoonful of honey.

bowel, or internally elsewhere in the body. According to herbalists, nettle leaf can be ground into a fine powder and used in the same way as snuff, to provide a handy, on-the-spot remedy for nose bleeds.

HELP FOR DIABETICS

Many herbalists recommend nettle in the treatment of diabetes. They claim that nettle reduces the level of sugar in the blood slightly, and that it can also lower the blood pressure. Nettle is also reputed to contain anti-asthmatic properties, and the juice of the plant is believed to help ease bronchial complaints.

NETTLE IN THE KITCHEN

In the spring, young nettle – high in iron content – can be cooked and eaten as a vegetable in much the same way as spinach or broccoli. The young plant cooks in just 2 to 3 minutes and the sting disappears as soon as the leaves are placed in boiling water.

POISON AND INSECT BITES

Ancient herbals advise the eating of nettle seeds as an antidote to poisoning by hemlock, henbane or deadly nightshade. Eating the seeds was also recommended as a means of obtaining relief from insect stings and mad dog bites!

STING AND FEVER RELIEF

One way of relieving nettle sting is to apply the juice of the nettle – provided it can be extracted without further stinging. Other, more common, antidotes are dock leaves – which grow alongside nettle, and rosemary, mint or sage leaves, all of which should be rubbed on the affected area.

In the Middle Ages it was believed possible to help cure someone of a fever by plucking a nettle by the roots and reciting the name of the sick person and the names of their parents.

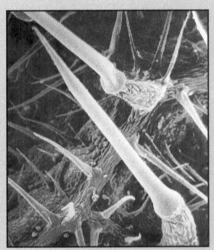

The fine, stinging nettle hairs.

NETTLE-WEAR

The name 'nettle' may be a derivative of the Anglo-Saxon word for a needle – noed – due to the plant's sharp sting. Or the name may be a reference to nettle's widespread use as a source of thread before the introduction of flax and hemp.

Even as late as the First World War, German soldiers wore tunics woven from 85 per cent nettle and 15 per cent Ramie (a tropical member of the nettle family).

ROMAN COMFORT

In Roman times, the nettle was used in a most unusual way by the flimsily attired soldiers of Caesar's armies. Before leaving the sunny climes of Rome, the soldiers were warned that 'the climate of Britain is so cold that is not to be endured'. Once the soldiers learned how unsuitable their uniforms were for the changeable seasons of the British Isles, they quickly discovered that by beating their bare legs with nettles, a warm, burning sensation followed that in some way compensated for the brevity of their tunics.

Similarly, the American Indians, when running long distances, used nettle to beat the backs of their legs until they became numb. This numbness enabled them to run all day.

TINCTURE OF NETTLE

To make a tincture (an alcoholic extract) of nettle, put 175 g (6 oz) fresh nettles into a jar and add 20 fl oz (1 pint) alcohol (it should be at least 30% proof; vodka is suitable) and seal the jar. Store it in a warm place and shake well twice a day. Two weeks later, decant the liquid into a dark bottle and extract as much liquid from the residue as possible (by pressing it through a metal sieve). Take a teaspoonful of the tincture with water at mealtimes.

NETTLE BEER

Nettle beer has long been valued as a tonic drink that also alleviates rheumatism and gout.

Take a good bucket-full of young nettle tops, wash them well (wear rubber gloves for this) and boil in 2.3 L (4 pints) water with 450 g (1 lb) sugar and 25 g (1 oz) ginger. Add 25 g (1 oz) cream of tartar and one washed and finely sliced lemon.

Let the mixture simmer for about 45 minutes, then pour off the liquid through a sieve into a further 2.3 L (4 pints) water (preferably bottled spring water) in a large china bowl, or better still, a wooden tub. Add 25 g (1 oz) yeast, and let the concoction ferment for at least 12 hours. Remove any accumulated scum from the surface; discard it and pour the beer into dark bottles. Do not over-fill the bottles or cork them too tightly, as they could

TEA TREE OIL

Australia's antiseptic alternative

*A gentle astringent that can be applied to the most sensitive skin
and bottled into an ideal First Aid kit for minor maladies*

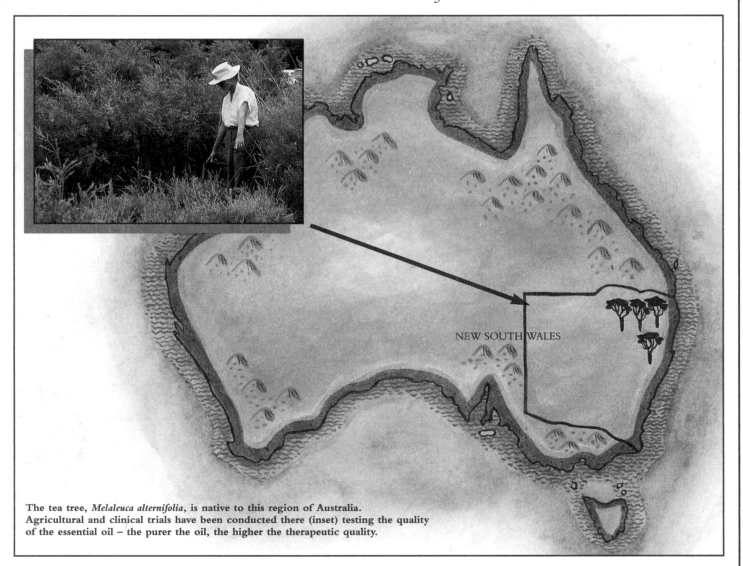

NEW SOUTH WALES

**The tea tree, *Melaleuca alternifolia*, is native to this region of Australia.
Agricultural and clinical trials have been conducted there (inset) testing the quality
of the essential oil – the purer the oil, the higher the therapeutic quality.**

Plant oils have been used through the centuries to flavour food, in perfumes and cosmetics, as well as for medicinal purposes. Essential oils can come from various parts of plants: some, such as lemon oil, come from fruits; some come from bark like camphor oil; some from flowers like the healing blue oil of camomile; while others come from leaves such as rosemary and tea tree oil.

Tea tree oil is a remarkable natural product that is native to Australia. It is distilled from the leaves of a medicinal tree, *Melaleuca alternifolia*, commonly known as the ma or tea tree. The 'tea' has nothing to do with the tea we drink. There are some 300 varieties of tea (or paperbark trees as

they are also known). The ma tree, found on the north coast of Northern New South Wales, is the one that is the source of this healing oil.

ABORIGINAL ANCESTRY
Oil from the tea tree was one of many herbal remedies used by Australian Aborigines long before the First Fleet arrived in 1788. But it was not until the 1920s that it was scientifically analysed as being a powerful natural healer. Considering data has since been accumulated confirming tea tree's benefits – one article that appeared in Australia by Dr Stephen Baker recommended the oil as being 'virtually hypoallergenic', and said 'it promotes

healing and is far more effective than some of the other germicidal preparations'. Tea tree oil is currently used by many medical herbalists and aromatherapists in various parts of the world and should become a standard first aid remedy in the home.

ANTISEPTIC PROPERTIES
Tea tree oil is a complex substance, containing at least 48 known organic compounds, which work together for maximum healing power. Although strongly antiseptic, tea tree oil is non-toxic and non-irritant. Low in cineole, a compound that has a stinging effect, it gives no more than a warm, tingling sensation when applied to wounds. Diluted it can be used on the most

133

ESSENTIAL OIL

At the first international Conference of Medical Herbalists held in London, in 1985, Dr Paul Belaiche, Head of the Phytotherapy (Natural Medicine) Department at the Faculty of Medicine in Paris, described tea tree oil as 'a new major essential oil in the range of anti-infectious aromatherapy.'

Essential oils do have remarkable healing properties. Massaged into the body they can help poor circulation, depression, nervous troubles, and other health problems. The ancient healing art of aromatherapy has become increasingly popular in recent times. You can also use essential oils at home or in massages, or aromatic baths for healing and relaxation. As with tea tree oil, many essential oils are powerful, natural antiseptics.

The expanding range of tea tree products – from shampoos to suppositories.

sensitive skins without causing reactions. What tea tree oil does it to act as a natural, powerful germicide and antiseptic. It penetrates deeply into the tissues, dispersing pus and cleaning wounds. It helps damaged tissue to heal, and prevents or clears up infection. Since it has a mild, local anaesthetic action it soothes pain at the same time.

FIRST AID OIL
Tea tree oil is a multi-purpose first aid remedy in a bottle. You can use it neat, or diluted, for cuts, bruises, minor burns and scalds. It's handy too for insect bites and

Leaf tips of *melaleuca alternifolia*.

stings, using the pure undiluted oil or a brand of tea tree antiseptic cream. Because it is non-irritant it is ideal as a first aid remedy for children.

HEAD TO TOE
Tea tree oil can literally be used from head to toe. For an itchy scalp try adding five drops of oil to your usual shampoo, or you can purchase medicated shampoo containing the oil. For the problem of smelly feet, bathe them each evening in warm water with ten drops of oil in it. The pure oil is helpful, because of its anti-fungal properties, for athlete's foot. Used as a rub it will also relieve muscular pains and strains.

SKIN SOOTHER
Tea tree oil, diluted in water, can be used as a face cleanser. For spots or acne, try washing with a dilute solution of the oil three times daily. It is helpful too for cold sores, dabbed on neat, and for skin rashes, when tea tree antiseptic cream may be used. This cream will also relieve sunburn and help prevent blisters. You could even use it on babies for treating nappy rash. Users of the oil have also reported its benefits in relieving dermatitis, and shingles.

INHALATION
Steam inhalations to which herbs or essential plant oils have been added can bring great relief for chest and nasal congestion. You can also rub the oil into the chest or back, or sprinkle a few drops on the pillow at bedtime to ease congestion (but ensure there is no possibility of rubbing the oil into your eyes).

ANTI-INFECTION
Some medical herbalists use tea tree oil in the treatment of urinary and vaginal

TEA TREE FOR TEETH

Dentists now believe that tooth-rotting power of foods depends very much on the type of food eaten and how clean one's mouth is. One dental expert has recommended cleaning the teeth before eating to remove the plaque that holds bacteria. One thing is for sure – the importance of daily oral hygiene. Tea tree can help here – a drop of the oil on your toothbrush with your regular toothpaste will help remove plaque and promote healthy gums.

infections. Minor vaginal infections may be cleared up using a douche of 5ml (1 teaspoon) of pure oil to each 600ml (1 pint) of water. Or add 5ml (1 teaspoon) to a sitz bath. For nail infections, bathe the infected area twice a day in the pure oil. For throat infections, gargle with a few drops of the oil in warm water.

TEA TREE PRODUCTS
Pure tea tree oil, and products containing it, are available from some health food shops and pharmacies. These include antiseptic tea tree oil cream, soap, and shampoo and hair conditioner containing five per cent tea tree oil in solution.

The family pet is not forgotten either. There is a special anti-itch pet shampoo available to keep coats glossy and free of ticks and fleas.

THYME
Thyme to relieve a cold

Aromatic and antiseptic – thyme has strong culinary and medicinal properties. It is an effective cleanser, both internally and externally.

Garden thyme, *Thymus vulgaris*, is native to the southern Mediterranean area, but is widely cultivated in kitchen garden on either side of the Atlantic. It is perhaps one of the best known culinary herbs and has been used in sauces and stuffings for fish and countless other dishes since ancient Greek and Roman times. As an important ingredient of bouquet garni, thyme aids the digestion of fat, and so is beneficial, as well as tasty, when used in cooking fatty meats and soups.

As a herbal remedy, it is best known for its antiseptic qualities – used both internally and externally – for the relief of colds and nervous headaches, skin irritations and rheumatism.

ANTISEPTIC ACTION

As a member of the Labiate family of plants, thyme is related to many other aromatic herbs, such as mint, lavender, rosemary and sage. Their distinctive aroma is due to the production of a class of chemical, called a 'volatile oil'. These oils are highly valued in commerce and the perfume industries, and are usually the most medically active ingredient present in the plant.

Thyme yields between two and three per cent volatile oil, depending on habitat and weather conditions. Of this oil, a percentage is thymol – which represents the strong antiseptic, deodorant and disinfectant element within the herb.

Thymol has been used in surgical dressings because of its germicidal action (killing germs and thus preventing infection).

Put thyme, parsley, marjoram and a bay leaf in muslin to make a bouquet garni.

BINDING AGENT

As well as a volatile oil, thyme contains tannins, a bitter principle called Anesin, and an unknown anti-spasmodic agent.

Tannins occur through the plant kingdom. They are contained within the entire rose family and many of the mint family. Tannins are perhaps best known for the black mark they leave on the inside of the teacup, if the tea has been taken black. When milk is added to tea it 'binds up' or 'hydrolyses' the tannins, thus making them ineffective and leaving a cleaner cup. Tannins do, however, have a useful purpose; they work as an astringent (acting

to contract tissues) – which can be of immense importance if you have the misfortune to succumb to a bout of diarrhoea. A few cups of black, thyme tea will often bring rapid relief by helping to alleviate the symptoms.

NO THYME FOR A COLD

Thyme acts specifically as a decongestant, especially in relation to the lungs and the mucous glands of the nose and throat. Therefore, if you take thyme regularly (either in food, or as a tea), it helps reduce the frequency of chest complaints such as flu, colds and bronchitis. This doesn't mean that thyme rids you of colds entirely, but that the number of colds that you experience decreases, the symptoms are milder and their duration shorter.

Thyme actually seems to strengthen the fabric of the lungs, and so is useful in combating whooping cough, and asthma. It also helps alleviate any shortness of breath.

MOTHER THYME

The French use thyme as a carminitive (digestive relaxant) to ease flatulence, dyspepsia and distension – it is the bitter principle that produces this effect. During the seventeenth century, thyme was used as a vermifuge (to expel intestinal worms) and its oil was hailed as an emmenagogue (to bring on menstruation). Culpeper places thyme under the auspices of Venus, and says 'it kills worms in the belly . . . provokes the terms (menstruation), gives safe and speedy delivery to women in travail (labour or childbirth) and brings away the after-birth'. Because thyme was so

TUNA AND THYME LOAF

Thyme goes well with most fish and meat dishes, but be careful not to underestimate its powerful aroma. This recipe serves 4. Take one 7 oz (200g) tin of tuna fish, drain off the juices and flake the flesh. Add two tablespoons of soft wholemeal breadcrumbs, two tablespoons of milk, a beaten egg, one tablespoon of chopped onions and a little crushed garlic. Sprinkle in one small teaspoon of dried thyme (more if the thyme is fresh), a little black pepper, sea salt and a generous squeeze of fresh lemon juice. Stir, and pack the mixture into a buttered loaf tin or casserole dish. Bake, uncovered in a pre-heated oven at 150C (300°F) for approximately one hour, increasing the oven heat for the last few minutes to brown. Serve with a white sauce.

effective in overcoming uterine problems, the ancient Romans and Greeks referred to it as 'mother' thyme.

Reference is also made by Culpeper to Thyme's ability to 'purge the body of phlegm', and as an external remedy for swellings, warts and gout.

GROWING THYME

Thyme prefers light, dry, hilly pastures and banks. It will manage in damper, heavier soil, but its aromatic content

THYME FOR TEA

To make a thyme tea, pour one pint (600ml) of boiling water on to one ounce (25g) of dried thyme and leave to infuse for 5-10 minutes. Un-fortunately, volatile oils live up to their name, and with heat tend to be lost in the steam. So, if it is possible make the tea in a thermos flask, or pot with a tight-fitting lid. A cupful can be drunk three to five times per day. It will help to ease a headache and relieve catarrh, if taken at the onset of symptoms.

It has been discovered that thyme is medicinally more effective when taken with other herbs, so as a suggestion you could try thyme tea with peppermint, elderflower or yarrow, plus a pinch of ginseng or a dash of cayenne.

Thyme tea with a spoonful of honey makes a more palatable cold cure for children and those with a sweet tooth.

BATH THYME

A thyme bath makes a refreshing tonic for rheumatic joints and skin complaints or irritations.

Run the hot water through a muslin bag of fresh or dried thyme, and the oil will flow into the bath and release its active components. Alternatively, decoct the herb; that is, by boiling it in a pan of water for five minutes. Strain the resulting liquid into the bath.

falls. It flowers from June to September, producing small, mauve and lipped blossoms. The stems, leaves and flowering tops can be used in the home, either fresh or dried. Collect them when the plant is in full bloom.

Sow thyme seeds in March or April when the weather is mild. Alternatively, take a cutting, or divide an established plant, in April or May. In the first year of growth it is a good idea to harvest only once, after which, two cuttings can be made each year, in June and August.

THYME FOR A NAME

The source of most plant names is a subject of much debate, and thyme is no exception to this rule. The origin of the name seems to date back to the ancient Greeks and Romans, but there are two suggestions as to its root. In Latin, fumos means 'smoke', as does thumos in Greek. Both the Greeks and the Romans burned thyme in their rooms to repel insects, and so it is from there that some believe the plant name originates.

Alternatively, thyme could be a derivative of the Greek word thumus meaning 'courage', because the ancient civilisations believed it could inspire this emotion. It was probably the Romans who introduced thyme into Great Britain, and by the Middle Ages, it was an accepted symbol of courage. At this time, ladies often embroidered a bee hovering over a spring of thyme on scarves that they gave their knights; and in 1663, a soup of thyme was advocated as a cure for shyness.

Bees seem to hold a great affection for thyme, and the honey that they produce from its pollen is said to taste delicious. The fine flavour of the honey from Mount Hymettus, near Athens, Greece, is attributed to the great abundance of thyme on the hillside.

ANTISEPCTIC MOUTH WASH

A cooled infusion of dried sage and thyme makes an easily prepared remedy for a sore throat or bad breath. Prepared as for thyme tea, but using half an ounce (15g) of each herb, this makes a soothing antiseptic gargle.

FACIAL STEAM

As a treatment for spots, blackheads or any kind of skin blemishes, thyme exhibits valuable antiseptic qualities.

Place a handful of thyme and the same quantity of sage into a bowl and pour over 1 litre (two pints) of boiling water. Put a towel over your head, keeping your head about 30 cm (12in) from the surface of the water, and remain like this for five to ten minutes. Wipe your face with clean cotton wool afterwards, and splash with cold water. Care must be taken to ensure that the steam isn't scalding, as this may burst small blood vessels under the skin's surface.

Thyme thrives indoors as a pot plant, within easy reach for use in the home. Hang fresh thyme in bundles to dry evenly by letting the air circulate.

WARNING

If you know that your skin is sensitive, do a patch test before trying any of the external remedies for thyme. It has been discovered that some people are allergic to thymol.

ZA'ATAR

Za'atar is a well-known Arabic condiment. It is a mixture of dried and powdered thyme, sesame seeds and salt that is usually eaten, mixed with olive oil, spread on bread.

A NOTHER THYME

Wild thyme (Thymus serpyllum), as the name implies, grows wild in Europe and Great Britain. Its medicinal applications are broadly identical to garden thyme (Thymus vulgaris) although its odour is weaker – which could imply that its active properties are less potent. The name serpyllum means 'creeping' (from the Greek) and refers to thyme's habit of spreading along the ground as it grows. Culpeper again places wild thyme under the auspices of Venus, but allots it to Aries (the astrological sign relating to the head). He recommends it for all the same conditions as garden thyme, as well as 'that troublesome complaint, the nightmare'.

THYME POULTICE OR DRESSING

A paste, or poultice, of moistened thyme leaves, applied to an affected area, will relieve the pain of an abscess, boil or swelling and encourage the healing process by stimulating blood flow to the area.

Aching or rheumatic joints can be treated using a thyme compress. This is made by soaking some lint, cotton wool or bandage in a thyme infusion and securing it over the painful area.

FOLKLORE AND TRADITIONS

Thyme has been mentioned in many contexts by a variety of authors from Pliny and Virgil through to Shakespeare. Pliny states that thyme, when burnt, puts all verminous creatures to flight (apart from bees). A muslin bag of lavender and thyme, hung in a wardrobe will not only freshen the clothes but repel moths too.

Among the ancient Greeks, thyme denoted grace and elegance, and to 'smell of thyme' was an accolade for those of style and courage. Greek and Roman men considered that applying thyme to their chests enhanced their manly virtues, and in medieval times, an intoxicating cordial made with thyme was said to bring courage and bravery.

At a later date, thyme was looked upon as a 'fairy flower' – the fairies were reputed to find thyme one of their favourite playgrounds. Charms made with thyme were worn, particularly in combination with mint and lavender, by girls in an attempt to find a sweetheart.

On a more sombre note, thyme has also been associated with death. It was planted on graves, especially in Wales; and the Order of Oddfellows adopted the custom of carrying sprigs of thyme at funerals to place in the graves of their dead comrades. A very old tradition says that thyme was one of the herbs that comprised the bed of the Virgin Mary. Jesus is also reputed to have slept on a bed of hay and thyme.

In southern France, a sprig of thyme is the symbol of extreme Republicanism, and tufts of thyme were sent with messengers to prove that the meeting was genuine.

As a herb associated with death, thyme can be found growing in graveyards.

TIGER BALM

Oriental cure-all

Used as frequently in the East as aspirin is used in the West, what makes this unassuming potion such a potent healer?

Tiger Balm is an extra-ordinary and unusual remedy, simple in its formulation, yet of world-wide repute. The name Tiger Balm is a trademark that is registered in every country. The hallmark of the logo on the distinctive octaganol jar is a leaping tiger, over which is positioned the Chinese character Hu, which means tiger.

A LEGENDARY START

The origins of Tiger Balm are buried in legend. In ancient times, a healing balm of similar ingredients is said to have been made for a Chinese emperor who suffered from persistent aches and pains. Although oriental herbalists and healers made it for centuries, using recipes that only differed slightly from each other, the balm became fairly obscure during the Ch'ing dynasty (c.1644-1911). By the end of this dynasty, many natural health treatments had been prohibited in an attempt to appear more Western in outlook. It was left to the Chinese herbalist Aw Chu Kin, who lived in Rangoon at the turn of the century, to resurrect the basic formula as it is sold today. Aw Chu Kin stayed close to the traditional remedy as it had been handed down through the ages. He used it frequently to treat a number of the disorders his many patients suffered from. Aw Chu Kin's remedy was not designed to be the market leader it is now. This ointment was simply a herbal remedy for the aches and pains of his usual customers. One of his sons, Aw Boon Haw, had more entrepreneurial flair than his father. He travelled through Malaysia, taking the balm with him. When he arrived in Singapore he saw that the balm had tremendous commercial possibilities, so, together with his brother, Aw Boon Par, he set up a manufacturing base and created the brand name Tiger Balm for the hitherto ubiquitous herbal mixture. The tiger, synonymous in the East with strength and vitality, seemed the obvious choice of name for such a powerful remedy.

As the Tiger Balm industry spread, demand for it grew throughout South East Asia. During the Second World War the brothers moved their manufacturing centre to Hong Kong. After their death during the 1950s their company, Haw Par Brothers, continued to grow and became a public company in Singapore in 1979. Tiger Balm Ltd is now 25 per cent publicly owned and 75 per cent owned by Haw Par Ltd.

ORIENTAL ANALGESIC

Tiger Balm is described as 'an all-natural analgesic rub'. A solid wax in its jar, it smooths easily and transparently into the skin wherever it is applied. It uses are endless, but primarily it is recommended for easing muscular aches and pain. People buy it for a huge variety of conditions, including relief from the pain of rheumatism, arthritis, lumbago, sciatica, sprains, bruises, headache, insect bites, stiff neck and bronchial disorders. Its applications vary according to where you are in the world. In South East Asia, for example, Tiger Balm is used widely for rubbing on the temples, to relieve headache and general tension. It is also common for the balm to be massaged into acupuncture points, where it can work directly on the subtle energy meridians. In the West, Tiger Balm is used more for rheumatic pain and pre-sport muscle warm-ups. Your body will certainly know when you use Tiger Balm. Although non-irritating, the sensation is that of an actively refreshing, deep-spreading warmth.

VITAL INGREDIENTS

Tiger Balm's pungent smell testifies to its strong natural oils, blended into a paraffin wax base. The following three active ingredients are effective as counter-irritants, rubefacients and mild anaesthetics:
• **Camphor** – from the wood of *Cinnamomum camphora* (*Lauraceae*).
• **Peppermint oil** – from the flowers of *Mentha piperita* (see MINT).
• **Cassia oil** – from the leaves and twigs of *Cinnamomum cassia*. Cassia oil is also known as cinnamon oil.
Two other ingredients offer additional benefits:
• **Cajeput oil** – from the leaves and twigs of *Melaleuca cajuputi*. This oil works as a vasodilator, improving blood circulation.

139

TIGER BALM GARDEN

萬水匯歸璟海銀濤收眼底

Wishing to repay their customers' loyalty, the Haw Par brothers built the Tiger Balm Garden in Singapore. Opened in 1930, it is a major attraction – full of strange and mystical statues from Chinese mythology.

TWO-STRENGTH POTENCY

Tiger Balm comes in two strengths. The regular variety is white and has a higher concentration of peppermint oil. The extra-strength Tiger Balm is amber, with a strong smell of cinnamon from its camphor and cassia contents.

Tiger-Balm has come a long way since its humble origins. It is now made under completely hygienic modern conditions and chemists conduct constant tests on all the raw materials to ensure that they maintain a high standard. Tiger Balm has been able to satisfy the strictest requirements of a number of international health organisations such as the Food and Drug Administration in the USA, the Bundesgesundheitsamt in Germany, and the Good Manufacturing Practice Standard established by the World Health Organisation.

MUSCLING IN

Tiger Balm has a particularly beneficial action on sore muscles. Muscles ache after exercise because chemical reactions that take place during muscular exertion produce a build-up of waste products, in particular lactic acid. Muscles that are over-stressed, either in sport, or in repetitive everyday actions, do not get a chance to clear themselves of these toxic wastes and are therefore unable to repair tiny stress-induced tissue tears. Increasing the blood supply to muscles when they are resting helps to clear the waste products and speed muscle repair. Because it enables the small blood vessels near the skin surface to dilate, Tiger Balm helps this mending process. Nutrients carried by the blood are able to flow freely to the deep muscle tissue and regenerate them. Applications two or three times a day are recommended for aching muscles; after massaging the balm into the muscles, cover them immediately to provide extra warmth.

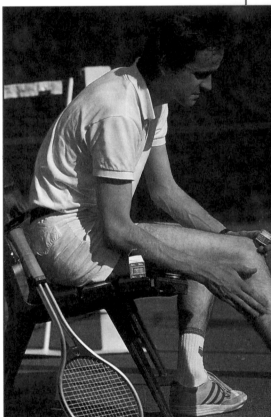

Providing relief for stressed muscles, Tiger Balm has helped to treat numerous athletes.

• **Menthol** – from the volatile oils of various species of *Mentha* (*labiatae*). Menthol has counter-irritant and anaesthetic qualities.

MEDICAL EFFECTS

1. Rubefacients are able to promote blood flow and create a sensation of warmth accompanied by surface skin reddening. They may also cause a slight numbness.
2. Anaesthetics partially, or completely, block out messages of pain, pressure and temperature change.
3. Vasodilators open the blood vessels and capillaries, releasing nutrients and oxygen to help the healing process. They can also enable dead cells and toxins to be eliminated.
4. Counter-irritants increase the circulation in the area being treated and cause vasodilation in the deeper layers of skin and muscle. Like anaesthetics, they can help to block out pain impulses to the brain.

Tiger Balm is available in both liquid and solid forms.

WHITE WILLOW BARK

Nature's aspirin

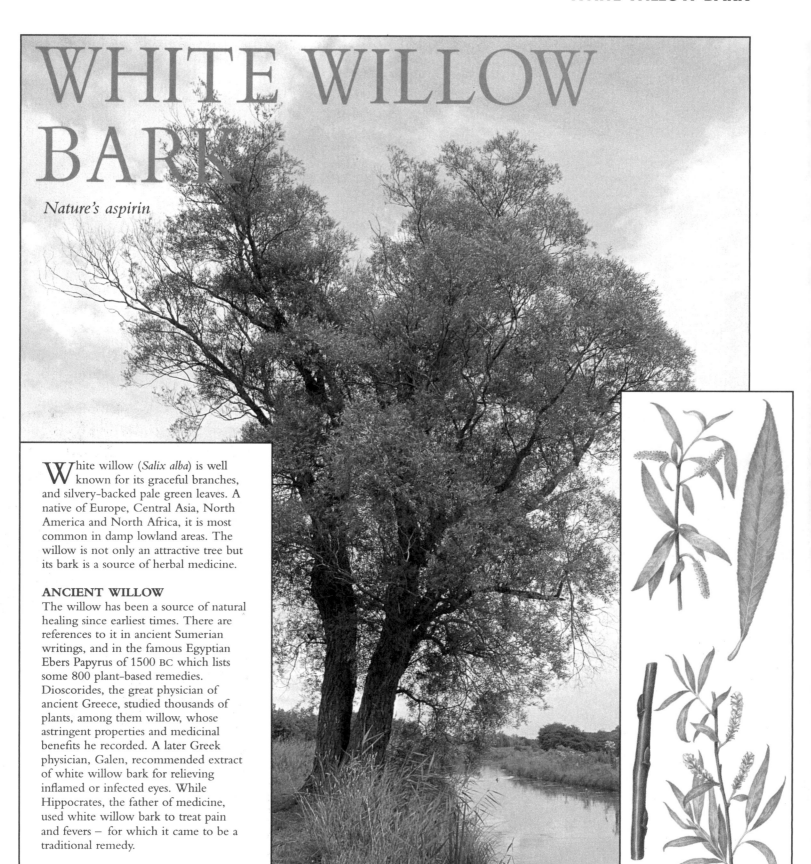

White willow (*Salix alba*) is well known for its graceful branches, and silvery-backed pale green leaves. A native of Europe, Central Asia, North America and North Africa, it is most common in damp lowland areas. The willow is not only an attractive tree but its bark is a source of herbal medicine.

ANCIENT WILLOW

The willow has been a source of natural healing since earliest times. There are references to it in ancient Sumerian writings, and in the famous Egyptian Ebers Papyrus of 1500 BC which lists some 800 plant-based remedies. Dioscorides, the great physician of ancient Greece, studied thousands of plants, among them willow, whose astringent properties and medicinal benefits he recorded. A later Greek physician, Galen, recommended extract of white willow bark for relieving inflamed or infected eyes. While Hippocrates, the father of medicine, used white willow bark to treat pain and fevers – for which it came to be a traditional remedy.

AGE-OLD REMEDY

Historically, in Britain the wood of the white willow was used to make household and dairy utensils. Its medicinal benefits were also put to good use. The English herbalists John Gerard and Nicholas Culpepr listed it and its various uses, including the treatment of fevers, colic, and sore eyes. A decoction of the bark was an old country remedy for pain and headaches. It was also prescribed by some country doctors as a drink, made by steeping the willow bark and twigs in water, for chills and fevers. This was a substitute for the more expensive cinchona bark imported from South America. During the 18th century white willow bark was used to ease the pain of rheumatism.

SCIENTIFIC DISCOVERY

White willow was used as a folk remedy through the centuries. Then in 1827 a French chemist, Leroux, succeeded in extracting the bark's active principle, which he called Salicin. From this salicylic acid was prepared. In 1852 there was a scientific breakthrough when these white crystals were produced synthetically. Eventually, a less irritant synthetic version was developed, called acetyl salicylic acid. Manufactured by the German company Bayer it became commercially available in 1899. This is better known to us as our most common drug, aspirin.

upsets and bleeding to dizziness and interference with the blood-clotting mechanisms. White willow bark offers a natural alternative.

BALANCE OF NATURE
Orthodox or allopathic medicine concentrates on finding, isolating, and

As a pain reliever it is thought to act to depress the central nervous system. As an anti-inflammatory agent it has a marked effect on inflamed rheumatic joints. This would seem to be due in part to white willow being an astringent herb, which means it has a binding action and is able to check inflammation, and soothe tissues.

RHEUMATISM AND ARTHRITIS
A main use for white willow bark in herbal medicine today is for the relief of rheumatism and arthritis – to reduce inflammation and relieve pain. Recommended dosage is 0.5–3g (¼–½ teaspoon) of the dried herb or the equivalent, three times a day. Often it is used in combination remedies for the same purpose.

Modern research has confirmed the traditional benefits of white willow for rheumatism and arthritis. One major research programme into the herb was carried out in the 1970s by a leading Swiss herbal medicine company. Results showed that in a great many cases, taking an extract of white willow reduced arthritic swelling.

AVAILABILITY
White willow bark is available from a number of herbal specialists, and you can buy it in capsule form, containing the dried, powdered bark, or as tablets. There are also various combination herbal remedies containing white willow. One of these is a herbal pain-killing tablet – specially good for headaches or hangovers. As well as poplar and willow barks it contains tonic and cleansing herbs.

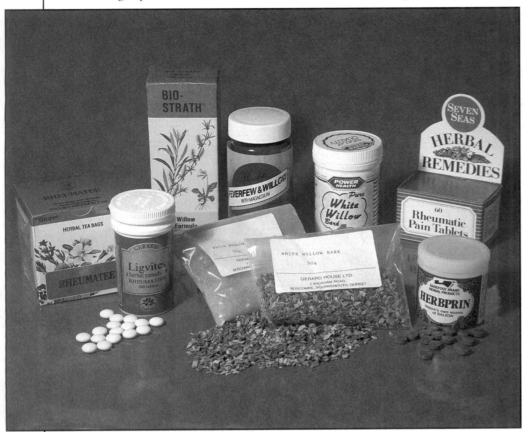

White willow comes in a variety of forms. As well as helping rheumatism and arthritis, it can relieve sciatica, lumbago and muscle pains.

NATURE'S ASPIRIN
The main active ingredient in white willow bark, salicin, is converted by the body into salicylic acid. So white willow has the same anti-inflammatory and pain-killing properties as aspirin, without any side-effects. It is estimated

then synthesising the active principle of plants. Herbalists have a different approach. They believe in using the whole of a plant, or a part like the leaves or bark, so that the natural balance of constituents is maintained. White willow, like other herbs, contains a number of substances which herbalists believe work together in a complementary way – to reinforce the healing action, and to check toxic elements which could cause side-effects.

MEDICINAL USES
Throughout its long history as a herbal remedy, white willow bark has had three main uses:
- to treat fevers
- to relieve pain
- to reduce inflammation

In the treatment of fevers and feverish condition, white willow helps to bring down high temperatures. This is probably due to its increasing the peripheral blood flow and encouraging sweating, so the body can dissipate the heat more efficiently.

RHEUMATISM REMEDIES
Rheumatism remedies come in tea, liquid, capsule and tablet form. One tea on the market combines nine different herbs, including willow bark, elder, primrose, and juniper berries, all working together to calm inflamed muscles and joints. Rheumatic pain tablets often combine the basic anti-rheumatic formula of popular, white willow, and prickly ash barks to reduce pain and inflammation, with herbs that can help cleanse the body of toxins.

The Swiss company who have done so much research into white willow have a liquid remedy, taken as drops in water. This combines willow with cowslip root and wild yeast.

HEART HELP?

Various research projects into the effects of aspirin have suggested that taking a daily dose of aspirin acts as a prophylactic against some types of heart attack. Given the known side-effects of manufactured aspirin, white willow bark remedies should be a much safer and effective alternative.

that 130 million tonnes of aspirin are swallowed by the Americans every single day. Yet even quite small doses can cause side-effects, from stomach

THE GENUINE BARK
There are a number of different indigenous species of the white willow tree to be found, and only the bark of a specific age is collected for natural remedies, so do not be tempted to collect the bark yourself!

YARROW

Cleanse your system with this versatile herb

With its pink or white flowers, yarrow is easily recognisable as one of our most common wayside plants. It grows on tall, upright stalks, with irregular, pungently-scented leaves, and at the top it has a large, flat head of many small flowers. The leaves are fine, fern-like and delicate and these make it popular for ornamental use. Yarrow grows in most temperate climates, including the UK, Europe and northern parts of the USA, where the white flower is more common. The plant is able to thrive on all but the most barren soils; however, it does need to be in a sunny position. Yarrow's Latin botanical name is *Achillea millefolium* – the god Achilles is said to have used it for healing. Millefolium means 'thousand-leaf', describing its dense leaves. Some of yarrow's many names include milifoil, nosebleed, staunchgrass, ladies' mantle, thousandleaf, butchers' wort and soldiers' wort.

BOOST TO THE BLOODSTREAM

Yarrow is a highly valued herb, both in the herbalists' repertoire and in popular use. It can be used as an alternative to hops in brewing, eaten fresh in salads, or as a cosmetic skin cleanser, especially for greasy skin. Yarrow acts as a vasodilator, expanding blood vessels and so regulating blood circulation around the body. Circulatory problems such as varicose veins and high blood pressure have responded well to treatment with yarrow.

The herb also acts as a diaphoretic, that is, it makes the body sweat and emit toxins. A hot infusion will be able to cool a fever. If taken at the first signs of a cold or influenza, yarrow has been known to relieve the symptoms within hours. It can also be taken when 'flu symptoms accompany cases of measles, chicken pox and even typhoid fever. The tannins contained in yarrow act astringently on the blood flow, thereby stopping bleeding. The plant also contains flavinoids which help to clear blood clots and dilate arteries.

Acting as a diuretic, yarrow helps to release fluid from the body. This makes it ideal for treating cases where too little urine is being expelled, or where there is a mucus discharge from the bladder. It is useful in the treatment of ailments such as cystitis (where it acts as a urinary antiseptic), and excess menstrual bleeding. Remember, however, that you should visit a practitioner if you have any vaginal or urinary discharges, menstrual problems, or cystitis. Yarrow can also be taken for haemorrhoids (piles). There are many cases of yarrow being administered

Alone or in conjunction with other herbs, yarrow helps to eliminate toxins, promote perspiration and improve blood circulation

Combined with other herbs, yarrow infusions can treat many conditions.

to facilitate the cure of wounds and surface skin inflammations. It was used routinely by soldiers and fighting men throughout the ages, who paid tribute to the plant's healing qualities by calling it soldiers' woundwort and knights' milifoil.

PLANT WITH A PAST

Like many herbs, yarrow played its part in pagan and esoteric rites and rituals. It is sacred to the horned god of pagan mythology, regarded as the male principle of the Universe. Yarrow was supposedly used to invoke the male aspect of the divinity in lunar celebrations. Astrologically, its planetary ruler is Jupiter, the god of love.

Traditionally, yarrow flowers were used at weddings, where they were worn by guests and added to bouquets. Yarrow was the plant chosen for the ancient ritual of handfasting, in which the hands of the male and female participants were bound together and not released until they celebrated the Great Rite. This was a sexual union in which the woman ritually embodied the feminine Goddess principle and the man represented the male God element. The rite was done purely for healing and spiritual transformation.

Another folk custom involving yarrow is to watch the yarrow patch in the garden or countryside, and make a wish when you see the first blossom of summer.

USING YARROW

All parts of the plant which grow above the ground are used. The plant is gathered between June and September when it is in flower. The most convenient way for the non–herbalist to use yarrow is in infusions. However, herbalists can also make it up into tinctures, ointments and powders. You can pick and dry your own yarrow, tying it up in bunches in a warm, dry place where plenty of air can circulate. If you do not wish to wait for home drying, you can buy dried yarrow from any reputable herbalist's, or obtain it by post from herbal suppliers.

Making an infusion:

Pour 300 ml (½ pt) of freshly boiled water onto 5 ml (1 tsp) of the dried herb and leave to infuse for 10 to 15 minutes. You can then drink this as often as required. In acute fevers, drink the infusion every hour. For menstrual problems and cystitis, circulatory problems, or as a diuretic, drink the infusion three times a day, increasing the dosage until you feel the benefit.

• Fevers

Combine yarrow with elder flowers and peppermint leaves that have been prepared in the same way (see ELDER; MINT). Use in equal proportions. You can also add to the infusion a shake of cayenne or ginger, or half a teaspoonful of grated fresh ginger root (see GINGER).

• High blood pressure

Yarrow combines well with infusions of hawthorn, lime blossom or mistletoe, again made in the same way (see HAWTHORN; MISTLETOE).

• Piles

Use as an enema following the advice of your practitioner. Ideally the bowels should already have been evacuated or cleared with an enema of plain water. Yarrow infusion can also be used as a douche for leucorrhoea (vaginal discharge) and cystitis.

• External bleeding

Traditionally, the juice was squeezed from leaves and stems. A strong infusion is probably more convenient: add 10 ml (2 tsp) of the dried flowers to 300 ml (½ pt) of boiling water, leave until cool, then apply to the site as a compress.

Yarrow sticks cast the hexagrams of the Chinese *I Ching* (Book of Changes).

Culpeper, the English herbalist, says that cattle will not eat yarrow if it grows on pasture, as the stalks are too dry. However, if sown on rather barren ground, cattle and horses will eat the tender leaves, leading to an increase in their offspring and milk yield.

YARROW AND THE I CHING

The use of yarrow stalks is also the original method of casting the I Ching, the ancient Chinese system of divination. The stalks have a strong connection with the symbols of the I Ching. They are said to form a link between heaven – the creative principle – and earth – the receptive principle. Numerically, the manipulation of the stalks involves the four seasons and the five states of change which are highly significant in the philosophy of the I Ching.

Fifty yarrow stalks of the same length are needed, and the complex process involves removing stalks from two heaped piles until you obtain a certain number in one hand. This number will indicate the numerical value of the lines of the appropriate I Ching hexagram, or reading.